G000299305

ASTON VILLA
REVIEW 1999

Published by Sports Projects Ltd

ACKNOWLEDGEMENTS

Aston Villa Review 1999
First published in Great Britain, July 1999,
by Sports Projects Limited

© 1999 Sports Projects Limited
188 Lightwoods Hill, Smethwick, Warley,
West Midlands B67 5EH.
email: info@sportproject.u-net.com
web: http://www.sportsprojects.com

ISBN 0 946866 50 3

Printed and bound in Great Britain

All rights reserved.
No part of this publication may be
reproduced, stored in any retrieval system or
transmitted, in any form or by any means,
without the written consent of the
publisher.

Editor: Jeffrey Prest.

Photographs: Bernard Gallagher,
Neville Williams, Dan Charity, Tom Morris,
Action Images, Empics and Terry Mealey.

Design, layout and graphics: Vic Millward,
Bernard Gallagher, Phil Lees and
Nadine Goldingay.

Special thanks to: Rod Evans, Mike Beddow,
Pam & Dave Bridgewater and Tony Leighton.

KEY

❑	Player booked
■	Player sent off
32	Figure in goals column indicates time of goal
†56	First substitute and time of substitution
†	First player substituted
‡56	Second substitute and time of substitution
‡	Second player substituted

Notes:

● *Players are listed in squad number order, except for the goalkeeper, who is always at the top of the list.*

● *Substitute goalkeepers are in squad number order, with (Gk) after their name.*

● *In friendly games, where several substitutes may have appeared, additional symbols are used in the following order: #, §, ††, ‡‡, ##, §§, ≠.*

Also available in this series:

Aston Villa Review 1993
ISBN 0 946866 09 0   Price: £7.95

Aston Villa Review 1994
ISBN 0 946866 19 8   Price: £8.95

Aston Villa Review 1995
ISBN 0 946866 23 6   Price: £8.95

Aston Villa Review 1996
ISBN 0 946866 32 5   Price: £8.95

Aston Villa Review 1997
ISBN 0 946866 39 2   Price: £8.95

Aston Villa Review 1998
ISBN 0 946866 46 5   Price: £9.95

A Jekyll and Hyde season

In most English households, media talk of Kevin Keegan starting a new era and sweeping the old order aside, has been music to the ears these last few months.

In Villa homes, however, such sentiments have a discordant irony to them, for even before Keegan took over the England team, Aston Villa supporters had ample experience of his transformative powers.

A bellyful, in fact.

We may never know what mental somersaults reduced Aston Villa from assured Premiership leaders to bewildered souls during the months of February and March 1999. What we do know is that when the game that started it came to a close, Kevin Keegan was holding the smoking gun.

His Fulham side's 2-0 win at Villa Park on 23rd January put one more year between Villa and their last FA Cup. Had that been the extent of it, it would have amounted to little more than a scratch on their season.

Instead, it was the start of a slippery slope that would plummet through 11 consecutive winless games. A new era all right.

Loss of key personnel, snowballing self-doubt and the old footballing truism that losing is a habit, turned a poor run into a monster.

Even at its peak, this wasn't a spectacular Villa team. It was neat, efficient and never knew when it was beaten. Just as importantly, in an age where no back page is complete without a Premiership 'personality' beating his breast and raging at the universe, it was a team that helped itself by generally keeping its head down and controversy out.

However valid his condition, it is a fact that Stan Collymore's problems with depression meant that his was the first head above the parapet. Factor in Ugo Ehiogu's dreadful eye injury and suddenly, Villa's wagons weren't as tightly circled as they had been.

Deprived of two high-calibre players, and with suspensions and other injuries starting to bite, the shallow squad which many had predicted would be their handicap was finally exposed.

Football, like America's 'gridiron' version, is more platoon-game than team-game these days and while it's bad news for those holding the purse strings, successful sides are now those to whom substitution routinely involves replacing one international with another.

Of course, had those 11 games without a win been scattered throughout the season instead of lumped together, Villa's season might not look quite so bad in retrospect. But then, the spur to make amends next season would be nowhere near as sharp.

That ghastly hiatus was an almighty slap in the face for a proud club. If lessons are learned, it is not inconceivable that this time next season we could look back at it as the making of John Gregory and his team.

Jeffrey Prest

CONTENTS

CONTENTS

Saturday 15th August 1998 • Goodison Park • 3.00pm

EVERTON 0 ASTON VILLA 0

Half-time 0-0 • Attendance 40,112

Referee Alan WILKIE (Chester-le-Street)
Referee's Assistants J. HOLBROOK and E. WALSH

Blue Shirts, White Shorts	Goals	Claret and Blue Shirts, Blue Shorts	Goals
1 Thomas MYHRE		1 Mark BOSNICH	
2 Alex CLELAND		2 Gary CHARLES	
3 Michael BALL ❑		3 Alan WRIGHT	
4 Olivier DACOURT ‡ ❑		4 Gareth SOUTHGATE (c)	
7 John COLLINS		7 Ian TAYLOR	
8 Nick BARMBY		10 Dwight YORKE	
9 Duncan FERGUSON (c)		11 Alan THOMPSON †	
11 John SPENCER †		12 Julian JOACHIM ❑	
12 Craig SHORT ❑		15 Gareth BARRY	
15 Marco MATERAZZI		17 Lee HENDRIE ❑	
23 Carl TILER		20 Riccardo SCIMECA ❑	

Substitutes		*Substitutes*	
5 Dave WATSON		8 Mark DRAPER †74	
10 Don HUTCHISON ‡75 ❑		13 Michael OAKES (Gk)	
13 Paul GERRARD (Gk)		16 Simon GRAYSON	
16 Michael BRANCH		22 Darius VASSELL	
29 Danny CADAMARTERI †63		26 Ben PETTY	

BEFORE	P	W	D	L	F	A	pts
Villa	0	0	0	0	0	0	0
Everton	0	0	0	0	0	0	0

AFTER	P	W	D	L	F	A	pts
Villa	1	0	1	0	0	0	1
Everton	1	0	1	0	0	0	1

FACTFILE

Ehiogu and Unsworth out through suspension... Immediate improvement on last season's nightmare start... All 84 league meetings between these clubs have been in the top flight... Villa goalless for first time in nine Premiership games... Unbeaten away run in Premiership now six games.

Bosnich penalty save is crucial

As if the uncertainty surrounding Dwight Yorke's future wasn't enough, Villa face a whirlwind of anticipation on Merseyside, where the arrival of Scottish quartet John Collins, Alex Cleland and management duo Walter Smith and Archie Knox has Evertonians believing that the good days are back.

A blast of bagpipes ushers the teams onto the sunlit field and lanky Everton striker Duncan Ferguson maintains the Rob Roy theme.

A marauding figure, whose height, power and deftness are in perfect unison, the Scot is the focus of most Everton attacks, laying off to the energetic John Spencer whatever scraps of possession he feels unable to exploit himself.

It threatens to make it a long afternoon for Villa, particularly when Spencer is adjudged to have been pulled down in the penalty area by Riccardo Scimeca in the eighth minute.

Collins hits the spot-kick to Mark Bosnich's right but the Australian, perhaps mindful that the Scottish international had done likewise with his penalty equaliser against Brazil in the World Cup, parries at the foot of the post and Everton can't capitalise on the rebound.

With Everton's newly-signed Frenchman, Olivier Dacourt, displaying a penchant for mixing it that belies his boyish looks, he and Collins dominate midfield and Bosnich is in action again in the 39th minute, diving at Nick Barmby's feet after a back-heel from Spencer sets up the former Spurs striker.

Dwight Yorke and Julian Joachim are quiet against the three six-footers at the heart of the Toffees' defence, but finally get behind them to latch onto a Riccardo Scimeca clearance in the 27th minute. Yorke, however, is unable to line up a shot.

Villa have another chance when home goal-keeper Myhre drops a looping Alan Wright cross but he recovers the ball before the visitors can pounce.

Bosnich palms a shot from Ferguson over the bar five minutes after the interval but Villa are now finding their feet. Both Yorke and Joachim evade their markers more readily, although Villa's midfield, where Alan Thompson is improving after an anonymous first half, struggles to get the ball behind Everton's defence.

Yorke's nine years with Villa end in an anti-climax. Myhre forces his 62nd minute shot past the post and although Dwight gets the ball into the net when the keeper fumbles a sloppy back pass shortly afterwards, the flag is up for offside.

Villa sense an unlikely win when Lee Hendrie appears to be tripped in the penalty box six minutes from time, but the referee shows no interest.

Everton continue to press, Ferguson and substitute Danny Cadamarteri linking to menacing effect, but by full-time Villa look better value for a point than they had 45 minutes earlier.

"Half-time couldn't come quickly enough for us," John Gregory agrees afterwards. "We weren't allowed to play in the first half. Southgate and Scimeca always seemed to be in the right place, though and we had a good second half with players backing each other up. Those were the hallmarks of our good run late last season."

Ian Taylor tracks back to cover Nick Barmby.

Sunday 23rd August 1998 • Villa Park • 4.00pm

ASTON VILLA 3 MIDDLESBROUGH 1

Half-time 1-0 • *Attendance* 29,559

Referee Paul ALCOCK (Redhill)

Referee's Assistants A. KAYE and N.E. GREEN

Claret and Blue Shirts, White Shorts		Goals
1	Mark BOSNICH	
2	Gary CHARLES	52
3	Alan WRIGHT ❑	
4	Gareth SOUTHGATE (c)	
5	Ugo EHIOGU	
7	Ian TAYLOR	
11	Alan THOMPSON	73
12	Julian JOACHIM ‡	6
15	Gareth BARRY	
17	Lee HENDRIE #	
20	Riccardo SCIMECA †	
	Substitutes	
8	Mark DRAPER #83	
13	Michael OAKES (Gk)	
16	Simon GRAYSON †68	
18	Fabio FERRARESI	
22	Darius VASSELL ‡80	

Sky Blue and White Striped Shirts, Navy Blue Shorts		Goals
1	Mark SCHWARZER	
2	Curtis FLEMING	
3	Dean GORDON	
5	Gianluca FESTA ❑	
7	Robbie MUSTOE	
8	Paul GASCOIGNE ‡	
10	Paul MERSON	
11	Alan MOORE †	
14	Phil STAMP	
16	Andy TOWNSEND (c)	
21	Craig HARRISON	
	Substitutes	
12	Mikkel BECK †60	61
13	Marlon BERESFORD (Gk)	
15	Neil MADDISON	
17	Vladimir KINDER	
19	Hamilton RICARD ‡60	

BEFORE		P	W	D	L	F	A	pts
	Villa	1	0	1	0	0	0	1
	Boro	1	0	1	0	0	0	1

AFTER		P	W	D	L	F	A	pts
3	Villa	2	1	1	0	3	1	4
17	Boro	2	0	1	1	1	3	1

FACTFILE

Collymore missing through injury... Villa's 100th Premiership victory... Middlesbrough have won only once in their last eight league games at Villa Park... Villa needed five games to score their first three goals of the season last year... Gary Charles' third goal in five seasons at Villa Park.

Life after Dwight is looking rosy

There's an air of uncertainty around a rain-soaked Villa Park as the hosts embark on *Life After Dwight*.

Three days after Dwight Yorke left for Old Trafford and David Unsworth ended his bed-and-breakfast Villa career by signing for Everton, John Gregory's problems still aren't over.

Striker Stan Collymore has limped out of training with an ankle injury, so Riccardo Scimeca plays up front, a position he once occupied in the Reserves.

The game is just six minutes old when his striking partner Julian Joachim eases the pressure on Scimeca and Villa in general, with a delightful goal. Receiving an Alan Wright cross on the edge of the box, Lee Hendrie scoops the ball over his head and into the path of Joachim, who strikes a crisp half-volley into the bottom corner.

Nerves are visibly settled. Alan Thompson sees a shot from 25-yards whiz just past Mark Schwarzer's right post a minute later and a Gareth Southgate effort is deflected for a corner.

A passive Middlesbrough are using Paul Merson as their principal striker, while Paul Gascoigne is shorn of his darting improvisation and reduced to a tidy, if unremarkable, distributor playing just in front of his defence.

Apart from intermittent probes by Merson, they offer little to set Villa back on their heels and Gary Charles is beginning to relish the space he will enjoy on the right flank all afternoon.

It looks like the visitors' day is done after 38 minutes, when Joachim is spun then hauled

Ugo slides in.

down in the box by Gianluca Festa, who is promptly booked for his trouble. So pumped up is Alan Thompson that he steps up ahead of newly-designated penalty-taker Lee Hendrie, only to see his gentle effort saved by Schwarzer, diving low to his right.

Shortly before half-time, Boro get a chance to make Villa pay, when a free-kick sets Merson free, but he fires past Mark Bosnich's right-hand post.

In the second half, as in the first, Villa find the net within seven minutes of kick-off, Ian Taylor's header flicking on a diagonal pass from midfield into the path of Gary Charles, who cuts in from the right past Dean Gordon and curls a shot inside the far post.

Middlesbrough nearly hit back two minutes later, when Merson finds Phil Stamp in wide open space on the left, but Bosnich easily saves his shot from the edge of the box.

Bryan Robson reshuffles his deck and finds the two of trumps when substitute strikers Mikkel Beck and Hamilton Ricard come on just before the hour. The visitors come alive, their first corner of the half after 61 minutes leading to a cross from Merson that Beck's head touches in at the near post.

It launches the game's most vibrant phase, yet Joachim is again involved in pulling the plug on Boro's hopes, despite being lone ranger up front after Scimeca departs.

Turning past Gordon with 17 minutes left, Joachim is pulled down by the defender and Alan Thompson, his free-kick assisted by a deflection, scores from 25 yards.

"The lads were determined to show that we are not a one-man team," says a justly buoyant John Gregory afterwards. We have lost an outstanding player, but life goes on."

Saturday 29th August 1998 • Hillsborough • 3.00pm

SHEFFIELD WEDNESDAY 0 ASTON VILLA 1

Half-time 0-1 • Attendance 25,989

Referee Keith BURGE (Tonypandy)

Referee's Assistants M.J. CAIRNS and S.R. BRAND

Blue and White Striped Shirts, Black Shorts	Goals	Claret and Blue Shirts, White Shorts	Goals
1 Kevin PRESSMAN		1 Mark BOSNICH	
2 Peter ATHERTON (c)		2 Gary CHARLES	
4 Wim JONK		3 Alan WRIGHT	
6 Des WALKER		4 Gareth SOUTHGATE (c)	
8 Benito CARBONE ❑		5 Ugo EHIOGU	
10 Andy BOOTH		8 Mark DRAPER †	
11 Paolo DI CANIO		9 Stan COLLYMORE	
15 Juan COBIAN †		11 Alan THOMPSON	
20 Andy HINCHCLIFFE		12 Julian JOACHIM	38
22 Emerson THOME		15 Gareth BARRY	
25 Petter RUDI		17 Lee HENDRIE	
Substitutes		*Substitutes*	
7 Guy WHITTINGHAM		13 Michael OAKES (Gk)	
12 Graham HYDE		16 Simon GRAYSON †78	
13 Matt CLARKE (Gk)		18 Fabio FERRARESI	
17 Lee BRISCOE		20 Riccardo SCIMECA	
27 Earl BARRETT †64		22 Darius VASSELL	

BEFORE		P	W	D	L	F	A	pts	AFTER		P	W	D	L	F	A	pts
3	Villa	2	1	1	0	3	1	4	2	Villa	3	2	1	0	4	1	7
9	Wednesday	2	1	0	1	3	1	3	12	Wednesday	3	1	0	2	3	2	3

FACTFILE

Ian Taylor misses game with knee injury... Villa go top of the table (albeit only for some 24 hours) for the first time since 14th August 1993... Villa now unbeaten in seven straight Premiership away games, six of them victories... Villa's best-ever start to a Premiership campaign.

Owls denied by 'Mean Machine'

Deep in the heart of Yorkshire, it's the Italian job that poses the biggest threat to Villa's unbeaten Premiership record.

One man may not make a team, but two can come close, as Paulo Di Canio and Benito Carbone demonstrate. The Italian duo are the spice in a Wednesday team that is otherwise purposeful without being spectacular.

Di Canio serves early notice of trouble ahead when he hovers along the 18-yard line after five minutes, finally curling in a cross that Andy Booth's head deflects wide of Mark Bosnich's left hand and into the net.

An offside flag preserves Villa's perfect defensive record away from home however, and the hosts will come no closer to scoring.

Starting his first competitive game since 3rd March, Stan Collymore is quickly in the thick of things, although this will be an afternoon in which he is more provider than predator, as he seeks to get some mileage under his belt.

He threatens to find Lee Hendrie with a 9th-minute cross, only for goalkeeper Kevin Pressman to head clear. Stan's first chance comes four minutes later when Hendrie threads a pass into his path with just the keeper to beat, only for Des Walker, Collymore's nemesis all afternoon, to take the ball off his toe.

One of several six-footers in Wednesday's team, Booth puts a free header wide of the post after 15 minutes and Carbone is miffed to be flagged for a marginal offside soon afterwards.

His side are bubbling now, and Villa are glad of a starring role at the heart of defence from Ugo Ehiogu, who heads clear a Carbone pass lofted towards Di Canio over the Villa lines.

Villa stun their opponents with the game's solitary goal seven minutes before half-time, when Collymore punches in a short cross towards Joachim, whose first intention is to play the ball through for Alan Thompson, making a run into the box.

Joachim miscues his effort, however, but as the ball remains in his vicinity, he resorts to Plan B, whipping the ball into the net past a diving Pressman from just inside the box.

Collymore lines up another 'assist' four minutes later, when his touch back from a Joachim cross is struck goalwards by Hendrie, only for Pressman to save in the top corner.

Shortly after the interval, Di Canio hits a spontaneous shot on the turn which Bosnich parries for a corner but the game's tide is beginning to ebb away from the hosts, as Villa start to dominate aerially in their own box.

Wednesday, nevertheless, wind up for a final assault in the closing minutes. Carbone is aggrieved not to get a penalty after contact with Wright, while Bosnich twice has to go where angels fear to tread to beat Booth to 50-50 balls.

The Australian then matches guts with grace when diving full-length across the face of his goal to parry another shot out of nothing from Di Canio.

Afterwards Bosnich praises "the best defence I've ever played behind," while John Gregory applauds the improvement in his goalscorer.

"A year ago, 20 or 30 minutes and Julian was done," says the Villa boss. "Now he can last 90 minutes."

Mark Bosnich – two clean sheets in three games.

Wednesday 9th September 1998 • Villa Park • 7.45pm

ASTON VILLA 1 NEWCASTLE UNITED 0

Half-time 0-0 • Attendance 39,241

Referee Graham POLL (Tring)
Referee's Assistants A.N. BUTLER and A.J. MARTIN

Claret and Blue Shirts, White Shorts	Goals		Black and White Striped Shirts, Black Shorts	Goals
1 Mark BOSNICH			1 Shay GIVEN	
2 Gary CHARLES			3 Stuart PEARCE	
3 Alan WRIGHT			7 Robert LEE (c)	
4 Gareth SOUTHGATE (c)			9 Alan SHEARER	
5 Ugo EHIOGU			11 Gary SPEED	
8 Mark DRAPER †			16 Laurent CHARVET	
11 Alan THOMPSON ‡			17 Stephen GLASS	
12 Julian JOACHIM			19 Steve WATSON	
15 Gareth BARRY			24 Nolberto SOLANO ‡	
17 Lee HENDRIE ❑	63pen		27 Philippe ALBERT	
20 Riccardo SCIMECA #			40 Andreas ANDERSSON †	
Substitutes			*Substitutes*	
7 Ian TAYLOR †67 ❑			2 Warren BARTON	
13 Michael OAKES (Gk)			5 Alessandro PISTONE	
16 Simon GRAYSON ‡80			8 Stéphane GUIVARC'H ‡69	
18 Fabio FERRARESI			14 Temuri KETSBAIA †58 ❑	
22 Darius VASSELL #86			23 Lionel PEREZ (Gk)	

BEFORE		P	W	D	L	F	A	pts
2	Villa	3	2	1	0	4	1	7
17	Newcastle	3	0	2	1	2	5	2

AFTER		P	W	D	L	F	A	pts
2	Villa	4	3	1	0	5	1	10
19	Newcastle	4	0	2	2	2	6	2

FACTFILE

Newcastle fresh from 4-1 defeat at home by Liverpool... Injured Stan Collymore's stop-start Villa career continues... Villa's first win over Newcastle since the Premiership formed... Villa's first win in four attempts over a team managed by Ruud Gullit... Lee Hendrie's first successful penalty for the senior side.

Hendrie penalty downs Magpies

For the second time in three seasons, Villa meet a Newcastle side getting acquainted with a brand new manager. Last time it was Kenny Dalglish, this time it's Ruud Gullit.

Newcastle are missing the suspended David Batty and the injured John Barnes and Dieter Hamann, while Villa have Riccardo Scimeca playing stand-in striker again, Stan Collymore having dropped out with a torn thigh muscle.

The manager of Villa's UEFA Cup opponents, Strømsgodset IF, looks on as the hosts give Newcastle the jitters in the 10th minute, when Julian Joachim looks to have been clipped by Shay Given as he takes the ball past the visiting goalkeeper.

No penalty is given, though, but Newcastle's sluggish back-four give Villa ample hope of finding the net eventually. Scimeca has a gilt-edged chance when a Gary Charles cross lets him in behind the defence after 12 minutes, but he side-foots wide. A minute later he's one-on-one with Steve Watson only for Given to clear for a throw-in.

Gullit has called Alan Shearer his 'Guns of Navarone' in pre-game newspaper reports but with none of his team-mates able to provide regular ammunition, 21 minutes elapse before Newcastle mount a decent attack, Gary Speed's low header from a free kick comfortably clearing the bar.

Having no joy from several promising attacks, Villa lose their momentum and with Newcastle's trademark panache currently a thing of the past, the game stagnates.

There's alarm for Villa when Gareth South-gate's 41st-minute clearance from his own penalty area ricochets off another player and bounces invitingly loose before Ugo Ehiogu sweeps it to safety.

The same pair combine at the other end a minute later following a corner, when Given punches Southgate's header upwards rather than away, but as the ball returns to ground, Ehiogu heads it over the bar.

The game has at last begun to open up as the second half gets under way and Villa need a masterly performance from Southgate to ensure Shearer's night of frustration continues.

The introduction of Temuri Ketsbaia lends Newcastle some overdue pep, but the Magpies' most promising period of the game deflates after 63 minutes when Julian Joachim is deemed to have been pulled down in the area by Stuart Pearce while shielding the ball.

Lee Hendrie spots Given making his move in the middle of his run-up and slots the penalty kick into the middle of the goal.

Finally snapping out of some dejected body language, Shearer tries to get United level again after 66 minutes, beating Bosnich to a cross. He can't ally aim to his speed, however, and Charles clears. There's greater danger for the Australian keeper when Ketsbaia works a one-two with Speed with 17 minutes to go, forcing Bosnich down to his left to hold onto Ketsbaia's shot from just outside the box.

Villa's new striker Paul Merson, signed from Middlesbrough just too late the previous day to be eligible to play, takes comfort from the clear-cut chances his new team are creating. Alan Thompson clips the bar with a shot from 20 yards after 76 minutes, while Scimeca is clearly starting to find his feet in his makeshift forward role.

A determined run from Shearer after 85 minutes threatens to jeopardise their efforts, however, as Britain's most expensive footballer just beats Gareth Barry to a ball that seemed destined for a throw-in. Shearer is clear but his pass for Stéphane Guivarc'h isn't penetrative enough and the visitors, for all their late pressure, are left still looking for their first win under new management.

Saturday 12th September 1998 • Villa Park • 3.00pm

ASTON VILLA 2 WIMBLEDON 0

Half-time 1-0 • *Attendance* 32,959

Referee David ELLERAY (Harrow-on-the-Hill)

Referee's Assistants H. WEBB and M.A. WILLIAMS

Claret and Blue Shirts, White Shorts		Goals	Dark Blue Shirts, Dark Blue Shorts		Goals
1	Mark BOSNICH		1	Neil SULLIVAN	
2	Gary CHARLES		2	Kenny CUNNINGHAM	
3	Alan WRIGHT		3	Alan KIMBLE	
4	Gareth SOUTHGATE (c)		4	Chris PERRY ❏	
5	Ugo EHIOGU		6	Ben THATCHER	
7	Ian TAYLOR ‡	57	8	Robbie EARLE (c)	
10	Paul MERSON #90	45	10	Andy ROBERTS #	
11	Alan THOMPSON †		11	Marcus GAYLE †	
12	Julian JOACHIM		15	Carl LEABURN ■45	
15	Gareth BARRY		16	Michael HUGHES ‡	
17	Lee HENDRIE		20	Jason EUELL	
	Substitutes			*Substitutes*	
8	Mark DRAPER ‡88		9	Efan EKOKU †79	
13	Michael OAKES (Gk)		13	Paul HEALD (Gk)	
16	Simon GRAYSON †74		17	Brian McALLISTER	
20	Riccardo SCIMECA #		18	Mark KENNEDY ‡83	
22	Darius VASSELL		24	Peter FEAR #90	

BEFORE		P	W	D	L	F	A	pts	AFTER		P	W	D	L	F	A	pts
2	Villa	4	3	1	0	5	1	10	1	Villa	5	4	1	0	7	1	13
4	Wimbledon	4	2	2	0	8	5	8	7	Wimbledon	5	2	2	1	8	7	8

FACTFILE

Third straight home win this season, something Villa never managed last term... Last season's Dons' 'double' avenged... Paul Merson debuts for Villa three weeks after playing here for Middlesbrough... Ian Taylor opens his account for season... Only once in 11 league meetings at Villa Park have these teams finished 0-0.

Merson debuts in tame contest

Wimbledon's recovery from three goals down to beat West Ham 4-3 in midweek, merely confirms Gareth Southgate's opinion that the Dons could prove Villa's toughest opponents to date this season.

Ultimately, however, Villa control with ease a disappointing game whose scope for improvement narrows markedly when the visitors' Carl Leaburn is sent off shortly before half-time.

Paul Merson makes his Villa debut and receives applause for his first touch, a raking pass on the turn to the right flank. One of Southgate's early touches isn't so auspicious, as he takes a shot full in the face, requiring lengthy treatment before carrying on.

After referee David Elleray changes his dark shirt, which was clashing with The Dons' navy blue, we're able to get down to some serious football. Villa make a brisk start and Alan Thompson, playing uncharacteristically deep in the early stages, strikes a 13th-minute half-volley from the edge of the box which is palmed away for a corner by Neil Sullivan.

Wimbledon respond and for much of the half look threatening on the break, despite Villa enjoying the greater share of possession.

With no height in the forward line to do justice to a flurry of crosses, however, the hosts are not creating the clear-cut chances they managed against Newcastle three days earlier, although Sullivan has to take the ball off Lee Hendrie's forehead as Merson whips in a 24th minute cross from the left.

Villa look to have reprised their Wednesday night route to goal, however, when Joachim gets the benefit of a close call and is deemed to have been impeded by Chris Perry in the penalty area in the 33rd minute.

John Gregory has a dilemma following Lee Hendrie's penalty success against Newcastle. Alan Thompson looked in daunting form from the spot during Friday's training session and it's the Geordie who gets the nod for this one.

Training's one thing, games another, however, as Thompson's effort slides comfortably wide of Sullivan's left post.

Villa get another chance on the stroke of half-time, when Ugo Ehiogu cuts into the area only to be tugged back by Leaburn, who is red-carded for a professional foul. Merson is entrusted with this penalty, but needs a rebound from Sullivan, diving to his left, before he can tuck the ball away to open Villa's account.

After the interval, Villa are soon chivvied by an impatient crowd as Wimbledon have the early opportunities through Robbie Earle.

What edge the visitors had is blunted by being a man down, however and they are put in their place in the 57th minute when Joachim centres from the right and Ian Taylor hooks home a volley from inside the box.

Twice denied good opportunities by an offside flag, Paul Merson has a frustrating half. After his knee takes the brunt of Perry's landing following a slide tackle by the ex-Middlesbrough player, Merson recovers, only to scoop a close-range shot over the bar after a break by Joachim three minutes before full-time. It's a promising debut, nevertheless, and he is warmly applauded when substituted shortly before full-time.

Gareth Southgate closes in on Marcus Gayle.

Tuesday 15th September 1998 • Villa Park • 7.45pm

ASTON VILLA 3 STRØMSGODSET IF 2

Half-time 0-2 • Attendance 28,893
Referee Hartmut STRAMPE
Referee's Assistants C. KADACH and H. NEUENSTEIN
Officials from Germany

Claret and Blue Shirts, White Shorts	Goals	Dark Blue Shirts, Dark Blue Shorts	Goals
1 Mark BOSNICH		30 Glenn Arne HANSEN	
2 Gary CHARLES	83	3 Thomas WÆHLER	
3 Alan WRIGHT		6 Kenneth KARLSEN (c) ❑ ■68	
4 Gareth SOUTHGATE (c)		7 Sander SOLBERG	
8 Mark DRAPER ‡		8 Ousman NYAN	
11 Alan THOMPSON ❑		10 Rune HAGEN ❑	
12 Julian JOACHIM		14 Hans Erik ØDEGAARD †	
15 Gareth BARRY		17 Lars GRANÅS	
16 Simon GRAYSON †		20 Anders MICHELSEN #	21
17 Lee HENDRIE		21 Pål SKISTAD	
21 Darren BYFIELD #		23 Morten KIHLE	
Substitutes		*Substitutes*	
7 Ian TAYLOR †37 ❑		1 Thomas ØDEGAARD (Gk)	
13 Michael OAKES (Gk)		2 Espen HORSRUD	
18 Fabio FERRARESI		5 Vegard STRØM ‡70	
20 Riccardo SCIMECA ‡67		13 Christer GEORGE †11 ❑ ‡ 23	
22 Darius VASSELL #80 90,90		15 Lasse OLSEN #87	
23 David HUGHES		16 Erland JOHNSEN	
28 Tommy JASZCZUN		22 Tor Arne SANNERHOLT	

FACTFILE

*The first time Villa have met Norwegian opposition in European competition...
At 0-1, Villa trail for the first time this season... Their fifth straight home win in
European competition... Gary Charles and Darius Vassell score their first goals for
Villa in Europe*

Super-sub spares Villa blushes

The theory that there are no easy games in international football may be due a wider application, after an injury-hit Norwegian club in mediocre form gives Villa their biggest scare of the season so far.

It takes two late goals from 18-year-old sub Darius Vassell to extricate Villa from a 0-2 hole that had turned Villa Park into the *House of Bewilderment* for a stunned crowd.

After Gary Charles begins the salvage with an 83rd minute goal from close range, Strømsgodset's staff shortage begins to take its toll.

Kenneth Karlsen had received his marching orders for a second bookable offence, having elbowed Riccardo Scimeca after 68 minutes. It deprives Strømsgodset of valuable height and throws a spanner in their efficient works.

As the home team's superior fitness begins to tell, their opponents wilt and Vassell strikes. Ninety minutes are up when he pounces on a mis-hit shot from Lee Hendrie to slam the ball into the net and he connects again in the poacher's zone three minutes later when Glenn Arne Hansen can only parry an Alan Thompson shot to the youngster's feet.

It is the climax that has threatened ever since Villa began the second half with 15 minutes of embarrassed reflection behind them and finally found the top end of their gear-box.

Even then, however, Strømsgodset ironically have a gilt-edged chance to nail down the win after 56 minutes.

Christer George, arguably their most effective player, despite only being introduced as a sub after 11 minutes, triggers another of the breaks that haunt Villa all evening and leaves Anders Michelsen with just Mark Bosnich to beat.

Bosnich spreads himself and his flailing leg nudges Michelsen's shot for a corner.

The Australian had previously been helpless to prevent the Norwegians from transforming the character of the tie in the first half.

He halts but can't hold Michelsen's fierce strike in the 15th minute and the striker slots home the rebound. Two minutes later and the tiny wedge of 'Godset fans in the Doug Ellis Stand are making all the noise as Rune Hagen cuts inside Gareth Barry and crosses for George to sidefoot the ball home.

Villa try frantically to restore normal service, but Strømsgodset defend tightly even when under pressure, allowing their opponents no time to settle on the ball. Strong claims for a 33rd minute penalty are turned away when Hendrie is tripped with the referee close at hand.

The half-time break works wonders, however, though young striker Darren Byfield is entitled to feel rueful after Villa's transformation. After several half-chances that on another night might have found the net, he makes way for Vassell in the 80th minute and is left feeling like the man who's pumped silver into a one-armed bandit all night only to watch someone else hit the jackpot with his first two coins.

Not that he's feeling sorry for himself afterwards. Like the rest of his team he knows only too well that thanks to his young team-mate's opportunism, Villa are heading to Norway with a toe in the second round instead of one foot in the grave.

Mark Draper and Lee Hendrie just miss out.

Saturday 19th September 1998 • Elland Road • 3.00pm

LEEDS UNITED 0 ASTON VILLA 0

Half-time 0-0 • *Attendance* 33,446

Referee Jeff WINTER (Stockton-on-Tees)

Referee's Assistants A. HOGG and D. DRYSDALE

White Shirts, White Shorts	Goals	Claret and Blue Shirts, Blue Shorts	Goals
1 Nigel MARTYN		1 Mark BOSNICH	
5 Lucas RADEBE (c)		2 Gary CHARLES ‡	
9 Jimmy Floyd HASSELBAINK		3 Alan WRIGHT ❏	
10 Bruno RIBEIRO ‡		4 Gareth SOUTHGATE (c)	
11 Lee BOWYER		5 Ugo EHIOGU	
12 David HOPKIN		7 Ian TAYLOR ❏	
18 Gunnar HALLE		10 Paul MERSON	
19 Harry KEWELL †		11 Alan THOMPSON †	
20 Ian HARTE		12 Julian JOACHIM	
21 Martin HIDEN		15 Gareth BARRY	
30 Robert MOLENAAR		17 Lee HENDRIE	
Substitutes		*Substitutes*	
4 Alf Inge HAALAND †76		8 Mark DRAPER †61	
6 David WETHERALL		13 Michael OAKES (Gk)	
7 Lee SHARPE ‡76		16 Simon GRAYSON ‡82	
8 Clyde WIJNHARD		18 Fabio FERRARESI	
36 Paul ROBINSON (Gk)		22 Darius VASSELL	

BEFORE		P	W	D	L	F	A	pts	AFTER		P	W	D	L	F	A	pts
1	Villa	5	4	1	0	7	1	13	1	Villa	6	4	2	0	7	1	14
3	Leeds	5	2	3	0	5	1	9	6	Leeds	6	2	4	0	5	1	10

FACTFILE

Villa's unbeaten away record in the Premiership extends to eight games...
They have not conceded an away goal for four and a half hours... Liverpool draw
with Charlton and Derby beat Leicester, turning next week's Villa v Derby game
into a top-of-the-table clash.

'Mean Machines' draw a blank

They play 'Nessun Dorma' before the game; 'None Shall Sleep'. Some feel that's a broken promise after an unspectacular contest that will have cut little ice with neutrals.

For the partisans, however, it's an absorbing footballing chess game between two well-matched teams whose manifestos, in fairness, were clear after both conceded only one goal in their opening five Premiership games.

Villa, well practised in coming off the ropes after their UEFA Cup adventure earlier in the week, almost repeat the feat when Julian Joachim is inches wide of securing three points inside the game's last ten minutes.

United's Robert Molenaar appears to lose a high ball in the sunshine that graces the whole game, letting in Joachim, who opts for the early strike as goalkeeper Nigel Martyn accelerates off his goal line.

Martyn is fractionally too slow to smother the shot but 'JJ' is fractionally wide and the ball goes the wrong side of the post.

It would have been ample compensation for as tough an afternoon's work as the Villa striker has seen this season, thanks to the unrelenting attentions of Leeds' South African central defender Lucas Radebe.

Joachim is forced repeatedly into midfield in an attempt to grab some unmolested possession but his defence make their own contribution to the stalemate, with Gareth Southgate frustrating Jimmy Floyd Hasselbaink at almost every turn.

After having weathered an uncomfortable first half, Villa see their doggedness nearly wasted on the stroke of half-time, as a few inches of timber save them twice within a matter of seconds. Ian Harte raps Mark Bosnich's left hand post with a long range shot and when a diving header from Lee Bowyer sends the rebound against the bar, Leeds fans old enough to remember Jim Montgomery's miraculous double save against them in the 1973 Cup Final, are left with a vague sense of *deja vu* as they head for the refreshment kiosks.

No-one is more frustrated during the interval than Bowyer, who had sent a shot just over the bar after 10 minutes and whose control of midfield in tandem with David Hopkin is making it a long afternoon for Villa's Alan Thompson.

Bosnich watches his compatriot Harry Kewell and Harte go close with long-range efforts in the second-half, while a combination of Alan Wright and errant shooting denies Hasselbaink twice when the Dutchman finds space at the far post. These turn out to be United's last real salvos of the game, as frustration and fatigue begin to take their toll.

Villa step into the breach and Ian Taylor flicks a header just wide of Martyn's post after 64 minutes. By the time Joachim's late effort goes the same way, Leeds are shaky and it takes the introduction of Lee Sharpe to revitalise them in the closing stages.

George Graham, in what turns out to be the latter stages of his reign at Elland Road, assures himself of a warm welcome whichever team he next brings to Villa Park when he damns Villa with faint praise afterwards, describing them as a 'nice little side'.

A nice little side that is four points clear of his own and at the top of the table.

Jimmy Hasselbaink is no match for Ugo.

Saturday 26th September 1998 • Villa Park • 3.00pm

ASTON VILLA 1 DERBY COUNTY 0

Half-time 1-0 • *Attendance* 38,007

Referee Steve DUNN (Bristol)

Referee's Assistants M.L. SHORT and G. TURNER

Claret and Blue Shirts, White Shorts		Goals	White Shirts, Black Shorts		Goals
1	Mark BOSNICH		1	Russell HOULT	
2	Gary CHARLES ❑		2	Horacio CARBONARI ‡	
3	Alan WRIGHT		4	Darryl POWELL	
4	Gareth SOUTHGATE (c)		8	Dean STURRIDGE	
5	Ugo EHIOGU		9	Paulo WANCHOPE	
7	Ian TAYLOR		10	Rory DELAP	
10	Paul MERSON	15	14	Lars BOHINEN	
11	Alan THOMPSON ‡		16	Jacob LAURSEN ❑	
12	Julian JOACHIM #		17	Spencer PRIOR (c)	
15	Gareth BARRY †		18	Lee CARSLEY	
17	Lee HENDRIE		25	Robert KOZLUK †	
	Substitutes			*Substitutes*	
8	Mark DRAPER ‡72		11	Kevin HARPER	
9	Stan COLLYMORE #87		21	Mart POOM (Gk)	
13	Michael OAKES (Gk)		20	Stefano ERANIO ‡83	
16	Simon GRAYSON †64		26	Jonathan HUNT	
22	Darius VASSELL		27	Francesco BAIANO †72	

BEFORE	P	W	D	L	F	A	pts	AFTER	P	W	D	L	F	A	pts
1 Villa	6	4	2	0	7	1	14	1 Villa	7	5	2	0	8	1	17
2 Derby	6	3	3	0	6	2	12	2 Derby	6	3	3	1	6	3	12

FACTFILE

A rude awakening for Jim Smith, who had admitted that after Derby rose to second place in the table, "I am truly starting to dream"... Villa achieve three straight Premiership clean sheets at home for the first time since 2nd November 1996... Paul Merson's first Villa goal from open play.

Three more hard-earned points

Villa v Derby - top of the table clash. It's comforting to know football still retains the ability to surprise.

This meeting of the *Unlikely Lads* produces a contest that is higher on tension than chances but Villa are happy with three points after another solid defensive display, made no easier by Gareth Barry hobbling off injured with nearly half an hour left.

Paul Merson secures the points after only 14 minutes, following a fortuitous ricochet that Derby manager Jim Smith later dubs 'the best pass of the game.'

Lee Hendrie gets involved in a midfield tussle that sees the ball struck hard at the legs of innocent bystander Lee Carsley. The Brum-born County midfielder serves Villa better than he ever did when cheering them on as a boy, as the ball ricochets from his shins into the path of Merson, who runs on to tuck his shot in the bottom right-hand corner.

It's a slap in the face for the visitors, for whom Paulo Wanchope had gone close with a long-range shot out of nowhere on four minutes that Mark Bosnich can only parry.

The goal sees the momentum shift to Villa, however, and when Gareth Southgate is allowed to advance almost the length of the pitch before taking a shot that's deflected for a corner, you suspect this is their day.

The captain is back in a more orthodox role to snuff out a Rory Delap cross after the Sutton Coldfield-born winger gets behind the Villa defence, and Southgate is

also on hand to intercept Dean Sturridge as the striker slips past Wright and Gareth Barry to cut in from the right in the 33rd minute.

With Newtown lad Sturridge buzzing against his second-favourite club and Wanchope's gangly frame threatening to cut loose from any position, the visitors have regained their composure after the goal.

Merson and Julian Joachim toil hard to fend off the attentions of a physical County defence, and their team-mates are struggling to mount cohesive attacks when breaking from midfield.

When all else fails, though, Villa's defence continues to hold the line. A misplaced pass from Alan Thompson seven minutes from the interval is pounced open by Lars Bohinen and after the Norwegian midfielder threads a pass through to Sturridge, it needs Gareth Barry to take the ball off the striker's toe just as he enters shooting range.

The pressure stays on Villa early in the second half, as an improvised shot on the turn from Wanchope whistles just over the bar and Mark Bosnich recovers to palm away over a shot from Delap that appeared to take him by surprise.

The hosts have to reshuffle after Gareth Barry collides with an advertising board while closing down another Derby attack. The teenager complains of a painful Achilles' tendon and Villa are taking no chances, sending on Simon Grayson in his place.

With Bosnich again in commanding form and his team-mates having more of the game than they enjoyed in the latter part of the first half, however, Villa consolidate their lead at the top of the table, leaving Jim Smith to bewail the lack of a final telling ball that has dogged his team's season.

Lee Hendrie outpaces Darryl Powell.

Tuesday 29th September 1998 • Marienlyst Stadium • 6.00pm

STRØMSGODSET IF 0 ASTON VILLA 3

Aggregate score 6-2
Half-time 0-2 • Attendance 4,835

Referee Dieter SCHOCH
Referee's Assistants M. FRIEBURGHAUS and A. RISPLENDENTE
Officials from Switzerland

White Shirts, Dark Blue Shorts	Goals	Claret and Blue Shirts, White Shorts	Goals
30 Glenn Arne HANSEN		1 Mark BOSNICH	
3 Thomas WÆHLER		2 Gary CHARLES †	
7 Sander SOLBERG #		3 Alan WRIGHT	
8 Ousman NYAN		4 Gareth SOUTHGATE (c)	
10 Rune HAGEN		5 Ugo EHIOGU	
11 Jostein FLO (c)		7 Ian TAYLOR ❏ #	
13 Christer GEORGE ‡		8 Mark DRAPER	
16 Erland JOHNSEN		9 Stan COLLYMORE	11,24,64
17 Lars GRANÅS		11 Alan THOMPSON ❏	
19 Erik HAGEN †		12 Julian JOACHIM ‡	
21 Pål SKISTAD		16 Simon GRAYSON	

Substitutes		*Substitutes*	
1 Thomas ØDEGAARD (Gk)		13 Michael OAKES (Gk)	
2 Espen HORSRUD		17 Lee HENDRIE	
5 Vegard STRØM #85		18 Fabio FERRARESI #70	
14 Hans Erik ØDEGAARD †66		20 Riccardo SCIMECA †51	
15 Lasse OLSEN ‡66		22 Darius VASSELL ‡66	
20 Anders MICHELSEN			
22 Tor Arne SANNERHOLT		*Villa named only five subs for this game.*	

> **FACTFILE**
>
> *Stan Collymore's first Villa hat-trick... Villa's first aggregate defeat of Scandinavian opposition in Europe... Their fourth clean sheet in the last six European away legs... Villa have now failed to progress beyond the first round only twice in eleven European campaigns... Three days afterwards, they draw Spanish side RC Celta Vigo for the second round.*

Stan stars amid the mountains

Once Villa had retrieved the two-goal deficit they faced in the first leg, there was always the possibility that the return in Norway might degenerate into anti-climax.

That it doesn't is due to all three Villa goals coming from the boot of Stanley Collymore, which gives the media the perfect hook on which to hang their reports

It also renews the faith of Villa fans anxious to see more regular returns on their club's £7m investment and hopefully sets the seal on Stan's return from a thigh injury.

Obliged to go in search of a goal, Strømsgodset are denied the luxury they enjoyed at Villa Park of being able to defend in depth. Ex-Chelsea defender Erland Johnsen returns from injury to give Collymore a few early clattering reminders of his presence, before fading into irrelevance, as does the daunting figure of Jostein Flo, leading the home team's forward line.

With a handsome cross shot into the far corner on 10 minutes, Collymore opens the second-leg scoring after cutting in from the left flank. It is to Villa physio Jim Walker he runs in celebration; a 'thank-you' for the man who has helped him through the grey days of inaction.

Having shown his inventiveness, the Villa striker shows his poacher's instincts when he's on hand to bury 'Godset in the 23rd minute, after keeper Glenn Arne Hansen can only divert a Mark Draper shot towards the Villa number 9.

In the 64th minute, Collymore rounds off his hat-trick when Julian Joachim scampers through the rain to cross a ball that seemed beyond him, leaving Stan with a formality just feet from the goal-line.

He is ideally placed to become the first Villan since Simon Stainrod in 1985 to notch four goals in a competitive fixture, when with 16 minutes left, Draper shoots and misses while of the opinion that a pass to the wide open Collymore would have led to an offside flag.

Though Villa always look favourites, 'Godset do have their moments during the first half. Christer George is again their principal architect. His 14th-minute shot at goal is deflected to Rune Hagen, whose own strike Mark Bosnich needs two attempts to control.

The Australian is at his best seven minutes later as he drops to his right to smother a free header from Flo, and when he plucks a deep corner out of the air with Flo in attendance behind him, it is the beginning of the end for the underdogs, with nine minutes left in the first half.

If there is a stain on the evening for the visitors, it is the bookings against Ian Taylor and Alan Thompson, which condemn both to a night off when Villa play the first leg of their second round in three weeks' time.

Strømsgodset have reason to be discouraged, but they defiantly refuse to throw in the towel and Bosnich twice has to punch clear after the home team have a corner in the game's dying stages.

No longer an unknown quantity, however, their menace is greatly diminished after the first leg. Villa will have tougher nights than this in Europe this season, but having come so close to an almighty cropper at the first hurdle, there is cause for quiet celebration at a job eventually well done.

Mark Bosnich sees off a 'Godset attack.

Saturday 3rd October 1998 • Highfield Road • 3.00pm

COVENTRY CITY 1 ASTON VILLA 2

Half-time 0-2 • Attendance 22,654

Referee Stephen LODGE (Barnsley)

Referee's Assistants D.S. BABSKI and D.S. BRYAN

Sky Blue, Dark Blue and White Shirts, Sky Blue Shorts	Goals		Claret and Blue Shirts, White Shorts	Goals
1 Magnus HEDMAN		1	Mark BOSNICH	
2 Roland NILSSON		2	Gary CHARLES ❑ ‡	
5 Richard SHAW		3	Alan WRIGHT	
6 Gary BREEN ‡		4	Gareth SOUTHGATE (c)	
8 Noel WHELAN ❑		5	Ugo EHIOGU	
9 Dion DUBLIN (c)		7	Ian TAYLOR ❑	29,39
11 George BOATENG		9	Stan COLLYMORE ❑	
12 Paul TELFER		10	Paul MERSON †	
26 Stephen FROGGATT		11	Alan THOMPSON ❑	
27 Marc EDWORTHY		15	Gareth BARRY	
30 Barry QUINN †		17	Lee HENDRIE	
Substitutes			*Substitutes*	
13 Jean-Guy WALLEMME ‡76		8	Mark DRAPER	
14 Trond SOLTVEDT †59 71		12	Julian JOACHIM †69	
15 Paul HALL		13	Michael OAKES (Gk)	
16 Steve OGRIZOVIC (Gk)		16	Simon GRAYSON ‡69	
18 Philippe CLEMENT		20	Riccardo SCIMECA	

BEFORE	P	W	D	L	F	A	pts	AFTER	P	W	D	L	F	A	pts
1 Villa	7	5	2	0	8	1	17	1 Villa	8	6	2	0	10	2	20
19 Coventry	7	1	2	4	4	12	5	19 Coventry	8	1	2	5	5	14	5

> **FACTFILE**
> *Ian Taylor scores twice in a game for first time in his Villa career... Villa concede goal for first time in 549 minutes of Premiership football... Coventry fail to beat their local rivals for twelfth time in 13 Premiership games... International programme means Villa are safe at top of table for next fortnight.*

Busy Taylor sews up three points

If there's a downside to Stan Collymore's mid-week hat-trick it's that it leaves him, Paul Merson and Julian Joachim fighting over the two slots in Villa's forward line.

A healthy situation for John Gregory, less so for Joachim, who's left clutching the short straw on the substitutes' bench.

The fulcrum of Villa's early season success, he can only wonder what might have been as Ian Taylor moves up into the attack to open his account for the season.

Two first-half goals from the midfielder give Villa a platform which Coventry struggle to undermine until a goal from substitute Trond Soltvedt sets up a tense last 19 minutes.

It's a fair result for the Sky Blues, who claim that Taylor's second goal was offside, yet ruin numerous promising attempts to cancel it out with some ineffectual work inside their opponents' penalty area.

They could have used some of the incisiveness shown by Taylor when he puts Villa ahead just before the half-hour mark. His midfield colleague Alan Thompson shone most in a breezy start by both teams, yet it's Taylor who pounces when Roland Nilsson can only stun a fierce cross from Gary Charles, effectively teeing it up for the Villa man to slam in his second goal of the season.

Eleven minutes later and a pass from Lee Hendrie releases Paul Merson in acres of space on the right hand flank. The striker fires over a cross that finds Taylor with all the time he needs to find the net. It's a bitter double blow for the hosts, still struggling to recapture the form with which they beat Chelsea in this same stadium on the opening day of the season.

Ex-Villa player Stephen Froggatt, embarking on a promising Coventry debut after signing from Wolverhampton Wanderers in midweek, shoots wide after a 28th minute cross from Dion Dublin.

He's on target in the closing stages of the first half, only to see Mark Bosnich save at the foot of the post. When Gareth Southgate clears a looping Dion Dublin header off the line, City are entitled to feel it's not their day.

Taylor twice has a sniff of his first Villa hat-trick in the opening 25 minutes of the second half, but each time Collymore's cross is just too far in front of him. Heavily-marked, Stan is confined to a provider's role but his roving brief at least frees up space for his team-mates.

Coventry's spirit is unquestionable, but with Villa defending tenaciously throughout the side whenever they lose possession, the hosts find fluency hard to come by.

They find reward for their endeavours in the 71st minute, when a Dublin back-heel from the by-line sets up Soltvedt to stab the ball home from short-range.

It sets up a tense final few minutes, but Villa are unabashed by the set-back. With Coventry stretched as they press forward, Simon Grayson has a goal disallowed for handball and fellow substitute Julian Joachim has the chance to put his case for full-time employment when Collymore puts him clear in the box. With the ball bobbling around his shins, however, Joachim can only scoop the ball over the bar.

Paul Merson pressurises the City defence.

Saturday 17th October 1998 • Upton Park • 3.00pm

WEST HAM UNITED 0 ASTON VILLA 0

Half-time 0-0 • Attendance 26,002

Referee Paul ALCOCK (Redhill)

Referee's Assistants P. BARNES and S. GAGEN

Claret and Blue Shirts, White Shorts	Goals	Turquoise Shirts with Black Trim, Black Shorts	Goals
12 Shaka HISLOP		13 Michael OAKES	
3 Julian DICKS (c)		2 Gary CHARLES	
6 Neil RUDDOCK †		3 Alan WRIGHT	
8 Trevor SINCLAIR		4 Gareth SOUTHGATE (c)	
10 John HARTSON		5 Ugo EHIOGU	
11 Steve LOMAS		7 Ian TAYLOR	
14 Ian WRIGHT ‡		9 Stan COLLYMORE ❏	
15 Rio FERDINAND		10 Paul MERSON	
18 Frank LAMPARD		11 Alan THOMPSON ❏	
19 Ian PEARCE		15 Gareth BARRY	
29 Eyal BERKOVIC		17 Lee HENDRIE	

Substitutes		*Substitutes*	
7 Marc KELLER		6 Steve WATSON	
9 Paul KITSON ‡80		8 Mark DRAPER	
16 John MONCUR		12 Julian JOACHIM	
20 Andrew IMPEY †73		16 Simon GRAYSON	
22 Craig FORREST (Gk)		30 Adam RACHEL (Gk)	

BEFORE		P	W	D	L	F	A	pts	AFTER		P	W	D	L	F	A	pts
1	Villa	8	6	2	0	10	2	20	1	Villa	9	6	3	0	10	2	21
6	West Ham	8	3	3	2	7	8	12	8	West Ham	9	3	4	2	7	8	13

FACTFILE

Villa undefeated away from home in 11 games (all competitions)... A clean sheet for the eighth time this season... Michael Oakes' first clean sheet in 12 starts since 9th April 1997 (2-0 v Wimbledon)... Villa's third 0-0 scoreline of the season equals their goalless draw tally for the whole of 1997-98.

Merson miss as good as a mile

If you've ever been invited to dinner by a couple who have patently been engaged in the mother of all rows just before your arrival, you'll know how Villa feel in the season's first visit to the capital.

West Ham slap on the hospitality and go through the motions of a football game but the fall-out from the training ground coming-together of John Hartson's boot and Eyal Berkovic's skull makes them a club distinctly ill at ease with itself.

The Welshman and the Israeli have publicly made their peace after the bust-up, but while Berkovic's probing passes to his forwards suggest the unfortunate chapter is closed, Hartson is a peripheral figure, his only notable contribution a side-footer headed to the top corner in the 9th minute before Michael Oakes intervenes to palm the ball over.

It's a rare outing for the back-up keeper, who buffs up his CV with a confident display while Mark Bosnich is sidelined by a shoulder injury sustained at Coventry

Oakes' cause is helped by a listless, error-ridden display from West Ham's forward line, which makes the superb performance from their striker-turned-wing-back Trevor Sinclair all the more ironic. While John Gregory later professes himself satisfied with a point, there is a nagging feeling that two more have just gone begging.

This becomes a stone-cold conviction when Paul Merson appears to under-estimate Shaka Hislop's reflexes in the 67th minute. Villa have been tight-

**Michael Oakes -
a clean sheet.**

ening the screw with several minutes' sustained pressure and when Hislop parries a Hendrie shot to Merson's feet, an open goal looms large. With the West Ham goalkeeper seemingly stranded, Merson opts for the nudge rather than the blast and has to hide his face in his hands as Hislop scrambles back to claw the ball to safety.

That closes Villa's window of opportunity for the afternoon. Hendrie has a second, and more convincing, penalty appeal of the afternoon turned down with eight minutes left, and it's another close shave for his marker Ian Pearce, who 10 minutes earlier had been fortunate not to be done for handball in his own area when labouring to bring a high ball under control in the nagging wind that mars the game.

The West Ham defender had earned some luck when twice beating Stan Collymore to low crosses into the danger area during the first half. It's a long afternoon for Stan in the face of Pearce's limpet-like attention, but while he may not be imposing himself on the game in the way Julian Joachim did at the start of the season, his effort cannot be faulted.

The hosts' best chances come in the first half. Neil Ruddock steps up from the back at a corner-kick to glance a free header narrowly past Oakes' far post with 26 minutes gone and Frank Lampard screws his shot wide just before half-time, with a considerably better placed Berkovic left despairing behind him after Hartson had headed the ball into the box.

The game turns ragged after Ian Wright fires the ball into the net in the 77th minute, only to be adjudged to have handled as he drove into the penalty area. Justice for Villa but further disappointment for a West Ham team to whom some good news wouldn't go amiss.

Tuesday 20th October 1998 • Estadio de Balaídos • 8.15pm

RC CELTA VIGO 0 ASTON VILLA 1

Half-time 0-1 • Attendance 30,000

Referee Oguz SARVAN

Referee's Assistants A. UGURDUN and H. DARICI

Officials from Turkey

Sky Blue Shirts, Dark Blue Shorts	Goals	Claret and Blue Shirts, White Shorts	Goals
1 Richard DUTRUEL		13 Michael OAKES	
2 Michel SALGADO		2 Gary CHARLES	
4 Fernando CACERES		3 Alan WRIGHT	
6 Iomar do Nascimento 'MAZINHO' (c)		4 Gareth SOUTHGATE (c)	
8 Valeri KARPIN #		5 Ugo EHIOGU	
9 Haim REVIVO †		8 Mark DRAPER ❏	
14 Luboslav PENEV		9 Stan COLLYMORE ❏	
19 Goran DJOROVIC		12 Julian JOACHIM	15
20 Alexandre MOSTOVOI		15 Gareth BARRY	
22 José María López 'JOSEMA' ‡		17 Lee HENDRIE	
23 Claude MAKELELE		20 Riccardo SCIMECA	

Substitutes		*Substitutes*	
3 Rafael BERGES		16 Simon GRAYSON	
5 Oscar VALES		18 Fabio FERRARESI	
7 TOMAS Hervás ‡62		22 Darius VASSELL	
10 Vladimir GUDELJ		23 David HUGHES	
11 Jorge CADETE #83		30 Adam RACHEL (Gk)	
13 José Manuel PINTO (Gk)			
18 Juan SANCHEZ †45		*Villa named only five subs for this game.*	

FACTFILE

Villa post back-to-back away wins in European competition for the first time since their European Cup-winning campaign... They have conceded one goal in their last nine hours of football... Julian Joachim's first goal for Villa in European competition... In his fourth European appearance, Michael Oakes is on the winning side for the first time.

Villa Euro stars stay on track

No-one can accuse Julian Joachim of not taking his chances. Even his manager admits the striker has done nothing to warrant his recent relegation to the substitutes bench, as competition for the two forwards' slots hots up, yet the former Leicester City man makes up for lost time with a vengeance in a ferocious away leg in north-west Spain.

Joachim grabs his third goal of the season just 15 minutes into the game, as Stan Collymore leaves his markers for dead with a burst of pace that takes him deep into Celta territory.

He slides the ball through to Joachim, who has just evaded the offside trap on the left. 'JJ' moves into the box and pushes the ball home off the body of Vigo keeper Richard Dutruel.

Appropriately enough for this part of the world, the goal is red rag to a bull. Celta, one of Spain's unsung teams who, like Villa, are riding unexpectedly high in their domestic league, had made a brisk start and merely redouble their efforts to get back on terms.

The result is a second half assault on the Villa goal which the visitors survive as much by luck as good judgment. For while no-one can question the Englishmen's efforts to protect their lead, a Celta side with its shooting boots on could have at least expected to end the game level. They make use of the space they keep finding in front of their visitors' back line and on several occasions see the whites of Michael Oakes' eyes. After 54 minutes, Gareth Southgate slices a clearance to Alexandre Mostovoi, who shoots over the bar from inside the penalty area.

Tomas Hervas peppers the vicinity of Oakes' goal throughout the second half without any joy and Ugo Ehiogu has to dive in with a timely block after a dummy and a backheel in Celta's

neatest move of the half, work a right wing cross over to Valeri Karpin with the goal in his sights.

Oakes tips a 30-yarder from Claude Makelele over the bar at the death, but it's Juan Sanchez who's left ruing his moment the most: eight minutes remain when a corner is headed down to him at the far post and he hooks his shot on the turn over the bar.

Villa, arguably, have earned the breaks. With Alan Thompson and Ian Taylor suspended, Riccardo Scimeca slots into midfield (and now needs only an appearance in the goalie's jersey to wrap up the season's 'Mr Versatility' award) while Mark Draper has to eschew his customary creative role for a tigerish display that Roy Keane would have been proud of.

His team has barely an attack worthy of the name in the second half, however, and this failure to break Celta's rhythm only increases the Spaniards' momentum.

With former Brazilian World Cup player Mazinho orchestrating from the back and wing-back Michel Salgado giving Gareth Barry headaches down the flank, Celta serve ample notice over 90 minutes that this tie is far from over.

Valiant Villa can be rightly proud of an excellent result, while their opponents are entitled to think they won't be so wasteful of opportunity when the teams reconvene at Villa Park.

Mark Draper threads his way between Tomas and Mazinho.

Saturday 24th October 1998 • Villa Park • 3.00pm

ASTON VILLA 1 LEICESTER CITY 1

Half-time 0-1 • *Attendance* 39,241

Referee Keith BURGE (Tonypandy)

Referee's Assistants M. RYAN and R. BURTON

Claret and Blue Shirts, White Shorts		Goals
13	Michael OAKES	
2	Gary CHARLES †	
3	Alan WRIGHT	
4	Gareth SOUTHGATE (c)	
5	Ugo EHIOGU ❑	68
7	Ian TAYLOR	
9	Stan COLLYMORE	
10	Paul MERSON ‡	
11	Alan THOMPSON	
15	Gareth BARRY	
17	Lee HENDRIE	
Substitutes		
6	Steve WATSON ‡83	
8	Mark DRAPER	
12	Julian JOACHIM †62	
16	Simon GRAYSON	
30	Adam RACHEL (Gk)	

Blue Shirts, Blue Shorts		Goals
1	Kasey KELLER	
3	Frank SINCLAIR	
6	Mustafa IZZET	
7	Neil LENNON ❑	
9	Emile HESKEY	
11	Steve GUPPY	
14	Robbie SAVAGE	
18	Matt ELLIOTT (c)	
19	Robert ULLATHORNE ❑	
27	Tony COTTEE	36
37	Theo ZAGORAKIS †	
Substitutes		
5	Steve WALSH	
10	Garry PARKER	
21	Graham FENTON	
22	Pegguy ARPHEXAD (Gk)	
25	Stuart WILSON †83	

BEFORE		P	W	D	L	F	A	pts
1	Villa	9	6	3	0	10	2	21
11	Leicester	9	3	3	3	9	9	12

AFTER		P	W	D	L	F	A	pts
1	Villa	10	6	4	0	11	3	22
12	Leicester	10	3	4	3	10	10	13

FACTFILE

Ugo Ehiogu's first goal since 22nd November 1997 (2-1 v Everton)...
Villa equal their highest home crowd of season so far...
First score-draw of season... Steve Watson makes debut as sub.

Ehiogu goal keeps Villa unbeaten

Something old, something new, something borrowed and something blue make up a Midlands derby which ends more satisfactorily for Villa than had seemed likely at half-time.

The old is a winless record against the blue shirts of Leicester that now runs to seven games. The new is Villa trailing in a Premiership game for the first time this season, following a Tony Cottee goal. The borrowed is an equaliser from occasional goalscorer Ugo Ehiogu, whose first goal in 42 outings bears witness to a Villa team that may have left some of its vigour behind on the Spanish coast but whose reserves of character remain undiminished.

Ugo's thumping header reveals a rare chink in a Leicester defence which for much of the contest looks like a mirror image of its Villa counterpart. To see their opponents, particularly the magnificent Matt Elliott, get a foot or head in the way of every Villa attack is a bitter taste of their own medicine for the Premiership leaders and a far cry from their confident start in torrential rain which gave every indication that Leicester would be worn down and picked off.

Kasey Keller has a case of the jitters when a 19th-minute backpass stops like a turtle with air brakes on the sodden turf and Stan Collymore bears down. The American goalkeeper's clearance strikes Stan's back and ricochets upwards but Leicester clear when it returns to earth.

Gareth Barry confidently joins the attack and when City have two men booked inside a minute, mid-way through the first half, fortune's tide in this fixture appears to be set.

When you've just fended off Leeds United's overtures to your manager, though, coming to grips with an awkward away game is no big deal. Martin O'Neill's animated presence on the touchline has a talismanic quality for Leicester these days and gradually his team begin to find their feet.

In the 36th minute Theo Zagorakis collects a cross on the by-line and pulls it back for the evergreen Cottee to open the scoring.

In arrears for the first time since Strømsgodset were in town, Villa knuckle down resolutely to preserve their 100% home record, but as the second half progresses they lack width and pace and they look a team refreshed when the arrival of Julian Joachim introduces both commodities.

Once Ugo heads home Lee Hendrie's corner, it's Leicester's turn to dig deep. Emile Heskey's battering-ram presence means Gareth Southgate has his hands full but the clear cut openings are more often Villa's.

Crosses from Joachim and Merson are just beyond the reach of their team-mates and when Robert Ullathorne commits to a long ball out of the Villa defence but fails to connect, only Elliott, glued to Collymore all afternoon, denies the striker a shot on target.

Stan has the chance for redress with five minutes left when he is on the end of a Watson cross, but it's just too high for him to plunder the goal he deserves and give the Geordie a dream debut.

The final scoreline, though, does justice to both teams. Home draws can never be satisfactory to would-be champions, but this one comes closer than most.

Julian Joachim and Theo Zagorakis.

Wednesday 28th October 1998 • Stamford Bridge • 7.45pm

CHELSEA 4 ASTON VILLA 1

Half-time 1-1 • Attendance 26,790

Referee Graham BARBER (Tring)

Referee's Assistants L.C. JONES and M. TINGEY

Blue Shirts, Blue Shorts	Goals	Claret and Blue Shirts, White Shorts	Goals
23 Dmitri KHARINE		13 Michael OAKES	
2 Dan PETRESCU ❑ ‡		2 Gary CHARLES #	
3 Celestine BABAYARO		3 Alan WRIGHT ‡	
8 Gustavo POYET		5 Ugo EHIOGU (c)	
9 Gianluca VIALLI ❑ # 32,67,85		6 Steve WATSON	
11 Dennis WISE ■88		7 Ian TAYLOR ❑	
12 Michael DUBERRY ❑		8 Mark DRAPER	10
19 Tore Andre FLO	71	12 Julian JOACHIM	
21 Bernard LAMBOURDE		16 Simon GRAYSON	
22 Mark NICHOLLS †		20 Riccardo SCIMECA †	
28 Jody MORRIS		21 Darren BYFIELD	
Substitutes		*Substitutes*	
13 Kevin HITCHCOCK (Gk)		11 Alan THOMPSON †57 ❑	
25 Gianfranco ZOLA		22 Darius VASSELL #75	
26 John TERRY ‡85		28 Tommy JASZCZUN ‡73	
27 Jon HARLEY #90		30 Adam RACHEL (Gk)	
29 Neil CLEMENT †76		31 Jlloyd SAMUEL	

Villa's first defeat in 16 matches (1-3 v Bolton 25th April)... Their first loss away since 3rd March (0-1 v Atlético Madrid)... They concede their greatest number of goals in a game since 17th January (0-5 v Blackburn Rovers)... Ugo Ehiogu dons the captain's armband... Draper's first goal since his brace against Spurs last Boxing Day... Villa go out of this competition at the first time of asking for the second straight year... Three days later, the return match in the Premiership is washed out thanks to a waterlogged pitch.

FACTFILE

Unbeaten record bites the dust

The District Line tube-trains may rumble all the way down to Wimbledon but on this occasion it's all change at Fulham Broadway as Chelsea and Aston Villa muster 14 team alterations between them at Stamford Bridge.

If it's another snub to an ailing competition, no-one can say Villa's unbeaten record this season ended on a tame note. Having taken the lead with a Mark Draper free-kick after nine minutes, the visitors are dismantled by a Gianluca Vialli hat-trick before Dennis Wise comes within inches of doing the same to Darren Byfield's ankles, earning himself a red card and ushering in a tempestuous ending to the game.

It's a confident performance by the Blues, but their unnecessary expenditure of emotion in the closing stages is not exactly the mark of a team that is quietly digging itself in for the long haul, and league-leaders Villa could be excused for focussing less intently on the blue shirts next time they look over their shoulder.

With the evening's complement of goals complete, Chelsea's Dan Petrescu had already left the field in a titanic rage at being substituted when Wise launches a two-footed tackle at Byfield in the closing minutes.

A clamorous inquest quickly convenes at the scene of the crime and Vialli, anxious that the Villa bench doesn't miss out, detaches himself to berate Villa physio Jim Walker in the dug-out.

The Italian is no less menacing in Dr Jekyll mode and with Steve Watson in the starting line-up and Simon Grayson coming into the middle of defence, Villa's back line inadvertently becomes the front row at a striker's masterclass.

If slotting home a pass from Bernard Lambourde after Ugo Ehiogu failed to clear, is all in a day's work for the Chelsea player-manager, his ability to make space and then ruthlessly exploit it are there for all to see as he adds the second and third instalments of Chelsea's first hat-trick of the season in the second half.

In between, Tore Andre Flo cashes in with a free header from a Wise free-kick after 69 minutes and only a superb save at full stretch by Michael Oakes prevents the Norwegian from collecting his second.

The Villa goalkeeper had kept out a Gustavo Poyet header as the striker crept in between two markers in the game's opening stages but he previously needed the bar to deny the same man, having parried a shot from Flo to Poyet's feet.

It turns out to be third time unlucky for Gustavo when Villa get one of their few sights of goal in the first half after Darren Byfield is fouled by Wise. Draper's free-kick finds a certain Uruguayan's head in the defensive wall and Poyet's deflection sends the ball unerringly into the top corner of the net.

It is one crumb of comfort for Villa, the other being that if you must lose heavily to the Blues, the SW6 version is the preferred option.

Following the game, John Gregory is quick to ensure that any seeds of doubt don't have the chance to put down roots. "It will be a totally different game on Saturday," he vows.

Fateful words, as it turns out.

Mark Draper – his free-kick put Villa into the lead.

Tuesday 3rd November 1998 • Villa Park • 7.45pm

ASTON VILLA 1 RC CELTA VIGO 3

Aggregate score 3-2 to Celta Vigo
Half-time 1-2 • Attendance 29,910
Referee Amand ANCION
Referee's Assistants H. KUMS and L.M. PAUL
Officials from Belgium

Claret and Blue Shirts, Blue Shorts		Goals	Sky Blue Shirts, White Shorts		Goals
13	Michael OAKES		1	Richard DUTRUEL	
2	Gary CHARLES †		2	Michel SALGADO ❑	
3	Alan WRIGHT		3	Rafael BERGES (c) ❑ ■57	
4	Gareth SOUTHGATE (c)		4	Fernando CACERES	
5	Ugo EHIOGU		6	Iomar do Nascimento 'MAZINHO' (c)	
7	Ian TAYLOR ❑		8	Valeri KARPIN ‡	
9	Stan COLLYMORE	29pen	14	Luboslav PENEV ❑ #	48
11	Alan THOMPSON #		18	Juan SANCHEZ †	26
12	Julian JOACHIM		19	Goran DJOROVIC	
15	Gareth BARRY ❑ ‡		20	Alexandre MOSTOVOI	34
17	Lee HENDRIE ❑		23	Claude MAKELELE	
	Substitutes			*Substitutes*	
8	Mark DRAPER †45 ❑		5	Oscar VALES	
16	Simon GRAYSON #82		7	TOMAS Hervás ‡68	
21	Darren BYFIELD		10	Vladimir GUDELJ	
22	Darius VASSELL ‡63		11	Jorge CADETE #76	
28	Tommy JASZCZUN		13	José Manuel PINTO (Gk)	
30	Adam RACHEL (Gk)		16	Dan EGGEN †58	
	Villa named only six subs for this game.		22	José María López 'JOSEMA'	

Back-to-back defeats for first time since February and first time in John Gregory's reign... Villa bow out in second round for fifth time in last seven UEFA Cup campaigns... First home defeat since Bolton (25th April), last team to score three at Villa Park... Collymore one goal shy of matching Villa's all-time individual scoring record in a European campaign (5: Gary Shaw and John Deehan).

FACTFILE

Lesson in poise from silky Celta

For the second time in a row, the home leg of Villa's UEFA Cup commitments provides a reminder that winning football matches isn't as easy as it may appear from a glance at the Premiership table.

This time, however, there is no late salvation. Celta Vigo are no Strømsgodset: slick and composed, they have the measure of their hosts the moment Lubo Penev puts them 3-1 ahead on the night just three minutes after the interval, and not even the sending off of their captain Rafael Berges eight minutes later can ruffle their feathers. The only consequence of Berges' departure, following a second bookable offence, is to diminish Villa's sense of injustice from the first half.

Stan Collymore had been perplexed to see his fourth minute header into the net from a Julian Joachim cross ruled offside, but that became a minor quibble when Celta's Juan Sanchez was allowed to open the scoring from what looked a far more clear-cut offside position after 25 minutes.

Eight minutes later, the Belgian referee's apparent aversion to physical contact had been displayed to ruinous effect when Ugo Ehiogu was whistled for an innocuous challenge just outside Villa's box. Alexandre Mostovoi, tormenting Villa this night just as he had in Spain, curled his free-kick around the right hand side of the wall and beyond Michael Oakes' reach.

Coming barely four minutes after a Stan Collymore penalty for a handball by

Mazinho looked to have steadied the boat, Mostovoi's goal boosts his side, whose first leg waywardness in front of goal is now history.

Alan Thompson deserves better luck when he worms his way into the Vigo box in the 55th minute, only for his shot to rebound from the post, straight to goalkeeper Richard Dutruel.

Collymore alone seems to possess the knack for the unexpected that flat-foots Celta's otherwise unflappable ten-man defence. He is beginning to impose himself on a game again instead of merely taking part.

This trait seems to suffuse the entire Villa team in the early stages, as they confidently stroke the ball around. Whether their decline is down to well-organised opponents or the demoralising unpredictability of the referee, will be this game's eternal enigma.

Defeat could have become embarrassment early in the second half, for after Oakes can only parry a Sanchez header to Penev for Celta's third goal, an error by Gareth Southgate lets in Mostovoi, only for his shot to be deflected for a corner.

Celta's rearguard action after the sending-off is conducted with rather more aplomb than Villa's salvage operation and two clearances in the vicinity of the goal-line from efforts by Collymore and Ehiogu are as close as the home side come.

"There's nothing about Celta I envy," John Gregory says afterwards. "They looked better-balanced and kept the ball better than us, but then we kept possession better in Spain than we did tonight. We worked hard to get into this competition and it's a disappointing end to what could have been a glorious night."

Alan Thompson – hit the post.

Saturday 7th November 1998 • Villa Park • 3.00pm

ASTON VILLA 3 TOTTENHAM HOTSPUR 2

Half-time 2-0 • Attendance 39,241

Referee Rob HARRIS (Oxford)

Referee's Assistants G. ATKINS and M. NORTH

Claret and Blue Shirts, White Shorts		Goals	White Shirts, Dark Blue Shorts		Goals
13	Michael OAKES		13	Espen BAARDSEN	
3	Alan WRIGHT		2	Stephen CARR	
4	Gareth SOUTHGATE (c)		6	Allan NIELSEN	
5	Ugo EHIOGU ❏		7	Ruel FOX ‡	
6	Steve WATSON		9	Darren ANDERTON	62pen
7	Ian TAYLOR ❏		12	Justin EDINBURGH †	
9	Stan COLLYMORE	47	14	David GINOLA ❏	
10	Paul MERSON		17	John SCALES	
14	Dion DUBLIN ❏ †	30,34	18	Steffen IVERSEN	
15	Gareth BARRY		23	Sol CAMPBELL (c)	
17	Lee HENDRIE		25	Stephen CLEMENCE #	
Substitutes			*Substitutes*		
8	Mark DRAPER †81		1	Ian WALKER (Gk)	
11	Alan THOMPSON		15	Ramon VEGA †45	75
12	Julian JOACHIM		20	Jose DOMINGUEZ	
16	Simon GRAYSON		21	Rory ALLEN #82	
30	Adam RACHEL (Gk)		22	Andy SINTON ‡45	

BEFORE	P	W	D	L	F	A	pts	AFTER	P	W	D	L	F	A	pts
1 Villa	10	6	4	0	11	3	22	1 Villa	11	7	4	0	14	5	25
9 Spurs	11	4	3	4	14	18	15	14 Spurs	12	4	3	5	16	21	15

FACTFILE

Dion Dublin enjoys most productive Villa debut since Stuart Gray scored twice in 4-2 win over Bradford City on 28th November 1987... The last three Villa v Spurs matches have produced 15 goals... Their eleventh league game unbeaten since the season began equals the all-time club record set in 1932-33.

Dion wins his Spurs on debut

He doesn't have the golden goal ticket and his head isn't circled in the 'Face in the Crowd' competition, but otherwise Dion Dublin dominates the game in his first day on duty for Aston Villa.

Not-so-proud owner of the quickest booking in the season so far, his foul incurring the referee's wrath after just 80 seconds, the £5.75m signing makes reparation with two goals and a third that's disallowed, to clear the UEFA Cup cobwebs and make it clear to George Graham that New Spurs, like Rome, won't be built in a day.

When Stan Collymore caps a bustling performance with his first Premiership goal this season to put the home side 3-0 up after 47 minutes, a rout is in the offing, with Spurs' defence turning in a performance almost worthy of charitable status.

The Londoners' resilience will go some way to soothing their new manager's disappointment, though. A Darren Anderton penalty and a Ramon Vega prod from a corner turn what should have been a stroll for Villa into a sweat.

A factor in this may be the re-jig that sees Paul Merson playing just behind Collymore and Dublin. If it lends Villa fluidity up front, it leaves the midfield thin and the engine room is high on effort but low on creativity.

Not that they need it today, for Tottenham are the soul of generosity. No matter how well-drilled a team may be in the offside trap, its inherent wafer-thin margin of error means that doom is never far off, and for all the ironic cheers as George Graham's latest defence steps forward with arms aloft and faces turned plaintively towards the linesmen, there are early signs that Tony Adams shouldn't start eating his heart out just yet.

It lends an air of inevitability to the opening goal. Spurs fail to clear a corner-kick on the half-hour and John Scales knocks the ball into the path of Dublin, who opens his Villa account from close-range.

This is merely the warm-up for the vaudeville which leads to his second just four minutes later, when one Tottenham player is caught tying his boot as a pass comes his way and then two more decide to leave the ball to each other. It rolls unhindered into Dublin's path and he takes it into the box before sliding it home.

Tottenham's best chances of the first half – a header flicked over the bar by Iversen, who later screws wide a promising rebound when Oakes saves from Ginola – appear academic when Collymore steals a yard on Sol Campbell two minutes into the second half to gather a Hendrie cross which he thunders home despite Campbell's desperate attempts to intervene.

Unbelievably, Spurs regain a stake in the contest when Ginola goes down over Ugo Ehiogu's outstretched leg and Darren Anderton converts from the penalty spot with 62 minutes gone.

15 minutes remain when Iversen flicks on a corner for Vega to sidefoot home and Villa's disbelief is compounded a minute later when an offside flag denies Dublin his hat-trick.

His team can't be denied their win, though. The great 1970 Brazilian side took the view that goals against were irrelevant as long as they went one better at the other end, a philosophy for which Villa suddenly look handsomely equipped.

Dion Dublin celebrates his first goal for Villa.

Saturday 14th November 1998 • The Dell • 3.00pm

SOUTHAMPTON 1 ASTON VILLA 4

Half-time 0-1 • Attendance 15,242

Referee Neale BARRY (Scunthorpe)

Referee's Assistants K. PIKE and P.V. NORMAN

Red and White Striped Shirts, Black Shorts		Goals	Claret and Blue Shirts, White Shorts		Goals
1	Paul JONES		13	Michael OAKES	
2	Jason DODD (c)		3	Alan WRIGHT	
4	Carlton PALMER		4	Gareth SOUTHGATE (c)	
5	Claus LUNDEKVAM †		5	Ugo EHIOGU	
6	Ken MONKOU		6	Steve WATSON	
7	Matthew LE TISSIER ❏ ‡	53	7	Ian TAYLOR	
8	Matthew OAKLEY		9	Stan COLLYMORE ❏ †	
10	Egil ØSTENSTAD		10	Paul MERSON ‡	77
14	Stuart RIPLEY		14	Dion DUBLIN	2,56,85
15	Francis BENALI		15	Gareth BARRY	
23	Scott HILEY		17	Lee HENDRIE	
	Substitutes			*Substitutes*	
12	Richard DRYDEN		8	Mark DRAPER †79	
13	Neil MOSS (Gk)		11	Alan THOMPSON	
16	James BEATTIE †45		12	Julian JOACHIM ‡83	
21	Andy WILLIAMS ‡76		16	Simon GRAYSON	
30	Hassan KACHLOUL		30	Adam RACHEL (Gk)	

BEFORE		P	W	D	L	F	A	pts	AFTER		P	W	D	L	F	A	pts
1	Villa	11	7	4	0	14	5	25	1	Villa	12	8	4	0	18	6	28
20	Saints	12	1	4	7	9	26	7	20	Saints	13	1	4	8	10	30	7

FACTFILE

Twelve games unbeaten, the best Villa start to a League campaign ever... John Gregory has a special team photo taken afterwards to record the event... Dion Dublin makes it five goals in two games... Villa's fourth straight league win at the Dell... Villa's first goal is only their second from a header all season.

History is made at The Dell

The most successful start to an Aston Villa League campaign is eventually achieved in some style but not without a little drama along the way.

A Dion Dublin hat-trick and a superb team goal finished by Paul Merson are punctuated by a vintage cameo from Matt Le Tissier that leaves the visitors briefly rocking at 1-1 against a struggling team driven on by desperation.

When Ugo Ehiogu slices a clearance against his own crossbar at 1-1, Villa's wheels seem to be coming off, yet that escape is in fact the turning point. Dublin nets his second goal two minutes later and Saints have no stomach for another come-back.

For all the party line about 'no easy games at this level', Southampton's defence against Villa's attack is a mismatch, the Saints heavy-footed and pedestrian against their sophisticated opponents. When Dublin has time to pick his spot with a header at just two minutes after three, the game has the makings of a contest every bit as one-way as its bottom v top status would suggest.

Aided by some useful crosses from Steve Watson, Villa have the aerial battle to themselves, although it's a low cross from Paul Merson that Southampton keeper Paul Jones just reaches in the 11th minute before an unmarked Dublin can pounce.

The home team begins to gain momentum as the midway point of the first half arrives. Stuart Ripley enjoys some freedom on the right, but his crosses don't always match his pace.

While Le Tissier seems to become increasingly discouraged as the game wears on, you ignore him at your peril and it needs a fine block by Oakes to deny him after Ken Monkou touches on a Hiley cross. The Villa goalkeeper is pressed into action shortly afterwards, when Saints captain Jason Dodd is on target from long-range.

Dodd reverts from midfield into his more customary defensive role after the interval, following the departure of the injured Claus Lundekvam, and Le Tissier puts Southampton level in the 53rd minute. Collecting the ball in Villa's penalty area, the former England player drags Southgate one way and then the next before firing home a low angled shot.

It is the start of the game's brief decisive stretch. Two minutes later, Ehiogu's blushes are spared by the woodwork and soon afterwards, a tussle between Hendrie and Monkou sends the ball into the path of Dublin, whose instinctive shot curls into the bottom right-hand corner from outside the box.

Such is Dion's domination that Villa can afford a peripheral game from Stan Collymore, although Dublin spurns a one-on-one with Jones in the 70th minute as the game becomes wide-open.

Twice, Ehiogu denies the promising James Beattie in the air before Gareth Barry finds Collymore with a diagonal cross-field ball. Stan crosses it from the right and Merson sweeps home the *coup de grâce* in an end-to-end manoeuvre that has lasted a matter of seconds.

While Saints' substitute Andy Williams adds a late spark to Southampton's forward line, Villa are home and Dublin's third goal, prodding home a nod down from a Hendrie corner, is merely window-dressing.

Having a ball – Dublin claims his hat-trick prize.

Saturday 21st November 1998 • Villa Park • 3.00pm

ASTON VILLA 2 LIVERPOOL 4

Half-time 0-2 • Attendance 39,241

Referee Peter JONES (Loughborough)

Referee's Assistants A. HOGG and D. BABSKI

Claret and Blue Shirts, White Shorts	Goals	White Shirts with Red Trim, White Shorts	Goals
13 Michael OAKES		1 David JAMES ❑	
3 Alan WRIGHT ‡		5 Steve STAUNTON	
4 Gareth SOUTHGATE (c)		6 Phil BABB ❑	
5 Ugo EHIOGU		9 Robbie FOWLER	7,58,66
6 Steve WATSON #		10 Michael OWEN ❑ #	
8 Mark DRAPER †		11 Jamie REDKNAPP ❑	
9 Stan COLLYMORE ❑ ■67		12 Steve HARKNESS †	
10 Paul MERSON		14 Vegard HEGGEM	
14 Dion DUBLIN	47,64	15 Patrik BERGER ‡	
15 Gareth BARRY		17 Paul INCE (c)	2
17 Lee HENDRIE		23 Jamie CARRAGHER	
Substitutes		*Substitutes*	
2 Gary CHARLES #87		4 Jason McATEER ‡65	
11 Alan THOMPSON †52		13 Karlheinz REIDLE #75	
12 Julian JOACHIM ‡75		19 Brad FRIEDEL (Gk)	
16 Simon GRAYSON		20 Stig Inge BJØRNEBYE †12	
30 Adam RACHEL (Gk)		25 David THOMPSON	

BEFORE	P	W	D	L	F	A	pts
1 Villa	12	8	4	0	18	6	28
12 Liverpool	13	4	4	5	20	17	16

AFTER	P	W	D	L	F	A	pts
1 Villa	13	8	4	1	20	10	28
9 Liverpool	14	5	4	5	24	19	19

FACTFILE

Villa's first reverse in the League since visitors Bolton Wanderers won 3-1 in April this year... First Villa sending off since Ugo Ehiogu dismissed against Arsenal on final day of last season... Most goals conceded in a home game since Blackburn Rovers won 4-0 on 13th August 1997.

Unbeaten run finally broken

The first of three daunting home games yields what looks like an emphatic defeat for Villa, yet the most exciting match of their season so far could easily have ended 5-4 in their favour.

That it ends 11-10 to Liverpool in terms of manpower is due to Stan Collymore being sent off after providing the sobering sub-plot to an afternoon of thrilling football.

The striker's claim that his ugly challenge early in the game was more about careless execution than malicious intent would have fallen on less-sceptical ears had the man stretchered off in consequence not been Steve Harkness.

The Liverpool defender was embroiled with Collymore in a racial abuse controversy last season and while Stan insists there was no element of pay-back in the foul, even his own manager isn't convinced.

It leaves Harkness with ligament damage when many feared a broken leg and Stan with a yellow card which could easily have been red. It turns out to be merely a stay of execution for the Villa striker, who departs in the 67th minute after responding to a reckless rap on the shin from Michael Owen by shoving him over.

Otherwise, it's a better day for strikers than backs. Seemingly anxious to eradicate three mediocre months in just 90 minutes, Liverpool tear into the Villa defence to go two up after seven minutes, courtesy of free headers by Paul Ince at a corner and Robbie Fowler escaping two defenders to convert a Jamie Redknapp cross. Villa must wait until shortly after the break to make inroads into the deficit, Jamie Carragher's slip in the area allowing Dion Dublin the time and space to hook a Steve Watson cross inside David James' near post in the 46th minute.

A driving run upfield by Vegard Heggem sets up Fowler to score with a first-time shot from the edge of the box 11 minutes later, but Villa get one last shot at saving the game when Dion makes it seven goals in three games, tapping home a low Collymore cross.

Fowler, however, is to be the last of the red-hot strikers. Not even Celta Vigo could match the pace with which he and Owen fracture Villa's defences and but for the identity of his victims, few would begrudge him his 14th goal in 11 games versus Villa, after a lengthy absence with a knee ligament injury.

Liverpool work space for Redknapp on the left and his cross finds an unmarked Fowler, who calmly completes his hat-trick.

Ah, but what might have been, even for a Villa side bleeding goals so freely. Two lunges at substitute Julian Joachim in the area yield but one penalty, which James saves at full length from Dublin. The latter clips a post when set up by Merson seven minutes before half-time and two minutes later, Stan Collymore heads agonisingly wide, just feet away from a gaping goal.

So Villa's unbeaten start to the league season stalls at game 13. "We lost it in the first seven minutes," muses John Gregory. "We went 1-0 down and tried to score two goals by five-past-three. You have to grind yourself back into the game. I was very proud of our second half, though; it was just a shame David James decided to have his best game of the season."

Stan Collymore fends off Jamie Carragher.

Saturday 28th November 1998 • City Ground • 3.00pm

NOTTINGHAM FOREST 2   ASTON VILLA 2

Half-time 2-0 • *Attendance* 25,753

Referee Gary WILLARD (Worthing)

Referee's Assistants P. VOSPER and I. BLANCHARD

Red Shirts, White Shorts	Goals	Turquoise Shirts with Black Trim, Black Shorts	Goals
1 Dave BEASANT		13 Michael OAKES	
4 Nigel QUASHIE ❑		3 Alan WRIGHT	
5 Steve CHETTLE (c)		4 Gareth SOUTHGATE (c) ❑	
6 Jon Olav HJELDE		5 Ugo EHIOGU	
7 Steve STONE		6 Steve WATSON	
8 Scot GEMMILL ❑ †		7 Ian TAYLOR	
11 Chris BART-WILLIAMS ❑ 32		10 Paul MERSON †	
14 Dougie FREEDMAN ‡ 44		12 Julian JOACHIM 58,64	
15 Craig ARMSTRONG		14 Dion DUBLIN	
17 Thierry BONALAIR		15 Gareth BARRY	
40 Pierre VAN HOOIJDONK ❑		17 Lee HENDRIE ❑	
Substitutes		*Substitutes*	
10 Andy JOHNSON †76		11 Alan THOMPSON †45	
13 Mark CROSSLEY (Gk)		16 Simon GRAYSON	
19 Jean-Claude DARCHEVILLE ‡84		20 Riccardo SCIMECA	
24 Christian EDWARDS		22 Darius VASSELL	
29 Marlon HAREWOOD		30 Adam RACHEL (Gk)	

BEFORE	P	W	D	L	F	A	pts	AFTER	P	W	D	L	F	A	pts
1 Villa	13	8	4	1	20	10	28	1 Villa	14	8	5	1	22	12	29
18 Forest	14	2	4	8	10	22	10	18 Forest	15	2	5	8	12	24	11

FACTFILE

Julian Joachim's first two-goal game in his Villa career... He'll hope to cement his place in the starting line-up when Collymore misses next game through suspension... Villa now embark on a three-game sequence that pits them against title rivals Manchester United, Chelsea and Arsenal.

Joachim frees a team in Notts

Cometh the hour, cometh the man... Julian Joachim is Villa's Mr Fixit once more as he salvages a point for Villa after they trailed 2-0.

Two opportunistic goals from the diminutive striker, standing in for a poorly Stan Collymore, are the pay-off for a half-time tactical switch that sees the visitors revert to a three-man midfield, a move they may well have considered even if Paul Merson hadn't hobbled out of the game at the interval with a back injury.

Sacrificing his role as a support player just behind the two strikers, John Gregory introduces substitute Alan Thompson in a deeper position and the extra man in midfield sounds the death knell for Nottingham's hopes.

Lee Hendrie and Ian Taylor might as well have been patrolling the Khyber Pass before the break, such is the extent to which they are swamped by a Forest midfield led by Scot Gemmill and Nigel Quashie.

It leaves the visiting defence exposed and after Pierre Van Hooijdonk misses a gilt-edged chance from a Steve Stone cross, Chris Bart Williams is the first to benefit, when he finds space on the left in the 32nd minute to score with a cross-shot from just outside the box.

The impressive Dougie Freedman makes it 2-0 from similar range, shortly before half-time, pulling away from his marker to convert a defence splitting pass from Van Hooijdonk.

In retrospect, the hosts could have done without half-time, which does for their afternoon what the midnight chimes did for Cinderella's evening.

Thompson, who admits afterwards that his recent relegation to the subs' bench was the 'kick up the backside' he needed, goes industriously about his duties and with Forest no longer defending in the same depth, Villa ease their way back into the contest.

It takes 14 minutes for their transformation to reach fruition. Steve Watson cuts into the penalty area but can only find a weak shot. Dave Beasant can't find a handle on the ball, however, and merely pushes it out to Joachim who tucks away his fourth goal of the season.

Forest have the chance to respond and put the game away within minutes, when Freedman breaks on the left but opts to shoot across the face of the goal while a team-mate is unmarked by the penalty spot.

Punishment is immediate, when a high foot from Joachim diverts Beasant's attention just enough for him to fluff a defender's backheader after Oakes' long kick. The Villa forward is first on the case as the ball breaks free and he pushes the ball into an open net.

Forest rally bravely but as they may have twigged by now, their luck is out. Van Hooijdonk, whose contribution to his team is inversely proportional to his popularity, sees

Making a point: Julian Joachim.

Gareth Barry block his header at the foot of the post in the final quarter of an hour and he strikes two impeccable 30-yard free kicks only for Oakes to get in the way of both of them.

The hitherto-prolific Dion Dublin has no such obstacles in his way when Alan Wright crosses in the dying seconds of the game, yet he somehow sends the ball wide with the goal at his mercy. '3-2 Villa' would have been nice but after this quintessential game of two halves, it wouldn't have been justice.

Saturday 5th December 1998 • Villa Park • 3.00pm

ASTON VILLA 1 MANCHESTER UNITED 1

Half-time 0-0 • Attendance 39,241

Referee Mike RILEY (Leeds)

Referee's Assistants K. HAWKES and J. ROSS

Claret and Blue Shirts, White Shorts	Goals	White Shirts with Black Trim, Black Shorts	Goals
13 Michael OAKES		1 Peter SCHMEICHEL	
3 Alan WRIGHT		2 Gary NEVILLE ❑	
4 Gareth SOUTHGATE (c)		3 Denis IRWIN ❑	
5 Ugo EHIOGU ❑		6 Jaap STAM	
6 Steve WATSON		7 David BECKHAM	
7 Ian TAYLOR		9 Andy COLE ‡	
11 Alan THOMPSON		15 Jesper BLOMQVIST †	
12 Julian JOACHIM	54	16 Roy KEANE (c)	
14 Dion DUBLIN		18 Paul SCHOLES	47
15 Gareth BARRY		19 Dwight YORKE ❑	
17 Lee HENDRIE		24 Wesley BROWN	
Substitutes		*Substitutes*	
16 Simon GRAYSON		5 Ronny JOHNSEN	
18 Fabio FERRARESI		8 Nicky BUTT ‡70	
22 Darius VASSELL		10 Teddy SHERINGHAM	
30 Adam RACHEL (Gk)		11 Ryan GIGGS †45	
32 Aaron LESCOTT		17 Raimond VAN DER GOUW (Gk)	

BEFORE		P	W	D	L	F	A	pts
1	Villa	14	8	5	1	22	12	29
2	United	14	8	4	2	30	16	28

AFTER		P	W	D	L	F	A	pts
1	Villa	15	8	6	1	23	13	30
2	United	15	8	5	2	31	17	29

FACTFILE

Julian Joachim overshadows the anticipated Dwight and Dion Show, scoring Villa's first goal against United in six games... Two goals in two games from Joachim, standing in for Stan Collymore, strengthen his claim to start against Chelsea... Alex Ferguson's first game without Brian Kidd at his side.

Joachim strikes for deserved point

In other circumstances, Julian Joachim might have looked a little sheepish. When a deflection off Denis Irwin's boot has transformed your low drive into a lob so deadly, not even Peter Schmeichel can find someone to blame as he retrieves the ball from the net, throwing your arms aloft and basking in the crowd's adulation wouldn't normally be the done thing.

To hell with that today, though. Joachim's 54th-minute stroke of fortune has levelled the score at 1-1 and never has the adage that good teams make their own luck seemed so valid.

A defence close to its miserly best is turning Dwight Yorke's return into a nightmare, an attack missing the injured Paul Merson and suspended Stan Collymore is matching United at every turn, and Alan Thompson, turning in the best performance of his Villa career to date, is denied only by the woodwork from a 25-yard free-kick just past the hour, the ball cannoning off the left-hand post of a helplessly stranded Peter Schmeichel.

At the start of a week that's tantamount to an MoT for Villa's title hopes, you'd be hard-pushed to find so much as a missing hubcap.

United today, Chelsea midweek, Arsenal next Sunday; nine days that should confirm John Gregory's men as pretenders or the real McCoy. Non-believers will have to reassemble at Stamford Bridge, however, for Alex Ferguson has rather more cause than Gregory to welcome the final whistle.

Villa spurn a chance to secure maximum points when Lee Hendrie and Ian Taylor get involved in a gentleman's excuse-me in the United penalty area following a brisk advance down the left flank after 22 minutes.

The duo's indecision as to who should apply the formality of the finishing touch, gives United's defence a precious split-second in which to clear, while a certain ex-Villan can only dream of such an opening.

The bleak mid-winter has arrived early for Dwight Yorke, who admits to being rattled by the ballyhoo surrounding his first appearance at Villa since he left for Old Trafford in August. There is little warmth in the welcome he receives from Villa fans and a visibly fired-up Ugo Ehiogu has suspended their friendship for 90 minutes as he leads a home defence hell-bent on preventing the nightmare scenario of a Yorke goal.

It adds up to an anonymous afternoon for Dwight, on the pitch he once regularly made his own personal fiefdom. With the more prominent Andy Cole similarly shackled once Gareth Barry clears his looping header off the line in the 25th minute, it's left to Paul Scholes to open United's account, two minutes into the second half.

Michael Oakes pushes away a cross from Cole, only for Scholes to bang home the rebound. To Villa's credit, however, it is the last effort of note their opponents enjoy for half an hour.

Joachim's pace and Thompson's zest leave United in backpedal mode for much of the second half, with a long-range Scholes effort eight minutes from time the visitors' sole riposte.

Julian Joachim levels the scores.

Wednesday 9th December 1998 • Stamford Bridge • 7.45pm

CHELSEA 2 ASTON VILLA 1

Half-time 1-1 • Attendance 34,765

Referee Alan WILKIE (Chester-le-Street)
Referee's Assistants G. BEALE and D.C. RICHARDS

Blue Shirts, Blue Shorts	Goals	Claret and Blue Shirts, White Shorts	Goals
1 Ed DE GOEY		13 Michael OAKES	
2 Dan PETRESCU		3 Alan WRIGHT	
3 Celestine BABAYARO ‡		4 Gareth SOUTHGATE (c)	
5 Frank LEBOEUF (c)		5 Ugo EHIOGU	
6 Marcel DESAILLY		6 Steve WATSON	
9 Gianluca VIALLI ❑		7 Ian TAYLOR	
12 Michael DUBERRY		11 Alan THOMPSON ❑	
14 Graeme LE SAUX		12 Julian JOACHIM †	
16 Roberto DI MATTEO ❑		14 Dion DUBLIN ❑	
17 Albert FERRER		15 Gareth BARRY ❑	
25 Gianfranco ZOLA †	29	17 Lee HENDRIE ❑	32
Substitutes		*Substitutes*	
8 Gustavo POYET ‡80		2 Gary CHARLES	
11 Dennis WISE		9 Stan COLLYMORE †83 ❑	
13 Kevin HITCHCOCK (Gk)		16 Simon GRAYSON	
19 Tore Andre FLO †67	90	32 Aaron LESCOTT	
21 Bernard LAMBOURDE		40 Matthew GHENT (Gk)	

BEFORE		P	W	D	L	F	A	pts
1	Villa	15	8	6	1	23	13	30
7	Chelsea	14	6	7	1	22	13	25

AFTER		P	W	D	L	F	A	pts
1	Villa	16	8	6	2	24	15	30
3	Chelsea	15	7	7	1	24	14	28

FACTFILE

Villa's 'week of destiny' turns sour with just one point from two games...
First away defeat in the Premiership since John Gregory became manager...
Tore Andre Flo finds the net for the third time in four games against Villa...
Lee Hendrie's first goal in 16 games.

Beaten by late, late Flo goal

Home life can't be easy for Tore Andre Flo this season. With his girlfriend being a Villa fan, you probably need an ice-pick to crack the frosty silences at dinner *chez* Flo, after his goal against the claret and blue in the Worthington Cup and now a far more significant strike to break a 1-1 Premiership deadlock deep into injury time.

Hanging on like novice surfers in the face of a relentless blue tide, Villa's rearguard action has become worth a point for its sheer longevity, when Frank Leboeuf heads on Roberto Di Matteo's 94th-minute corner kick and Flo heads home above the flailing arms of Michael Oakes.

For Chelsea, it's a fitting reward at the end of a second half that they had comfortably won on points, although fate looked to have decreed a draw when Graeme Le Saux's shot in the 90th minute hit the inside of the post yet somehow bounced back into play.

No such problems with the laws of physics for Gianfranco Zola an hour earlier. He has pace and swerve in perfect unison when his free-kick from the edge of the box opens Chelsea's account after Gareth Southgate had brought down Di Matteo.

Villa have a response every bit as sophisticated just 90 seconds later, however, Lee Hendrie twisting and turning on a sixpence before drilling home a low shot past Ed De Goey.

Despite the scoreline, the hosts already have the run of play at this stage, even though there's a defensive look to their midfield unit of Dan Petrescu, Di Matteo, Marcel Desailly and Celestine Babayaro.

Thanks to Julian Joachim's pace, however, Villa are dangerous on the break on the few occasions when they manage to clear their lines. The striker has a chance to give them the lead in the 10th minute, when he shoots wide with just De Goey to beat after being sent clear by Dion Dublin.

It is a morsel of comfort, as Chelsea show every sign of continuing where they left off in October's 4-1 Worthington Cup win. Hat-trick hero that night, Gianluca Vialli torments Villa anew, volleying wide and then bringing a fine save out of Michael Oakes just before half-time.

It's useful practice for the young goalkeeper, who comes under attack from more Europeans than Margaret Thatcher after the interval.

Villa are already digging-in in earnest by the time Leboeuf hits the bar with a header from a Di Matteo corner in the 58th minute, then substitute Flo announces his arrival with a cross to the Spaniard Albert Ferrer, who warms Oakes' fingers with a shot from the edge of the box.

Di Matteo's 25-yard effort is pushed aside before Gustavo Poyet adds a Latin-American dimension to the barrage, his overhead kick being tipped away by Oakes. That merely sets up Di Matteo's telling corner, however, and another passing cloud over Tore Andre Flo's love life.

Smart work from Lee Hendrie tied the scores.

Sunday 13th December 1998 • Villa Park • 3.00pm

ASTON VILLA 3 ARSENAL 2

Half-time 0-2 • Attendance 39,217

Referee Stephen LODGE (Barnsley)

Referee's Assistants D. DRYSDALE and M. TINGEY

Claret and Blue Shirts, White Shorts	Goals	Yellow Shirts with Navy Blue Trim, Navy Blue Shorts	Goals
13 Michael OAKES		1 David SEAMAN	
3 Alan WRIGHT ❑		2 Lee DIXON ❑	
4 Gareth SOUTHGATE (c) ❑		4 Patrick VIEIRA	
5 Ugo EHIOGU		5 Steve BOULD (c)	
6 Steve WATSON		7 Nelson VIVAS	
7 Ian TAYLOR		8 Fredrik LJUNGBERG ❑ †	
11 Alan THOMPSON ❑		9 Nicolas ANELKA	
12 Julian JOACHIM ‡	62	10 Dennis BERGKAMP ❑	14,45
14 Dion DUBLIN	65,83	11 Marc OVERMARS	
15 Gareth BARRY †		14 Martin KEOWN	
17 Lee HENDRIE		15 Ray PARLOUR ‡	
Substitutes		*Substitutes*	
2 Gary CHARLES		12 Christopher WREH	
9 Stan COLLYMORE †53		13 Alex MANNINGER (Gk)	
16 Simon GRAYSON ‡86		18 Gilles GRIMANDI †67	
22 Darius VASSELL		20 Matthew UPSON	
40 Matthew GHENT (Gk)		21 Luis BOA MORTE ‡89	

BEFORE	P	W	D	L	F	A	pts	AFTER	P	W	D	L	F	A	pts
1 Villa	16	8	6	2	24	15	30	1 Villa	17	9	6	2	27	17	33
5 Arsenal	16	6	8	2	15	7	26	6 Arsenal	17	6	8	3	17	10	26

FACTFILE

Villa's first win in four matches... They lead the Premiership again, 24 hours after Manchester United knocked them off the top for the first time since 12th September... Dion Dublin now has nine goals in seven games...Villa remain unbeaten in their last eight games against the Gunners (all competitions).

Gunners suffer second half blitz

There are countless turning points in the season for any Championship-winning side, but if Villa are in that enviable position come next Spring, you fancy this one will take some beating.

Dr Jekyll to Mr Hyde was a subtle mood-swing in comparison to Villa's half-time transformation from timid forelock-tuggers to the swaggering dictators who overturn a 2-0 half-time deficit against the reigning champions.

Rising to the occasion is Dion Dublin, who after three games without a goal, reinforces his credentials as the man for a crisis with two goals, after Julian Joachim begins the fight-back.

Credit is also due to substitute Stan Collymore, who rattles the Gunners' serene defence in the same way as he made Celta Vigo earn their crust here a month earlier. This time, however, the waves he makes have goals at the end of them. His flick to Lee Hendrie sets up the midfielder for a square pass across the Arsenal area to Joachim, whose coolly stroked goal from the outside of his boot belies the hour of Villa trepidation that preceded it.

Hendrie has an effort well saved at the foot of his post by Dave Seaman before Dublin takes centre stage in the 65th minute.

An attempted shot by Alan Thompson is going well wide until Dublin's leg intervenes to stab the equaliser past Seaman amid unheeded calls for offside from the visitors' defence.

It is a far cry from the first half, when a passive Villa side were outrun and out-thought by an Arsenal team supposedly suffering its own crisis of confidence in recent weeks.

Thirteen minutes have elapsed when a Nicolas Anelka header puts Dennis Bergkamp through on the right and he forces an angled shot past Michael Oakes into the far corner from the edge of the box.

Villa spend the rest of the half plotting their response, but with Dublin's preference for attacking from deep positions leaving Joachim isolated, they lack the ideas and the options to trouble their opponents.

The chants for Stan have already begun when Anelka takes the ball to the byeline before slotting a pass back into the path of Bergkamp whose first-time shot finds the target on the stroke of half-time.

A parachute drop during the interval goes horribly wrong when one of the parachutists, Flt.-Sgt Nigel Rogoff, has problems with his approach and collides with the roof of the Trinity Road Stand before falling to the ground, sustaining serious injuries. It puts a dampener on the afternoon for players and spectators alike, but Villa's professionalism sees them mentally regroup to take the game by the throat.

The Gunners rally briefly at 2-2, Bergkamp forcing a good save from Oakes from a free-kick on the edge of the area and Parlour shooting just wide of the far post on a counter-attack.

An extraordinary afternoon reaches an extraordinary climax with seven minutes left, however, Dion Dublin finding himself in space unheard of in an Arsenal penalty area as an Alan Thompson corner drops at his feet. When your price-tag says '£5.75m', you don't miss from there. Now how does that 'Great Escape' theme go again?

Dion Dublin beats David Seaman to score the winner.

Monday 21st December 1998 • The Valley • 8.00pm

CHARLTON ATHLETIC 0 ASTON VILLA 1

Half-time 0-1 • Attendance 20,043

Referee Steve DUNN (Bristol)

Referee's Assistants M. CAIRNS and M. SHORT

Red Shirts, White Shorts		Goals
1	Sasa ILIC	
2	Danny MILLS ▢	
3	Chris POWELL	
4	Neil REDFEARN	
5	Richard RUFUS	3og
7	Shaun NEWTON †	
8	Mark KINSELLA (c)	
9	Andy HUNT	
11	John ROBINSON	
19	Steve JONES ▢	
23	Carl TILER ▢	
	Substitutes	
10	Clive MENDONCA †70	
12	Steve BROWN	
15	Keith JONES	
26	Paul KONCHESKY	
28	Simon ROYCE (Gk)	

Turquoise Shirts with Black Trim, Black Shorts		Goals
13	Michael OAKES	
3	Alan WRIGHT	
4	Gareth SOUTHGATE (c)	
5	Ugo EHIOGU	
6	Steve WATSON ▢	
7	Ian TAYLOR ▢	
9	Stan COLLYMORE †	
11	Alan THOMPSON ▢	
12	Julian JOACHIM	
14	Dion DUBLIN	
17	Lee HENDRIE	
	Substitutes	
2	Gary CHARLES	
16	Simon GRAYSON	
20	Riccardo SCIMECA †55	
22	Darius VASSELL	
30	Adam RACHEL (Gk)	

BEFORE	P	W	D	L	F	A	pts
1 Villa	17	9	6	2	27	17	33
16 Charlton	17	3	7	7	22	27	16

AFTER	P	W	D	L	F	A	pts
1 Villa	18	10	6	2	28	17	36
16 Charlton	18	3	7	8	22	28	16

FACTFILE

At half-time referee Steve Dunn, who suffered hamstring damage, is replaced by Gary Willard, the fourth official... Villa's first clean sheet since winning at Celta Vigo on 20th October... Their first back-to-back wins for five weeks... Victory takes them back to the top of the Premiership, three points clear of Chelsea.

Festive cheer the hard way

The headline writers must hold off with their 'Christmas Cracker' standby until Boxing Day, as Villa and Charlton Athletic grind out a mundane affair at the Valley, two very different ships passing in the night.

For the visitors, a Richard Rufus own goal after three minutes is the kind of break you get when you lead the Premiership. For Charlton, their season heading south after a promising start, it is further proof that it never rains but it pours.

Dion Dublin collects a long ball out of defence from Gareth Southgate and sends in a low cross from the bye-line to the right of the goal. There aren't many team-mates in the box, but Rufus' right thigh is enough, a glancing contact angling the ball beyond the reach of goalkeeper Sasa Ilic.

Confirmation that Charlton's rut is indeed a valley arrives just three minutes later. Winless in all but one of their last eight Premiership games, their forward Steve Jones flops to the floor inside Villa's area after contact with Southgate. Referee Steve Dunn rightly doesn't want to know but a team whose luck was in might have got the nod.

Villa have a hard-luck story of their own which looks to have more weight behind it when Julian Joachim 'scores' in the 77th minute, only to fall victim to a very late flag for a questionable offside, the striker's pace that sends him clear of the defence too good to be true in the eyes of the linesman.

Villa would have been glad of the two-goal cushion. Charlton may be in the mire but there's no self-pity in the nagging assault they launch on their opponents' goal for much of the game.

John Robinson recovers a ball that looked to have run out of play in the 32nd minute, but his cross from the left bisects two incoming forwards and Villa clear. The ball arrives from the left flank again, nine minutes later, and ex-West Brom forward Andy Hunt heads narrowly over the bar.

Villa have had their moments since the goal but their best arrives on the stroke of half-time, when an overhead kick from Dion Dublin is headed off the line by Mark Kinsella.

The football may not be terribly festive but the off-field activities are pure pantomime. A second-half male streaker has an unhealthy interest in the Villa defence, and the referee leaves the field with an injury at half-time resulting in an off-duty ref being summoned from the crowd as a replacement for the fourth official. Rules being rules, the re-start is delayed while a spare pair of boots are found for him.

Once the evening's business resumes, Alan Wright clears off the line from a Charlton corner. After Joachim's spell in the limelight, Alan Curbishley's men crank up a final surge in the last ten minutes, forcing fine saves from the increasingly assured Michael Oakes, while Danny Mills heads against the bar from a left wing corner.

With Ugo Ehiogu commanding in the air, however, Villa's defence holds out to secure the points.

Ian Taylor and Ugo close in on Mark Kinsella.

Saturday 26th December 1998 • Ewood Park • 6.00pm

BLACKBURN ROVERS 2 ASTON VILLA 1

Half-time 1-0 • *Attendance* 27,536

Referee Dermot GALLAGHER (Banbury)

Referee's Assistants A.N. BUTLER and D. HORLICK

Blue and White Halved Shirts, White Shorts	Goals		Claret and Blue Shirts, Blue Shorts	Goals
13 John FILAN		13	Michael OAKES ■55	
2 Jeff KENNA		3	Alan WRIGHT	
3 Callum DAVIDSON ❑		4	Gareth SOUTHGATE (c)	
4 Tim SHERWOOD (c)	88	5	Ugo EHIOGU	
6 Stephane HENCHOZ †		6	Steve WATSON	
8 Kevin GALLACHER #	45	7	Ian TAYLOR ‡	
9 Chris SUTTON ‡		11	Alan THOMPSON	
11 Jason WILCOX ❑		12	Julian JOACHIM #	
17 Billy McKINLAY		14	Dion DUBLIN	
23 Christian DAILLY		17	Lee HENDRIE †	
31 Keith GILLESPIE		20	Riccardo SCIMECA ❑	81

Substitutes			*Substitutes*	
10 Kevin DAVIES ‡68 ❑		2	Gary CHARLES	
12 Damien DUFF #74		8	Mark DRAPER	
16 Marlon BROOMES †45 ❑		9	Stan COLLYMORE ‡70	
19 Damien JOHNSON		16	Simon GRAYSON #82	
22 Alan FETTIS (Gk)		30	Adam RACHEL (Gk) †57	

BEFORE	P	W	D	L	F	A	pts
1 Villa	18	10	6	2	28	17	36
18 Blackburn	18	3	5	10	17	26	14

AFTER	P	W	D	L	F	A	pts
2 Villa	19	10	6	3	29	19	36
16 Blackburn	19	4	5	10	19	27	17

FACTFILE

Second consecutive defeat in which Villa are denied inside the dying minutes... Riccardo Scimeca scores his first goal for the first team... Michael Oakes is the first Villa keeper to be sent off since Mark Bosnich at Leeds United on 29th April 1995... Rovers win their third straight league game against Villa.

Oakes off as Christmas sours

They plundered nine goals from Villa last season and not even a relegation dogfight can stop Blackburn Rovers from again planting a major thorn in their opponents' side.

Three points lost to a club recently in disarray is bad enough, but when Michael Oakes is sent off for allegedly handling the ball outside his area, Villa's despondency is laced with a fury which is fully justified.

The game is in its 55th minute, and Blackburn's 1-0 lead just 10 minutes old, when the Villa keeper runs out to gather a high ball at the edge of the box. His momentum takes him across the line, but TV replays suggest that he had released the ball in time and the mere fact that he was clearly making every effort to do so makes referee Dermot Gallagher's ensuing red card look like overkill.

With young Adam Rachel coming on as Oakes' replacement to make his first team debut and Lee Hendrie sacrificed to the subs' bench to make it possible, the sending off looks like being a pivotal moment. It is, but not in the manner you'd expect. Far from subsiding to defeat, 10-man Villa rely on the steam coming out of their ears to power them into contention for the first time in the game.

They had been jammed in neutral while Blackburn slipped into overdrive for most of the first half. Had Oakes been gone at that point, the shots from Chris Sutton, Jason Wilcox and Keith Gillespie which he superbly kept out, might have already seen Rovers home and hosed by half-time.

Instead, they make do with a solitary goal from the head of Kevin Gallacher on the brink of half-time.

It's cancelled out with nine minutes left in the game, when Riccardo Scimeca scores with a shot from just inside the Rovers area. Players who have handed in transfer requests can become dead weight, but Scimeca, given a fresh run in the first team, is playing with the air of a man who's got something off his chest and feels much better for it.

His goal is the climax to a 35-minute period of domination following Oakes' departure that promises to give Adam Rachel one of the easier Premiership debuts on record.

Steve Watson and Alan Thompson link to leave the latter with a shot that goes just wide of the goal, while Dion Dublin later goes close with a header from an Alan Wright cross. And when Ian Taylor makes way for Stan Collymore with 21 minutes left, you sense Villa are poised for the kill.

Instead, Rovers get their second lucky break of the game with just two minutes left. Tim Sherwood's control of a Kevin Davies pass seems to be more about arm than chest as he runs into the box, but there is no whistle and the Blackburn midfielder jubilantly wraps up the points with an angled shot.

Three days later, referee Dermot Gallagher admits an error was made and the red card is annulled. While his candour is commendable, it can do nothing to alter the result.

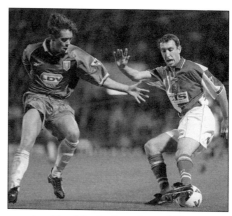

Lee Hendrie shadows Jason Wilcox.

Monday 28th December 1998 • Villa Park • 3.00pm

ASTON VILLA 2 SHEFFIELD WEDNESDAY 1

Half-time 1-1 • Attendance 39,217

Referee Graham BARBER (Guildford)

Referee's Assistants M.A. WILLIAMS and A.J. GREEN

Claret and Blue Shirts, White Shorts	Goals	Blue and White Striped Shirts, Black Shorts	Goals
13 Michael OAKES		33 Pavel SRNICEK	
3 Alan WRIGHT		2 Peter ATHERTON (c)	
4 Gareth SOUTHGATE (c)	7	4 Wim JONK	
5 Ugo EHIOGU	84	6 Des WALKER ❑	
6 Steve WATSON		8 Benito CARBONE	8
7 Ian TAYLOR †		10 Andy BOOTH	
12 Julian JOACHIM		18 Dejan STEFANOVIC ❑ ■20	
14 Dion DUBLIN		20 Andy HINCHCLIFFE ❑	
15 Gareth BARRY		22 EMERSON	
17 Lee HENDRIE		25 Petter RUDI ❑ †	
20 Riccardo SCIMECA ‡		26 Niclas ALEXANDERSSON ‡	
Substitutes		*Substitutes*	
2 Gary CHARLES		1 Kevin PRESSMAN (Gk)	
8 Mark DRAPER †52		16 Ritchie HUMPHREYS †88	
9 Stan COLLYMORE ‡52		17 Lee BRISCOE ‡88	
16 Simon GRAYSON		24 Jim MAGILTON	
30 Adam RACHEL (Gk)		32 Danny SONNER	

BEFORE	P	W	D	L	F	A	pts
2 Villa	19	10	6	3	29	19	36
15 Wednesday	19	6	4	9	20	20	22

AFTER	P	W	D	L	F	A	pts
1 Villa	20	11	6	3	31	20	39
15 Wednesday	20	6	4	10	21	22	22

FACTFILE

Villa achieve the 'double' over an opponent at the first time of asking this season... Gareth Southgate's first goal for Villa since 21st August 1996... First time Villa have relied exclusively on goals by defenders to win a game since Ugo Ehiogu's goal beat Everton on 4th September 1996.

Defence best form of attack

In spite of employing some £14m worth of strikers, Villa are indebted to their defence for shrugging off a gritty Wednesday team, as Gareth Southgate and Ugo Ehiogu bag goals at either end of the game to get their team back to winning ways.

Having come alive against Blackburn Rovers after Michael Oakes' dismissal two days earlier, Villa find out what it's like to be on the receiving end of 'Ten-Man Syndrome', as Wednesday close ranks following the sending off of Dejan Stefanovic.

The big Yugoslav hits the showers with just 20 minutes gone, after clipping Julian Joachim as the latter threatens to win the race for a through-ball by Lee Hendrie. To his credit, Joachim revives the lost art of staying on one's feet as long as humanly possible, but the damage has been done in referee Graham Barber's eyes and Stefanovic gets the fatal second yellow card, his first having come after another foul on Joachim.

One-nil and one man up, Villa look in good shape for the three points, having taken the lead on seven minutes when a free-kick emerges from a penalty-box melee for Southgate to fire in a low shot.

It's a short-lived advantage, however. Benito Carbone finds himself wide open in Villa's 18-yard box just a minute later as the ball is headed down from a cross to the far post. It rears up to an awkward height, but with his ability and all the time in the world, the Italian converts it tidily past Michael Oakes.

The visitors dig in, their size and hustling presence frustrating Villa as it had for so long at Hillsborough back in August. The hosts gradually draw the sting out of Wednesday's danger on the break and push their opponents' defence closer to breaking point as the game progresses but it's only in the closing stages that Sheffield's rearguard action breaks down.

Six minutes remain when an Alan Wright corner is met by an unmarked Ugo Ehiogu, who heads the ball into the middle of the net with Srnicek unsighted.

It's justice of sorts for the big defender, whose new year resolution is to find the scoresheet more often. He had bundled in another corner 12 minutes into the second half, only for an infringement to negate his efforts.

Villa had pressed on, however, looking odds on for a winner as holes began to appear in their opponents' undermanned and over-stretched defence.

Sheffield goalkeeper Pavel Srnicek parries the ball for a corner as Dion Dublin nods a Mark Draper cross goalwards in the 59th minute. Three minutes later, Srnicek is called upon again and tips over a long range Stan Collymore drive.

Villa fans are entitled to think it may be one of those days, nine minutes from time, when Joachim cuts in from the left and fires a shot against the top of the far post.

Up steps Ugo soon afterwards, however, and an awkward opponent is dispatched by the odd goal for the second time this season.

Heads we win: Ugo's late winner hits the back of the net.

Saturday 2nd January 1999 • Villa Park • 3.00pm

ASTON VILLA 3 HULL CITY 0

Half-time 1-0 • *Attendance* 39,217

Referee Scott MATHIESON (Stockport)

Referee's Assistants M. RYAN and A.R. WOOD

Claret and Blue Shirts, White Shorts	Goals	Amber and White Striped Shirts with Black Sleeves, Black Shorts	Goals
13 Michael OAKES		1 Steve WILSON	
3 Alan WRIGHT		2 Mark GREAVES †	
4 Gareth SOUTHGATE (c)		3 Gregor RIOCH ❏	
5 Ugo EHIOGU		4 Justin WHITTLE	
6 Steve WATSON ‡		5 Matt HOCKING	
8 Mark DRAPER †		6 Mike EDWARDS	
9 Stan COLLYMORE	45,67	7 Warren JOYCE #	
12 Julian JOACHIM	51	8 David D'AURIA (c)	
15 Gareth BARRY		9 David BROWN ❏ ‡	
17 Lee HENDRIE #		10 Craig FAULCONBRIDGE	
20 Riccardo SCIMECA		11 Ben MORLEY	
Substitutes		*Substitutes*	
2 Gary CHARLES ‡70		12 Richard PEACOCK †55	
16 Simon GRAYSON †58		13 Brian McGINTY ‡55	
22 Darius VASSELL		14 Stephen HAWES #86	
30 Adam RACHEL (Gk)		15 Lee ELLINGTON	
32 Aaron LESCOTT #76		16 Adam BOLDER	

Villa progress beyond the FA Cup Third Round for the eighth successive season... Stan Collymore now has six goals in four cup games this season... 5'6" Julian Joachim's first headed goal since 28th March 1998 v Everton!... Aaron Lescott comes on as sub for his first-team debut... Alan Thompson could be out for the rest of the month, after damaging ankle ligaments in a training-ground accident in the week leading up to this game.

Stan double torpedoes Hull

If Stan's 'the Man' at Premiership level, he is more like 'The Executioner' when lesser clubs are pitted against Aston Villa.

After Stan Collymore's hat-trick had put Strømsgodset firmly in their place earlier this season, the Villa striker shows a similar lack of compassion in scoring twice to end Hull City's flickering dreams of Cup glory.

Goal number one is a welcome relief for the hosts, who aren't exactly ruling the roost after 45 minutes of busy over-achievement from the team propping up the entire Football League.

The first crack appears on the stroke of half-time. A diagonal run from the right by Steve Watson sees the ball played to Lee Hendrie who scoops it over the City defence for Collymore to kill with his head before touching home the game's first goal.

Those stats boffins who insist that goals just before half-time aren't as psychologically momentous as tradition maintains, still have some persuading to do. For all the vociferous backing of their hordes of supporters, you can almost hear the air going out of the Tigers as they head for the dressing-room, a feeling confirmed when Julian Joachim kills the game six minutes after the restart.

Collymore is again instrumental, striking a superb curling cross from the left which Joachim's forehead nails with aplomb.

With Villa now firmly in their stride, Joachim returns the favour 16 minutes later, beating Mike Edwards and Gregor Rioch on the right hand side and putting in a low cross which the unmarked Stan sidefoots home with the greatest of ease.

No-one could begrudge the goal-count sticking at three, for Hull don't deserve a rout. For the whole of the first half, they find an extra gear that makes a mockery of their league position and if Rioch's booking for a foul on Steve Watson after just seven seconds is a fair indicator of the rigours that await Villa's midfield, the Tigers also look to play some football.

Justin Whittle is a tidy performer at the heart of their defence, while in midfield, player-manager Warren Joyce makes a useful prompter for the enterprise of forwards Craig Faulconbridge and Ben Morley.

Too little inspiration around the Villa penalty box, however, coupled with too many free-kicks conceded around their own, eventually wear the visitors down as the game progresses, and to quote one of their visiting radio reporters, their style becomes too "hit and hope", to be effective.

This constitutes a minor reprieve for Villa, who occasionally cruise a little too leisurely once they feel their work is done. Shortly after going 2-0 down, the Tigers pounce on a lazy Villa pass played across their own half and David Brown's cross is nudged against Oakes by Faulconbridge, who is unable to get to the rebound for a second attempt.

18 minutes from time, a Joyce free-kick takes Villa's defence by surprise and Oakes has to tip David D'Auria's header over for a corner. These, however, are mere crumbs of comfort for City's vociferous travelling fans. The day out is theirs but the result, emphatically enough, is Villa's.

Three's a crowd for one Hull player.

Saturday 9th January 1999 • Riverside Stadium • 3.00pm

MIDDLESBROUGH 0 ASTON VILLA 0

Half-time 0-0 • Attendance 34,643

Referee Uriah RENNIE (Sheffield)

Referee's Assistants H. WEBB and P. CANADINE

Red Shirts, White Shorts	Goals	Turquoise Shirts with Black Trim, Black Shorts	Goals
1 Mark SCHWARZER		13 Michael OAKES	
2 Curtis FLEMING ❑		3 Alan WRIGHT	
3 Dean GORDON		4 Gareth SOUTHGATE (c)	
4 Steve VICKERS		5 Ugo EHIOGU	
5 Gianluca FESTA		6 Steve WATSON	
6 Gary PALLISTER		7 Ian TAYLOR	
8 Paul GASCOIGNE ❑		12 Julian JOACHIM	
10 Brian DEANE		14 Dion DUBLIN	
15 Neil MADDISON		15 Gareth BARRY ❑	
16 Andy TOWNSEND (c)		17 Lee HENDRIE	
19 Hamilton RICARD ❑ †		20 Riccardo SCIMECA †	
Substitutes		*Substitutes*	
12 Mikkel BECK †84		8 Mark DRAPER	
13 Marlon BERESFORD (Gk)		9 Stan COLLYMORE	
14 Philip STAMP		16 Simon GRAYSON †70	
22 Mark SUMMERBELL		22 Darius VASSELL	
28 Robbie STOCKDALE		30 Adam RACHEL (Gk)	

BEFORE		P	W	D	L	F	A	pts
1	Villa	20	11	6	3	31	20	39
8	Boro	20	7	9	4	32	26	30

AFTER		P	W	D	L	F	A	pts
2	Villa	21	11	7	3	31	20	40
9	Boro	21	7	10	4	32	26	31

FACTFILE

Villa have now lost only one of their last five league games at Middlesbrough... They register back-to-back clean sheets for the first time since winning at Celta Vigo... But they fail to score for the first time in 16 games...Villa become the first visitors not to concede a goal at the Riverside since the opening day of the season.

Tees-ed and tormented

It's always the way. You beam a game to 18 countries around the world and a goalless draw is virtually guaranteed.

The global neutrals probably take rather less from a dour if hectic game than the 34,643 who provide the Riverside Stadium with its record attendance. For the Villa contingent especially, it's a reassuring point gained by their team after a searching examination.

The home side steps up the pressure after an even first half. Despite being booked for catching Lee Hendrie with a trailing arm on the stroke of half-time, an influential performance from Paul Gascoigne bodes well for the rest of Middlesbrough's season. Unfortunately, he is the only member of their team who can find the calibre of cross to stretch Villa to their limits.

Hamilton Ricard, still arguably the most under-rated striker in the Premiership at present, probes Villa's defence throughout, but is ultimately forced to share the honours with Ugo Ehiogu in one of the game's principal match-ups.

Villa have the better of the second half's early stages, but the momentum switches to their opponents once ex-Villan Andy Townsend scoops a shot over the bar following a Ricard cross shortly past the hour mark.

As Dion Dublin is increasingly seen in his *alter ego* of central defender, Michael Oakes tips over a shot from a corner and Ehiogu survives penalty appeals as the ball passes dangerously close to his hand in the 67th minute.

It's Gareth Southgate's turn to sweat just five minutes later. He had saved Villa's bacon when blocking a Brian Deane shot on the line five minutes before half-time, but he now comes close to undoing the good work when he slices a Ricard cross narrowly over his own bar.

Back in the forward line, Dublin provides brief respite when he collects a cross from the left at goalkeeper Mark Schwarzer's near post. The close attentions of Gianluca Festa prevent him from turning sufficiently to hit the target and Boro are swiftly back onto the offensive with 12 minutes to go.

The ball breaks out of midfield to Gascoigne, whose advance is solidly blocked by Southgate before Oakes pushes Dean Gordon's follow-up shot around the foot of the post. Gordon has another narrow miss in the game's dying minutes, heading a Gascoigne cross wide.

The traffic had been more two-way in the first half. While Deane sees his diving header fly just wide of Oakes' post with 14 minutes gone, Schwarzer has already been pressed into action when Villa attack down the left to set up Julian Joachim for a shot that the keeper saves to his right. The Australian isn't so sure-handed six minutes later, though, when fumbling a corner-kick, but Ian Taylor is unable to benefit from the loose ball.

When the bounce deceives Ehiogu after 26 minutes, Ricard looks set to benefit, but Ugo recovers with a timely tackle as the Colombian bears down on the Villa box. Ricard is denied by Michael Oakes shortly before half-time, the Villa keeper prodding his chip over the bar.

Gianluca Festa robs Dion Dublin.

Monday 18th January 1999 • Villa Park • 8.15pm

ASTON VILLA 3 EVERTON 0

Half-time 1-0 • Attendance 32,488

Referee Neale BARRY (Scunthorpe)

Referee's Assistants P. SHARP and D. BRYAN

Claret and Blue Shirts, White Shorts		Goals
13	Michael OAKES	
3	Alan WRIGHT	
4	Gareth SOUTHGATE (c)	
5	Ugo EHIOGU	
6	Steve WATSON	
7	Ian TAYLOR ‡	
12	Julian JOACHIM	40,51
14	Dion DUBLIN ❑ †	
15	Gareth BARRY	
17	Lee HENDRIE #	
20	Riccardo SCIMECA	
	Substitutes	
8	Mark DRAPER #80	
9	Stan COLLYMORE †45	
10	Paul MERSON ‡58	78
16	Simon GRAYSON	
30	Adam RACHEL (Gk)	

White Shirts, Blue Shorts		Goals
1	Thomas MYHRE ❑	
2	Alex CLELAND ❑ ■11	
3	Michael BALL	
4	Olivier DACOURT	
5	Dave WATSON (c)	
8	Nick BARMBY	
10	Don HUTCHISON	
14	Tony GRANT †	
15	Marco MATERAZZI	
19	John OSTER ‡	
26	Ibrahima BAKAYOKO #	
	Substitutes	
16	Michael BRANCH #82	
21	Mitch WARD †68	
29	Danny CADAMARTERI ‡82	
35	Steve SIMONSEN (Gk)	
36	Jamie MILLIGAN	

BEFORE		P	W	D	L	F	A	pts
2	Villa	21	11	7	3	31	20	40
14	Everton	21	5	9	7	13	21	24

AFTER		P	W	D	L	F	A	pts
2	Villa	22	12	7	3	34	20	43
15	Everton	22	5	9	8	13	24	24

FACTFILE

Villa's biggest margin of victory in the Premiership since winning 4-1 at Southampton on 14th November... Everton now with just one League win at Villa Park in 14 visits... Joachim's ninth and tenth goals of the season assure him of his best-ever season total as a Villa player, beating the eight he scored last term.

Joachim fires Villa back on track

How Everton would love Villa's problems. Drop a point occasionally; briefly relinquish the lead in the Premiership table, suffer the prophets of doom in the letters pages: yes, it still looks like bliss from where the Goodison Park disciples are sitting.

They could tell you the real story of dashed hopes. The same people who savoured a new dawn when Villa kicked off their campaign at the blue end of Stanley Park back in August.

Breezy, purposeful and seemingly stacked with skill, you watched Everton that day and felt that whatever the season held for them, a relegation struggle wasn't included.

Boardroom upheaval and a forward line that only rarely disturbs the scoreboard have decreed otherwise, however, and the Everton side that assembles at Villa Park for the return match is a poor imitation of its summertime version.

Not helped by injuries, the visitors are hampered further by the departure of full-back Alex Cleland with only 10 minutes gone.

The ink is barely dry in the referee's notebook following Cleland's trip on Julian Joachim, before the former Rangers man is entwining his legs around Dion Dublin's. Although replays suggest the Scot has got a piece of the ball, he can have little complaint after tempting fate so brazenly.

Everton's regroup leaves Ivory Coast striker Ibrahima Bakayoko in solitary confinement up front and, for all his graft, spitting in the wind. You suspect Villa are just one goal away from maximum points.

That it takes a while to come is a source of concern which the home fans aren't slow in articulating. Their team soaks up a 15-minute spell in which Everton work off their frustration with a series of clattering challenges, but the unlocking of the visitors is a laborious process, with Marco Materazzi outstanding at the heart of the Toffees' defence.

The breakthrough eventually happens in grand style after 40 minutes, Joachim controlling and volleying home Ian Taylor's knockdown of a Lee Hendrie free-kick.

Everton nearly respond just two minutes later, when Bakayoko's pressure almost turns Gareth Southgate's clearance into a lob over his own goalkeeper, but Michael Oakes tips the ball over the bar.

Villa unveil a candidate for their goal of the season title five minutes into the second half, when Ian Taylor's first time pass is threaded through to Joachim by Lee Hendrie and the striker zips clear of the defence before blasting a cross-shot past Thomas Myhre to put Villa two up.

Paul Merson comes on with just over an hour to go for his first appearance in nine games and takes just 19 minutes to rehabilitate himself, connecting with a Steve Watson header from a Joachim cross to make it 3-0.

It's much easier than it looked at one point and afterwards John Gregory reminds the Villa fans of the need for patience.

"Everton had the same number of men in their half after the sending off as before," he points out. "People thought we had to win the game straight away and became impatient."

The close attentions of Marco Materazzi can't stop Paul Merson getting a shot on goal.

Saturday 23rd January 1999 • Villa Park • 3.00pm

ASTON VILLA 0 FULHAM 2

Half-time 0-2 • *Attendance 35,260*

Referee David ELLERAY (Harrow-on-the-Hill)
Referee's Assistants R.J. BEEBY and D.S. BRYAN

Claret and Blue Shirts, White Shorts	Goals	Yellow Shirts with Black Trim, Black Shorts	Goals
13 Michael OAKES		1 Maik TAYLOR	
3 Alan WRIGHT †		2 Wayne COLLINS	
4 Gareth SOUTHGATE (c)		3 Rufus BREVETT	
5 Ugo EHIOGU ❑		4 Simon MORGAN	8
6 Steve WATSON ❑		5 Chris COLEMAN (c)	
7 Ian TAYLOR		6 Kit SYMONS	
10 Paul MERSON		7 Steve HAYWARD	44
12 Julian JOACHIM		8 Paul BRACEWELL	
15 Gareth BARRY		9 Geoff HORSFIELD	
17 Lee HENDRIE ❑		10 Paul PESCHISOLIDO †	
20 Riccardo SCIMECA		11 Steve FINNAN ❑	

Substitutes		*Substitutes*	
16 Simon GRAYSON		12 Neil SMITH †82 ❑	
18 Fabio FERRARESI		13 Andre ARENDSE (Gk)	
22 Darius VASSELL †58		14 Paul TROLLOPE	
23 David HUGHES		15 John SALAKO	
30 Adam RACHEL (Gk)		16 Barry HAYLES	

FACTFILE

Villa goalless at home for first time since 11th March 1998 (0-1 v Barnsley)... They bow out of FA Cup at home for second year running... Villa's first FA Cup defeat by non-Premiership opponents since First Division Bolton put them out in 1994... First FA Cup exit to a club at least two divisions below them since Aldershot in 1964.

Michael Oakes – desperately unlucky with a wickedly deflected free-kick which gave the Cottagers their second goal.

Aston Villa Review 1999

Home town duo sink Villa hopes

Walsall native Steve Hayward once roared Aston Villa on from the terraces; Northfield-born Simon Morgan played for the club as a youngster. Not that you'd know it from this stunning Cup upset, when their goals are the local anaesthetic that leaves Villa numb.

Before either man kicks a ball, another former paying customer at Villa Park inadvertently has a hand in the day's events, when Stan Collymore skips the game, claiming just hours before kick-off that he is not fit to play, due to a condition that will manifest itself as nervous exhaustion 48 hours later, when he embarks on a course of stress counselling.

If Villa's players claim that his 11th-hour withdrawal was not a factor in what follows, their body language suggests otherwise, as virtually to a man, they spend 90 minutes apparently running through quicksand in their most insipid performance of the season so far.

Fulham, whose big-time aspirations wouldn't exactly suffer from a scalp such as Villa's, need no further incentive. Morgan heads home a Hayward corner at the near post after just eight minutes and Hayward himself is the next to bite the hand that fed him, when his free-kick shortly before half-time enjoys a juicy deflection that takes Michael Oakes out of the game and his team along with it.

Making the embarrassment even worse for home fans is that both goalscorers are the remnants of 'old Fulham', pre-Fayed and pre-Keegan, when the Cottagers knew their place and 2-0 leads at the home of a Premiership front-runner were the stuff of fantasy.

Those days seem a while ago now, as Welsh international defenders Kit Symons and Chris Coleman blunt Villa's edge up front, while striker and former bricklayer Geoff Horsfield

makes the difference between Conference and Premiership football seem little more than extra noughts on the pay-slip, as his physical game chips away at Villa's back line.

Alongside him, ex-Blues striker Paul Peschisolido pays his respects to St Andrew's with a performance of nagging enterprise against their great rivals. Only the woodwork spares Villa deeper blushes when he latches onto a Coleman header to the near post following a 24th-minute corner.

None of this flatters the Londoners, who make the running almost for the entirety of the game with a performance of verve and audacity.

In what rare moments of respite they can find after their bright start dwindles, Villa encounter a goalkeeper in similar form to his team-mates. Twice in the space of eight minutes during the first half, Maik Taylor's legs block Julian Joachim's shot after the Villa man has been neatly picked out by a pass from Lee Hendrie.

Taylor saves his best moment for the 85th minute, when an arcing dive tips a header from namesake Ian Taylor over the bar. A piece of unruffled aplomb, it is Fulham's afternoon in miniature.

"We didn't have the ability, technique or guile to break them down," is John Gregory's blunt post-game assessment. Still, we consoled ourselves on the way home, it's only one game.

Darius Vassell causes problems for Fulham.

Saturday 30th January 1999 • St. James' Park • 3.00pm

NEWCASTLE UNITED 2 ASTON VILLA 1

Half-time 2-0 • Attendance 36,766

Referee Rob HARRIS (Oxford)

Referee's Assistants A. KAYNE and I. BLANCHARD

Black and White Striped Shirts, Black Shorts		Goals	Claret and Blue Shirts, White Shorts		Goals
1	Shay GIVEN		13	Michael OAKES	
2	Warren BARTON		3	Alan WRIGHT	
4	Didier DOMI		4	Gareth SOUTHGATE (c)	
6	Steve HOWEY		5	Ugo EHIOGU †	
9	Alan SHEARER (c)	3	6	Steve WATSON ‡	
11	Gary SPEED		7	Ian TAYLOR	
12	Dietmar HAMANN		10	Paul MERSON ❏	60
14	Temuri KETSBAIA ❏ †	26	12	Julian JOACHIM	
17	Stephen GLASS		15	Gareth BARRY	
24	Nolberto SOLANO ‡		17	Lee HENDRIE ❏	
34	Nikolaos DABIZAS		20	Riccardo SCIMECA	
	Substitutes			*Substitutes*	
3	Stuart PEARCE		16	Simon GRAYSON †40	
13	Steve HARPER (Gk)		22	Darius VASSELL ‡84	
28	Aaron HUGHES		23	David HUGHES	
29	Garry BRADY ‡82		25	Alan LEE	
40	Andreas ANDERSSON †62		30	Adam RACHEL (Gk)	

BEFORE		P	W	D	L	F	A	pts	AFTER		P	W	D	L	F	A	pts
2	Villa	22	12	7	3	34	20	43	3	Villa	23	12	7	4	35	22	43
14	Newcastle	22	6	7	9	26	31	25	13	Newcastle	23	7	7	9	28	32	28

FACTFILE

Villa's sixth successive defeat at St James' Park... They have taken one point from their last three away games; their leanest run on the road so far this term... They fall to third in the Premiership table for the first time since 23rd August... Alan Lee on the substitutes' bench for the first time

Late rally fails to save the day

At the end of a week in which he could have done with being a social worker, psychiatrist and faith healer to boot, John Gregory fits in a spot of football management at St James' Park, and watches Alan Shearer provide a pointed reminder of what you're missing when you have one multi-million pound striker out injured and another being treated for stress.

Gregory has spent the week fielding questions about Stan Collymore, who has checked into a clinic as part of his stress-counselling programme. Between this, rallying the troops and resigning himself to the nagging groin strain that has eliminated Dion Dublin, the Villa manager looks a weary man.

As somebody once pointed out, the trouble with football is that Saturday afternoons keep coming around. Out on that unforgiving turf, there is no scope for 'spin' or hard-luck stories; you stand or fall on the reality of your resources and as Shearer's dominant performance almost mockingly illustrates, Collymore and Dublin are sorely missed.

Along with Julian Joachim, Paul Merson works tirelessly on the Villa forward line, but asking him to play the thankless role of target man is like hitching a Derby winner to a plough. Bumped and bored by the physical attentions of central defenders Steve Howey and Nicos Dabizas, he is in no position to win anything other than intermittent possession for his team-mates.

Bagging the goal of the

No happy homecoming for Steve Watson.

game with a 25-yard drive after an hour is fitting reward for his persistence but only briefly does it threaten to be more than a consolation.

Shearer, goalless in his previous 10 Premiership games, has left Villa trailing after just three minutes, losing his marker Gareth Barry to force home a straightforward header from a Stephen Glass cross. Going close several times after the interval and with another goal disallowed beforehand, he could easily have had a hattrick, which would have been a just return for the commanding way he leads United's line both on the floor and in the air.

There's a real possibility of a rout when another Glass centre finds a Villa-free zone at the near post for Temuri Ketsbaia to make it 2-0 after 26 minutes. Glass and Gary Speed are providing a stream of crosses for Shearer to chase and Newcastle clearly sense the chance to shake the dust of a mediocre season off their boots.

With Ugo Ehiogu forced to bow out after his head and Shearer's boot come into contact in pursuit of a high ball, Villa drop Riccardo Scimeca back from midfield into his customary defensive role. Too late, the visitors start sealing off some of the inroads United had been making into their half.

After Steve Watson has received a touching ovation from his old club's fans following his substitution, Alan Wright almost catches United goalkeeper Shay Given cold when his spinning volley in the 85th minute takes a wicked bounce off the turf close to the goal-line.

This is United's day, however, and to Messrs. Collymore and Dublin, the message is clear. Get well soon.

Saturday 6th February 1999 • Villa Park • 3.00pm

ASTON VILLA 1 BLACKBURN ROVERS 3

Half-time 0-1 • *Attendance* 37,404

Referee Keith BURGE (Tonypandy)

Referee's Assistants P. NORMAN and M. DEARING

Claret and Blue Shirts, White Shorts		Goals	Blue and White Halved Shirts, Blue Shorts		Goals
13	Michael OAKES		13	John FILAN	
3	Alan WRIGHT		3	Callum DAVIDSON	
4	Gareth SOUTHGATE (c)	32og	5	Darren PEACOCK	
6	Steve WATSON		9	Chris SUTTON	
7	Ian TAYLOR		11	Jason WILCOX	
10	Paul MERSON		16	Marlon BROOMES	
12	Julian JOACHIM	69	17	Billy McKINLAY (c)	
14	Dion DUBLIN		27	David DUNN	64
15	Gareth BARRY †		32	Ashley WARD	62
16	Simon GRAYSON		33	Matt JANSEN †	
20	Riccardo SCIMECA		34	Jason McATEER	
	Substitutes			*Substitutes*	
11	Alan THOMPSON †78		1	Tim FLOWERS (Gk)	
22	Darius VASSELL		10	Kevin DAVIES	
27	Michael STANDING		12	Damien DUFF †81	
31	Jlloyd SAMUEL		20	Gary CROFT	
39	Peter ENCKELMAN (Gk)		23	Christian DAILLY	

BEFORE		P	W	D	L	F	A	pts	AFTER		P	W	D	L	F	A	pts
3	Villa	23	12	7	4	35	22	43	4	Villa	24	12	7	5	36	25	43
17	Blackburn	23	5	7	11	22	30	22	15	Blackburn	24	6	7	11	25	31	25

FACTFILE

Gareth Southgate scores first own goal of his career... Rovers join Celta Vigo and Liverpool as only opponents to score at least three goals at Villa Park this season... Julian Joachim's first goal in a losing cause this term... Alan Thompson returns after six games out with an ankle injury.

Few cheers in Rovers' return

Last season, Blackburn opted for the bludgeon. This season, they have used the rapier. The damage inflicted, however, is pretty much the same.

Their 2-1 defeat of Villa at Ewood Park and a 3-1 victory today may look mild compared to the 5-0 and 4-0 routs they inflicted last term but they could yet prove pivotal in Villa's fortunes.

The Boxing Day loss in Lancashire triggered a phase that has now seen Villa collect seven points from a possible 18 – a pace more commonly found around the relegation zone than the glamour end of the table – and now goals from Ashley Ward, David Dunn and a Gareth Southgate own goal plant Villa firmly in the mire with a third straight defeat.

Maddeningly, it could all have been very different, for when Southgate inadvertently beats his own keeper while trying to head away a Dunn cross after 32 minutes, it mars an otherwise promising Villa start.

Blackburn goalkeeper John Filan has already produced the first of several fine saves to keep out a shot from Julian Joachim, and Dion Dublin and Paul Merson have also had good looks at the Blackburn goal as the game starts at a brisk tempo.

Unabashed by going behind, the home side plough on as before. In a 10-minute spell either side of the interval, Dublin heads wide and then shoots against the near post after a Steve Watson effort is blocked by Marlon Broomes.

Everyone is piling forward for Villa at this stage and a third come-from-behind home win this season looks eminently possible, until Ashley Ward's killer goal in the 62nd minute.

Facing his own goal with Chris Sutton in attendance, Riccardo Scimeca opts to play his way out of trouble rather than depositing the ball in the Trinity seats. Punishment is immediate, even if Sutton appears to hold his man as he barges his way into possession. The Blackburn striker, rejuvenated today after a spell out of the team through injury, screws the ball back into the penalty area for Ward to shoot home. One minute later, the traumatised hosts are buried when Gareth Barry's header from a cross gets only as far as Dunn, who gleefully smacks home goal number three.

Whatever the season holds for Aston Villa, there may be no lower moment than the chant of 'Are you Burnley in disguise?' that rises from the Blackburn seats.

Villa at least respond quickly, one of the many delightful headers Dublin has scattered around him all afternoon finally meeting the finish it deserves, as Joachim runs onto it and fires home for a glimmer of hope with 21 minutes left.

This is not to be Villa's day, though. You know it when Filan covers yards in the blink of an eye to bat away an 80th-minute Alan Thompson free-kick. You know it when the goalkeeper's despairingly raised leg is enough to stop Ian Taylor netting the rebound. You know it when the industrious Simon Grayson heads over a Joachim cross when it looks easier to score. Such is life when your losing run is three games and counting.

Ashley Ward and Alan Wright.

Wednesday 17th February 1999 • Villa Park • 7.45pm

ASTON VILLA 1 LEEDS UNITED 2

Half-time 0-2 • Attendance 37,510

Referee Dermot GALLAGHER (Banbury)
Referee's Assistants P. SHARP and S. BRAND

Claret and Blue Shirts, White Shorts		Goals	White Shirts, Blue Shorts		Goals
13	Michael OAKES		1	Nigel MARTYN	
3	Alan WRIGHT		4	Alf Inge HAALAND	
4	Gareth SOUTHGATE (c)		5	Lucas RADEBE (c)	
6	Steve WATSON		6	David WETHERALL	
7	Ian TAYLOR		7	Willem KORSTEN	
10	Paul MERSON		9	Jimmy HASSELBAINK ❑	8,32
12	Julian JOACHIM		12	David HOPKIN	
14	Dion DUBLIN ‡		18	Gunnar HALLE	
15	Gareth BARRY †		19	Harry KEWELL	
17	Lee HENDRIE		20	Ian HARTE	
20	Riccardo SCIMECA	75	40	Matthew JONES †	
	Substitutes			*Substitutes*	
9	Stan COLLYMORE ‡71		8	Clyde WIJNHARD	
11	Alan THOMPSON †65		16	Danny GRANVILLE †80	
16	Simon GRAYSON		22	Tommy KNARVIK	
31	Jlloyd SAMUEL		36	Paul ROBINSON (Gk)	
39	Peter ENCKELMAN (Gk)		39	Alan SMITH	

BEFORE		P	W	D	L	F	A	pts
4	Villa	24	12	7	5	36	25	43
7	Leeds	24	9	9	6	36	24	36

AFTER		P	W	D	L	F	A	pts
4	Villa	25	12	7	6	37	27	43
5	Leeds	25	10	9	6	38	25	39

FACTFILE

Villa's first four-game losing streak since losing the initial four games of last season... Leeds' first win at Villa Park in eight years and their first goals in six visits... Villa concede the opening goal for the fourth successive game and go to half-time 2-0 down for the third time in four matches.

Jimmy Floyd hassles backs

At Elland Road in September, Villa virtually snuffed him out. If Jimmy Floyd Hasselbaink bears grudges, he now settles this one with a vengeance, producing 90 minutes of torment for defenders that proves the difference between the teams.

"Being at home, we had to press forward more this time and I think that suited his game, playing on his own and counter-attacking," explains Gareth Barry, one of several Villa men who's spent the evening executing textbook tackles on a man who was no longer there.

Hasselbaink's strength and ability to turn on a sixpence net him two goals that might easily have been four. Riccardo Scimeca over-commits to a Leeds throw-in after just seven minutes and Hasselbaink takes over, outpacing Barry before drilling home the opening goal.

Twenty-four minutes later, he hits a long-range free kick which Michael Oakes can only slightly divert in its journey to the top corner.

Such finishing is all Villa need, in an opening half where their industrious opponents give every impression of having 15 men on the field. Leeds pour through midfield with ease when attacking and the pressure they impose when defending contributes to an innocuous Villa performance, in which only Paul Merson offers much in the way of creativity.

It takes Villa 19 minutes to work a clear-cut opening, but Lee Hendrie is inches short of Julian Joachim's low cross when just a touch would have levelled the scores.

There's an even closer shave at the other end, when the ball's bounce deceives Alan Wright and Hasselbaink pounces. He has the beating of Oakes but his shot comes back off the post.

Such ominous vibes would discourage most sides two goals in arrears but Villa merely show once again that if the Premiership was all about doggedness, they would already be organising the civic reception.

United are on the back foot for much of the second half as Villa surge forward. With Lucas Radebe an imposing presence at the centre of Leeds' defence, Scimeca uses one of the few clear-cut headers enjoyed by his team to peg a goal back for Villa in the 75th minute, from an Alan Thompson corner.

Vibrant as Villa now look, however, Hasselbaink and Harry Kewell constantly threaten to kill them off on the counter-attack. Twice in the opening 10 minutes of the half, Hasselbaink and then Willem Korsten slice through the defence, only to be unable to find a shot with the goal at their mercy.

Villa look to cause similar mischief when they introduce Stan Collymore, once again at their disposal during a break from his stress counselling. It would seem necessity is also the mother of compassion, as he comes on to a reception far warmer than he may have expected.

While he throws himself into the game, it is Joachim and Ian Taylor who spurn the best chances of an equaliser and the home side are left second-best to a team that was reportedly exposed by Spurs just four days earlier. Which is precisely Villa's predicament at present: the race is hotting up around them, yet they are still trying to engage first gear.

Julian Joachim outjumps Gunnar Halle.

Sunday 21st February 1999 • Villa Park • 4.00pm

WIMBLEDON 0 ASTON VILLA 0

Half-time 0-0 • Attendance 15,582

Referee Paul ALCOCK (Sevenoaks)

Referee's Assistants T. GREEN and M. NORTH

Dark Blue Shirts, Dark Blue Shorts	Goals	Claret and Blue Shirts, White Shorts	Goals
1 Neil SULLIVAN		13 Michael OAKES	
2 Kenny CUNNINGHAM		3 Alan WRIGHT	
4 Chris PERRY ❑		4 Gareth SOUTHGATE (c)	
5 Dean BLACKWELL		6 Steve WATSON	
6 Ben THATCHER †		7 Ian TAYLOR	
8 Robbie EARLE (c)		10 Paul MERSON	
9 Efan EKOKU ‡		12 Julian JOACHIM †	
10 Andy ROBERTS		14 Dion DUBLIN	
11 Marcus GAYLE		15 Simon GRAYSON ❑	
12 Neal ARDLEY		17 Lee HENDRIE	
20 Jason EUELL		20 Riccardo SCIMECA	
Substitutes		*Substitutes*	
3 Alan KIMBLE †36		1 Mark BOSNICH (Gk)	
7 Ceri HUGHES		9 Stan COLLYMORE †76	
13 Paul HEALD (Gk)		11 Alan THOMPSON	
15 Carl LEABURN ‡88		16 Gareth BARRY	
18 Mark KENNEDY		31 Jlloyd SAMUEL	

BEFORE		P	W	D	L	F	A	pts
4	Villa	25	12	7	6	37	27	43
9	Wimbledon	24	9	8	7	29	35	35

AFTER		P	W	D	L	F	A	pts
4	Villa	26	12	8	6	37	27	44
9	Wimbledon	25	9	9	7	29	35	36

FACTFILE

Villa's fifth goalless draw of the season, all of them having come away from home... Their first goalless draw with the Dons since 1990... They keep a clean sheet for the first time since their last victory, the 3-0 win over Everton on 18th January

Villa hang on to end losing run

With substitute Mark Bosnich returning to the team-sheet for the first time in nearly five months, Michael Oakes could be forgiven for feeling under more pressure than usual, as he makes his 23rd straight appearance between the sticks.

As if it wasn't bad enough, a Villa team which can't buy a win at present faces a fixture that has prefaced the departure of its last two managers. The wind is blowing and the chewed-up midwinter turf is capable of turning any bounce into an off-break.

Credit to Oakes, then, for providing a timely reminder of how he has grown into the keeper's job, with a sterling second half performance as Wimbledon snap out of an ineffectual first period.

With Oakes largely reduced to pacing his area, anyone watching those initial 45 minutes after a month on a desert island would need some persuading that Villa are a side in a rut, as the visitors knock the ball about with an aplomb that reduces the Dons to virtual spectators.

Just two minutes have elapsed when Dion Dublin breaks clear of the Don's defence to launch a lob that keeper Neil Sullivan is at full stretch to tip over.

Sullivan is in action again 14 minutes later, reacting quckly to steal the ball from Simon Grayson's toe, but in between Ian Taylor misses a golden opportunity when an attempted Wimbledon clearance rolls straight to him inside the

Simon Grayson enjoys a rare place in the starting line-up.

penalty area and he shoots high over the bar.

Once a delightful sequence of passes has resulted in a Paul Merson strike that whistles just past the post, the hosts decide it's time they were joining in.

Half-time is two minutes away when Neal Ardley chests down a deep cross from the right before unleashing a shot that Oakes saves, smartly falling to his right.

If you can ever have a turning point in a goalless draw, this is it. Perked up by a few doubtlessly well-chosen words of encouragement from Joe Kinnear, Wimbledon assume the instigators' role after the break, while Villa, whom you suspect need to lead a game again to return to their old selves, become passive.

Having previously failed to reach a cross dangerously close to the visitors' goal, Efan Ekoku is denied only by an Oakes cavalry charge out of his box four minutes into the second half.

The Villa goalkeeper produces his best save of the match to keep out a 25-yarder from Marcus Gayle just before the hour and then enjoys the good fortune he's earned when Ekoku can find neither power nor aim to reward the Jason Euell cross that lands on his head just feet from the goal-line.

In virtual role-reversal since the first half, Villa's riposte amounts to a long range shot from Simon Grayson that Sullivan saves and a header that Dion Dublin may feel he could have done rather better with.

By then, the game has degenerated into uninspiring fare, but a point by any means is beautiful to behold for the visitors. As the old Chinese proverb observes, a journey of a thousand miles must begin with a single step.

Saturday 27th February 1999 • Villa Park • 3.00pm

ASTON VILLA 1 COVENTRY CITY 4

Half-time 0-1 • *Attendance* 38,799

Referee Uriah RENNIE (Sheffield)

Referee's Assistants P. CANADINE and R. GOULD

Claret and Blue Shirts, White Shorts		Goals	Sky Blue, Dark Blue and White Shirts, Sky Blue Shorts		Goals
13	Michael OAKES		1	Magnus HEDMAN	
3	Alan WRIGHT		2	Roland NILSSON	
4	Gareth SOUTHGATE (c) ❏		3	David BURROWS	
6	Steve WATSON ‡		4	Paul WILLIAMS ❏	
7	Ian TAYLOR †		5	Richard SHAW	
10	Paul MERSON		7	Darren HUCKERBY †	
12	Julian JOACHIM		10	Gary McALLISTER (c)	
14	Dion DUBLIN ❏	55pen	11	George BOATENG	51,84
15	Simon GRAYSON ❏		12	Paul TELFER	
17	Lee HENDRIE ❏		26	Steve FROGGATT	
20	Riccardo SCIMECA		28	John ALOISI ❏	25,72
	Substitutes			*Substitutes*	
1	Mark BOSNICH (Gk)		9	Muhamed KONJIC	
8	Mark DRAPER †31 #		14	Trond SOLTVEDT	
9	Stan COLLYMORE #56		27	Marc EDWORTHY	
16	Gareth BARRY ‡44		40	Gary McSHEFFREY †90	
31	Jlloyd SAMUEL		43	Chris KIRKLAND (Gk)	

BEFORE	P	W	D	L	F	A	pts	AFTER	P	W	D	L	F	A	pts
4 Villa	26	12	8	6	37	27	44	5 Villa	27	12	8	7	38	31	44
18 Coventry	26	6	6	14	24	37	24	17 Coventry	27	7	6	14	28	38	27

FACTFILE

Dion Dublin's first goal since his two-goal heroics against Arsenal on 13th December... This turns out to be the final game in Michael Oakes' uninterrupted run of appearances since first deputising for the injured Mark Bosnich on 17th October at West Ham

Darkest hour against Sky Blues

A progressively threadbare crowd as the game winds down to its inevitable conclusion, says it all, as Villa hit rock-bottom against a Coventry side recording its first-ever league win at Villa Park at the 25th time of asking.

The visitors' growing self-belief is in painful contrast to their opponents, who look like a team uncertain where its next decent break is coming from, once Coventry take the lead after 24 minutes.

Former Villa player Steve Froggatt fires in a low pass to the near post. John Aloisi, who is to prove a seamless replacement for the injured Noel Whelan, leaves Riccardo Scimeca for dead and hooks the ball home.

The goal had looked on the cards, with Coventry's Darren Huckerby making regular sorties down the right in the early stages, it is the game's defining contrast. While every Coventry attack is a voyage of hope, Villa advance with the hesitancy of men trying to sneak raw meat through a safari park.

This naturally has a telling effect on the chances tally. City have vociferous claims for a penalty waved away in the 27th minute when Huckerby and Scimeca collide and they fail to capitalise when Simon Grayson is dispossessed in midfield with his defenders out of position.

Villa must wait until four minutes before half-time for their first clear-cut opening, Magnus Hedman saving well from a long drive by Steve Watson. A minute later, Dion Dublin nearly levels from a Watson cross but Paul Williams blocks his shot.

Compounding Villa's injury problems, Steve Watson badly sprains an ankle while making the pass, although the injury initially looks rather worse, and he is stretchered off to be replaced by Gareth Barry.

The hosts' hopes of a second-half rally are dashed just five minutes after the break, when Huckerby cuts into the penalty area and pulls the ball back for Boateng, who evades Riccardo Scimeca to blast the ball high into the net.

There is at least a quick riposte from Villa, Dublin's 54th-minute spot-kick punishing his old club after Julian Joachim was tripped by Richard Shaw.

Stan Collymore is introduced shortly afterwards and for a 12-minute spell, Villa suggest that the team we know and love may just be one good result away. Transformed by the goal, they begin to find space and produce the kind of crisp, purposeful passing that powered them to the Premiership's summit in the first half of the season.

If Gordon Strachan's sudden appearance on the touchline suggests Coventry have a game on their hands, it also has the desired effect on his team.

Froggatt sends over a free-kick from the left in the 72nd minute and Aloisi nips in front of Southgate to score from close-range.

Collymore hits the post from a narrow angle nine minutes from time, pouncing on the rebound after Hedman parries a Dublin shot, but it's Coventry who have the last shout two minutes later, Boateng beating Villa's flat defence to a ball out of midfield and lobbing the ball over Michael Oakes and into the net.

Haven't we met before? Dion Dublin soars above his former team-mate.

Wednesday 10th March 1999 • Pride Park • 7.45pm

DERBY COUNTY 2 ASTON VILLA 1

Half-time 2-1 • Attendance 26,836

Referee Gary WILLARD (Worthing)

Referee's Assistants M. SHORT and I. BLANCHARD

White Shirts, Black Shorts	Goals	Claret and Blue Shirts, White Shorts	Goals
1 Russell HOULT		1 Mark BOSNICH	
3 Stefan SCHNOOR		3 Alan WRIGHT	
4 Darryl POWELL ❏		4 Gareth SOUTHGATE (c) ❏	
6 Igor STIMAC		8 Mark DRAPER	
9 Paulo WANCHOPE ❏ †		9 Stan COLLYMORE ❏	
14 Lars BOHINEN ❏		10 Paul MERSON ❏	
16 Jacob LAURSEN		12 Alan THOMPSON	44
17 Spencer PRIOR (c) ❏		14 Dion DUBLIN	
20 Stefano ERANIO		15 Gareth BARRY	
24 Deon BURTON	22	17 Lee HENDRIE ❏	
27 Francesco BAIANO	18	20 Riccardo SCIMECA †	
Substitutes		*Substitutes*	
2 Horacio CARBONARI		12 Julian JOACHIM †76	
11 Kevin HARPER †88		13 Michael OAKES (Gk)	
12 Malcolm CHRISTIE		23 David HUGHES	
19 Steve ELLIOTT		31 Jlloyd SAMUEL	
21 Mart POOM (Gk)		32 Aaron LESCOTT	

BEFORE		P	W	D	L	F	A	pts
5	Villa	27	12	8	7	38	31	44
9	Derby	27	9	11	7	26	25	38

AFTER		P	W	D	L	F	A	pts
5	Villa	28	12	8	8	39	33	44
6	Derby	28	10	11	7	28	26	41

FACTFILE

Mark Bosnich's first game since injuring his shoulder against Coventry City on 3rd October... Alan Thompson's first goal since the second game of the season on 23rd August... Leeds United's 2-0 defeat of Spurs leaves them four points clear of Villa in 4th place; the final European qualification berth

Shaky start sees Euro hopes fade

Time was when Villa were justifiably entitled to a fantasy or two about competing in next season's Champions' League. Even if the doom-sayers were right in predicting that their push for the Premiership title couldn't last, they looked a good bet for one of the two runners-up slots that would guarantee at least a shot at pre-qualifying for Europe's premier club competition.

Two goals in 22 minutes from Derby County, however, and suddenly even UEFA Cup quali-fication seems a shaky proposition, as Villa are emphatically punished for a listless opening half hour.

Mark Bosnich returns from injury and is a tonic but not an antidote as Francesco Baiano slots home a cross from Italian compatriot Stefano Eranio in the 22nd minute, four minutes before Jamaican striker Deon Burton dispatches a well executed back-heel from Baiano high into the roof of the net from just outside the penalty area.

For a new look Villa line-up, it's the same old problem. Dion Dublin has been seconded to central defence and Stan Collymore starts his first game since the Third Round FA Cup tie against Hull City, but they and their team-mates are again left chasing a match that threatens to outrun them when Burton nudges a Paulo Wanchope cross inches wide of the post, shortly after his goal.

Some crass showboating by County's Igor Stimac stirs up the visitors for an unexpected riposte shortly before half-time. The Croatian defender tauntingly bounces the ball on his foot deep in his own half and while he is pub-licly chastised by his manager Jim Smith after the game, a fuming Alan Thompson hands down summary judgment beforehand, when he tears at the Derby defence before rifling in a goal from 20 yards.

Any momentum stemming from this retort is unfortunately dissipated by the half-time break, for while Bosnich is quickly back into the groove, twice saving superbly from Paulo Wanchope early in the second half, it will be 28 minutes after the re-start before Villa mount another *bona fide* assault on the County goal, a reverse pass from Lee Hendrie running into Gareth Southgate's path for a shot that is well saved by Russell Hoult.

Collymore has the ball in the net a minute later, only to be penalised for a charge on Hoult, and Villa have their last chance two minutes before full-time, when Thompson again advances from midfield before chipping over the defence, but Hendrie is unable to find a shot on goal.

While John Gregory is critical of his team's start to the game, he says they were more like themselves in the second half and he also has praise for Stan Collymore.

"If you measure that alongside some of his performances, he can take a lot from it," says the Villa manager. "He played with a bit of devil in him."

Geordie jolt – Alan Thompson briefly rattled Derby with his second goal of the season.

Saturday 13th March 1999 • White Hart Lane • 3.00pm

TOTTENHAM HOTSPUR 1 ASTON VILLA 0

Half-time 0-0 • Attendance 35,963

Referee Peter JONES (Loughborough)

Referee's Assistants A.S. HOGG and M. TINGEY

White Shirts, Dark Blue Shorts		Goals	Claret and Blue Shirts, White Shorts		Goals
1	Ian WALKER		1	Mark BOSNICH	
2	Stephen CARR		3	Alan WRIGHT	
6	Allan NIELSEN		4	Gareth SOUTHGATE (c)	
9	Darren ANDERTON		8	Mark DRAPER ❑	
10	Les FERDINAND ❑		9	Stan COLLYMORE	
11	Chris ARMSTRONG ‡		10	Paul MERSON †	
14	David GINOLA †		12	Alan THOMPSON ❑	
15	Ramon VEGA		15	Gareth BARRY ❑	
19	Mauricio TARICCO #		17	Lee HENDRIE ❑	
23	Sol CAMPBELL (c)		20	Riccardo SCIMECA	
24	Tim SHERWOOD	89	26	Steve STONE ❑	
	Substitutes			*Substitutes*	
13	Espen BAARDSEN (Gk)		12	Julian JOACHIM †67	
18	Steffen IVERSEN †79		13	Michael OAKES (Gk)	
20	Jose DOMINGUEZ ‡79		21	Darren BYFIELD	
22	Andy SINTON #79		24	Mark DELANEY	
32	Luke YOUNG		31	Jlloyd SAMUEL	

BEFORE		P	W	D	L	F	A	pts	AFTER		P	W	D	L	F	A	pts
5	Villa	28	12	8	8	39	33	44	5	Villa	29	12	8	9	39	34	44
11	Spurs	28	8	12	8	33	34	36	10	Spurs	29	9	12	8	34	34	39

FACTFILE

Villa have now lost three straight games at White Hart Lane by the odd goal...
Five games have elapsed since a Villa striker scored in open play...
Villa debut for Steve Stone following his transfer from Nottingham Forest...
First appearance on team-sheet for Mark Delaney.

Sherwood late show stuns Villa

The last time Aston Villa saw Tim Sherwood, he was barrelling through their defence at Ewood Park to score the Boxing Day winner with a minute left. We're now heading towards Easter and Sherwood has swapped his Blackburn shirt for the white of Tottenham. Otherwise, it's as you were.

60 ticks are left on the clock when the midfielder transforms a low-key performance by being the final buffer in a spate of goalmouth pinball. Mark Bosnich can't hold a shot from Steffen Iversen, Sherwood's diving header hits the post, Alan Wright's attempted clearance hits his goalkeeper, the rebound finds Sherwood. Game over.

If the timing is cruel, the scoreline is vindication for those who maintain that fortune favours the brave. Though Gareth Southgate and Riccardo Scimeca defend doggedly and Mark Bosnich turns in another tidy performance in goal, Villa are a shadow of their former selves at the creative end of the pitch.

Their confidence shot, their forays into Spurs' half have no spark of conviction and an 'after you' mentality whenever they have goal at their mercy does not bode well in the quest for maximum points.

Stan Collymore and Paul Merson endure a fruitless afternoon against Spurs' central defenders, Sol Campbell and Ramon Vega, the extent of which is obvious when Merson is replaced by Julian Joachim with 22 minutes to go.

With their opponents' goal looking increasingly impregnable, Villa's only option is to ensure their own is similarly unviolated, and well before the final whistle, the afternoon becomes a case of holding what they have, rather than going for broke.

They survive an appeal for a penalty when Riccardo Scimeca appears to shove Les Ferdinand after an hour but Spurs' biggest grievance is their inability to make use of a stream of crosses from David Ginola.

No-one leaves White Hart Lane with greater relief than Villa's debutant Steve Stone. Back at the ground where he was sent off on his last visit, Stone suffers an even worse fate this time around: marking Ginola.

Forced to fill the wing-back role in the absence of the injured Steve Watson, Stone is lightly toasted by the flying Frenchman, before assistance arrives in the shape of Mark Draper. Between them, they harness Ginola as effectively as you can, but after his arrival from relegation-threatened Nottingham Forest, Stone can only be thankful that the latest crisis in which he finds himself doesn't have Division One at the end of it.

Adding salt to Villa's wounds are two incidents involving midfielder Alan Thompson, who is brought down by Spurs' goalkeeper Ian Walker in circumstances which John Gregory felt warranted the keeper's sending off. The Villa manager also claims that Thompson was head-butted in injury-time by Steffen Iversen without any of the four officials noticing it.

When you're in the mire as Villa are at present, however, those are the breaks; a point amply proved by Sherwood's second coming.

Debutant – Steve Stone.

Sunday 21st March 1999 • Villa Park • 11.30am

ASTON VILLA 0 CHELSEA 3

Half-time 0-0 • Attendance 39,217

Referee Graham BARBER (Tring)

Referee's Assistants Mrs W. TOMS and D.C. RICHARDS

Claret and Blue Shirts, White Shorts	Goals	Yellow Shirts, Yellow Shorts	Goals
1 Mark BOSNICH		1 Ed DE GOEY	
3 Alan WRIGHT		2 Dan PETRESCU †	
4 Gareth SOUTHGATE (c)		5 Frank LEBOEUF	
6 Steve WATSON		6 Marcel DESAILLY ❏	
10 Stan COLLYMORE ‡		7 Bjarne GOLDBAEK	85
11 Alan THOMPSON ❏		11 Dennis WISE (c) ❏	
14 Dion DUBLIN †		14 Graeme LE SAUX	
15 Gareth BARRY		17 Albert FERRER ❏	
17 Lee HENDRIE #		19 Tore Andre FLO ‡	59,90
20 Riccardo SCIMECA		25 Gianfranco ZOLA	
26 Steve STONE		28 Jody MORRIS	
Substitutes		*Substitutes*	
7 Ian TAYLOR #83		12 Michael DUBERRY	
8 Mark DRAPER		13 Kevin HITCHCOCK (Gk)	
10 Paul MERSON †74		21 Bernard LAMBOURDE †78	
12 Julian JOACHIM ‡74		22 Mark NICHOLLS ‡90	
13 Michael OAKES (Gk)		24 Eddie NEWTON	

BEFORE		P	W	D	L	F	A	pts	AFTER		P	W	D	L	F	A	pts
3	Chelsea	28	14	11	3	41	23	53	3	Chelsea	29	15	11	3	44	23	56
5	Villa	29	12	8	9	39	34	44	6	Villa	30	12	8	10	39	37	44

FACTFILE

Villa's third defeat by Chelsea this season, with Tore Andre Flo finding the net on each occasion... The Londoners have now won on their last four visits to Villa Park, with Villa's last goal in this fixture coming on 28th December 1994... They are now on the brink of a record sixth consecutive home defeat.

In form Flo puts Villa to sword

No fixture has been more redolent of strife this season than 'Villa v Chelsea'. The Blues inflicted Villa's first defeat of the season with a 4-1 thumping in the Worthington Cup; a water-logged Stamford Bridge forced them to abandon the next meeting, when Villa and most of their fans were already at the stadium, then they scored with virtually the last touch of the game to deny John Gregory's men a point in December.

All that pales into insignificance this morning, however, when a commanding Chelsea performance clearly illustrates how far Villa now trail the Premiership's elite.

In a fixture re-jigged to cater for those with inexplicable cravings for live televised football at 11.30am on a Sunday, Villa spend an hour of the game in containment mode, before folding like a house of cards the minute Tore Andre Flo opens the scoring in the 59th minute.

Outpacing the defence on the right hand side, the Norwegian steps inside to curl a shot into the far corner of Mark Bosnich's goal.

With Villa only able to hint at any sort of response, the game is made safe after 85 minutes, when the impressive Bjarne Goldbaek, set free down the right by Flo, beats Bosnich with a shot to the near post.

It is nothing more than the visitors have threatened since an opening 15 minutes in which the home goalmouth resembles Dodge City. Two crosses are agonisingly beyond the reach of Gianfranco Zola, while Flo also has his moment, forcing Bosnich to save with his legs after a piercing pass from Goldbaek.

While Chelsea are deft and assertive, Villa are a jumble of misplaced passes and their best hope lies in a stormy period just before half-time.

Clattered by Alan Thompson early in the game, Dennis Wise's short fuse is already alight when the game degenerates into a midfield kicking battle and testosterone briefly replaces tempo in Chelsea's gameplan.

The hosts shape their best chance of the game when a Thompson cross finds Dion Dublin's head in the 41st minute, forcing a smart save at the foot of his post from Ed De Goey.

The interval comes just in time to smooth the Londoners' furrowed brows, however, and if Villa need proof that this is not their day, it comes in the form of two stray passes by the normally watertight Gareth Barry, the second forcing Bosnich to save with his legs from the advancing Zola in the 65th minute.

But for their keeper, indeed, Villa's embarrassment could have been far worse. After Julian Joachim intercepts a Marcel Desailly back-pass only to see his shot go wide of the post, Chelsea resume the offensive and Bosnich is at full length to stop a Zola shot from 25 yards.

He is powerless to stop Flo making it 3-0 on the stroke of full-time, however. The striker makes a diagonal run across the penalty area to collect a Jody Morris chip over the defence, which he then angles into the net.

Crisp and imaginative, the move sums up Chelsea's morning – and Villa's deficiencies – to a tee.

Stan still – Chelsea defender Graeme Le Saux keeps Stan Collymore in check.

Friday 2nd April 1999 • Villa Park • 7.45pm

ASTON VILLA 0 WEST HAM UNITED 0

Half-time 0-0 • Attendance 36,813

Referee Gary WILLARD (Worthing)

Referee's Assistants K. PIKE and M. DEARING

Claret and Blue Shirts, White Shorts	Goals	White Shirts, White Shorts	Goals
1 Mark BOSNICH		12 Shaka HISLOP	
3 Alan WRIGHT		6 Neil RUDDOCK	
4 Gareth SOUTHGATE (c)		8 Trevor SINCLAIR ❏	
6 Steve WATSON		9 Paul KITSON	
7 Ian TAYLOR		10 Paolo DI CANIO	
8 Mark DRAPER ❏		11 Steve LOMAS (c)	
11 Alan THOMPSON †		13 Marc Vivien FOE	
12 Julian JOACHIM		15 Rio FERDINAND †	
14 Dion DUBLIN		18 Frank LAMPARD	
26 Steve STONE		19 Ian PEARCE	
34 Colin CALDERWOOD		20 Scott MINTO	
Substitutes		*Substitutes*	
7 Paul MERSON †86		4 Steve POTTS †8	
8 Michael OAKES (Gk)		7 Marc KELLER	
10 Gareth BARRY		16 John MONCUR	
12 Riccardo SCIMECA		22 Craig FORREST (Gk)	
13 Jlloyd SAMUEL		29 Eyal BERKOVIC	

BEFORE		P	W	D	L	F	A	pts
5	West Ham	30	13	7	10	34	39	46
6	Villa	30	12	8	10	39	37	44

AFTER		P	W	D	L	F	A	pts
5	West Ham	31	13	8	10	34	39	47
6	Villa	31	12	9	10	39	37	45

FACTFILE

Villa go three games without scoring for the first time since 1st November 1997... Colin Calderwood makes debut at the centre of defence... News that spare UEFA Cup place will go to Newcastle on the basis of their FA Cup run rather than to fifth-placed team in Premiership, removes much significance from this fixture.

Promising start to Easter week

If Villa aren't exactly flavour of the month with local clergy – following up a Sunday morning game with one on Good Friday – their stock with their own supporters is at least rising again, after they finally call a halt to a run of five straight home defeats with a battling performance that deserves maximum points.

Dion Dublin beats Marc Vivien Foe to a Steve Watson cross in the 40th minute, only to see his header come back from the post. That makes it just about even on the fortune front, with the Hammers having had their own set-back after four minutes, when Rio Ferdinand is stretchered off with damage to his ankle ligaments following a challenge from Mark Draper that earns the Villa man a yellow card.

The enforced alteration to their line-up isn't easily absorbed by the Londoners and they must wait until the closing stages of the first half to fashion a clear-cut chance on goal, when Foe breaks away to send in a shot that Paolo Di Canio deflects into the goal from the far post, only to be ruled offside

For once, it is Villa who enjoy the lion's share of the game. In the turmoil that follows a 13th-minute Alan Thompson corner into the visitors' area, Gareth Southgate pokes the ball goalwards, only for Steve Lomas to block on the line.

Dublin then forces a good save from West Ham keeper Shaka Hislop, with a shot from 20 yards, before Ian Taylor has two opportunities denied in the space of a minute, shortly after the half-hour mark.

First, Foe gets in the way of a shot from the Villa midfielder, who then just fails to make contact with a Mark Draper cross that fizzes across the face of goal.

West Ham are more composed after the interval and Mark Bosnich has to react quickly to save a deflected shot from Frank Lampard, who is subsequently involved in a smart move with Paul Kitson and Di Canio that leaves the Italian free for a shot which he puts over the bar, with Bosnich hurtling out to meet him.

Snapped into action by this flurry, Villa produce the best move of the game, when Draper and Dublin produce a nice exchange of passes before the ex-Coventry man scoops the ball over two defenders to set up Julian Joachim, who's unmarked 10 yards from goal. Agonisingly, however, Joachim's shot goes inches wide of the post.

There's a narrow miss at the other end when Mark Bosnich gets caught in no-man's land at the by-line, allowing Scott Minto to peel away from him and fire a shot into the side-netting from a narrow angle.

After shots from Taylor and Dublin go close, it's Kitson who almost wins the last laugh for the visitors in injury time, but his shot is too close to the Villa goalkeeper.

Ian Taylor – unlucky, on several occasions, not to give Villa the lead.

Tuesday 6th April 1999 • Filbert Street • 7.45pm

LEICESTER CITY 2 ASTON VILLA 2

Half-time 0-1 • *Attendance* 20,652

Referee Stephen LODGE (Barnsley)

Referee's Assistants P.V. NORMAN and R. BURTON

Blue Shirts, White Shorts	Goals	Claret and Blue Shirts, Blue Shorts	Goals
1 Kasey KELLER		1 Mark BOSNICH	
3 Frank SINCLAIR ❑		3 Alan WRIGHT	
7 Neil LENNON		4 Gareth SOUTHGATE (c)	
9 Emile HESKEY		6 Steve WATSON †	
11 Steve GUPPY ❑		7 Ian TAYLOR	
13 Arnar GUNNLAUGSSON †		8 Mark DRAPER ❑	
14 Robbie SAVAGE	63	12 Julian JOACHIM	49
18 Matt ELLIOTT (c) ❑		14 Dion DUBLIN	
19 Robert ULLATHORNE		17 Lee HENDRIE	2
24 Andy IMPEY		26 Steve STONE	
27 Tony COTTEE	71	34 Colin CALDERWOOD ❑	
Substitutes		*Substitutes*	
15 Pontus KAAMARK		10 Paul MERSON	
17 Charlie MILLER †59		13 Michael OAKES (Gk)	
20 Ian MARSHALL		15 Gareth BARRY †75	
22 Pegguy ARPHEXAD (Gk)		22 Darius VASSELL	
37 Theo ZAGORAKIS		24 Mark DELANEY	

BEFORE		P	W	D	L	F	A	pts	AFTER		P	W	D	L	F	A	pts
6	Villa	31	12	9	10	39	37	45	6	Villa	32	12	10	10	41	39	46
13	Leicester	29	9	10	10	30	37	37	14	Leicester	30	9	11	10	32	39	38

FACTFILE

Villa surrender a 2-0 lead for the first time since their 2-2 draw at home to Arsenal on 7th September 1996... They string back-to-back unbeaten games together for the first time since beating Everton 3-0 on 18th January.

A two goal lead is squandered

They've been beaten 4-2 by Chelsea, 6-2 by Manchester United, 5-0 by Arsenal and are slipping dangerously close to the relegation zone, but give Leicester City a pop at Aston Villa and you can bank on them playing out of their skins.

Villa fail to beat Leicester in the League for the eighth consecutive game. Yet to be beaten by Villa in the Premiership, the Foxes need a Houdini act of two goals in the last 27 minutes to preserve their record, after their visitors appeared set for their first win in nearly three months, at 2-0.

It's hard to imagine how Villa could have plotted their rehabilitation any better. When Lee Hendrie drives home the opening goal from an acute angle following a Julian Joachim cross, (his first goal since scoring at Chelsea on 9th December), they have the calming and novel experience of leading a game, after just 78 seconds.

The dividend is some of the best football Villa have produced since their halcyon days before Christmas, even if they have to wait until five minutes after the break to rediscover the killer punch in front of goal.

Alan Wright sends over a cross to the far post which Ian Taylor nods down to ex-Leicester player Julian Joachim, who shoots on the turn from close-range through a crowded goalmouth and well wide of Kasey Keller's despairing left

Lee Hendrie – a goal in 78 seconds.

hand, to put his team apparently out of sight. Villa's gremlins are not so easily evicted, however. What should have been the cue for a 40-minute holding job inexplicably triggers all the self-doubt of recent weeks instead and the hosts take full advantage.

Frank Sinclair had already stung Mark Bosnich's palms as the latter pushed aside a 20-yard piledriver from the former Chelsea player in the first half, but City step up the tempo after Joachim's goal, and subject their opponents' defence to incessant pressure that finally pays off in the 63rd minute.

After a long clearance, Robbie Savage spots Bosnich off his line and punishes the Australian with a perfect chip from 25 yards.

With Villa still trying to regroup, Tony Cottee ties the game up just nine minutes later when he stoops to put a header beyond Bosnich after a cross from Steve Guppy.

Both teams have a stab at maximum points in the closing stages. After a promising four-man move, Emile Heskey is just inches away from getting his toe to a low cross by Cottee, while for Villa, Julian Joachim is wide with a header after 88 minutes.

John Gregory describes his team as "devastated" afterward the match, but takes heart from the fact that they held out for the last 18 minutes when 2-2 might have easily become 3-2 to Leicester.

"...in the last 15 minutes of the game we played with a lot of passion and threw bodies in the way of everything," he says. "I don't think we would have got through that period three weeks ago."

Saturday 10th April 1999 • Villa Park • 3.00pm

ASTON VILLA 3   SOUTHAMPTON 0

Half-time 1-0 • *Attendance* 32,203

Referee Neale BARRY (Scunthorpe)

Referee's Assistants A. KAYE and D. MORRALL

Claret and Blue Shirts, White Shorts	Goals	Red and White Striped Shirts, Black Shorts	Goals
1 Mark BOSNICH		13 Neil MOSS	
3 Alan WRIGHT		2 Jason DODD (c)	
4 Gareth SOUTHGATE (c)		4 Chris MARSDEN	
6 Steve WATSON		5 Claus LUNDEKVAM ❏ ■39	
7 Ian TAYLOR		6 Ken MONKOU ❏	
8 Mark DRAPER ‡	13	7 Matthew LE TISSIER	
11 Alan THOMPSON †		9 Mark HUGHES †	
12 Julian JOACHIM	66	10 Egil ØSTENSTAD #	
14 Dion DUBLIN #	89	22 David HUGHES	
26 Steve STONE		23 Scott HILEY	
34 Colin CALDERWOOD		33 Patrick COLLETER ‡	
Substitutes		*Substitutes*	
10 Paul MERSON ‡57		14 Stuart RIPLEY #85	
13 Michael OAKES (Gk)		15 Francis BENALI †53	
15 Gareth BARRY #89		16 James BEATTIE	
17 Lee HENDRIE †5		27 David HIRST ‡72	
22 Darius VASSELL		32 Michael STENSGAARD (Gk)	

BEFORE	P	W	D	L	F	A	pts	AFTER	P	W	D	L	F	A	pts
6 Villa	32	12	10	10	41	39	46	5 Villa	33	13	10	10	44	39	49
19 Saints	32	8	6	18	28	57	30	19 Saints	33	8	6	19	28	60	30

FACTFILE

Villa's first win since beating Everton on 18th January... Southampton come away from Villa Park winless for the ninth time in 10 league games... Claus Lundekvam is the first player to be sent off at Villa Park since Everton's Alex Cleland in January.

Majestic Merson sees off Saints

If this season should represent Southampton's Premiership swansong, no-one will miss them more than Aston Villa.

The Saints were the last brittle hurdle that Villa cleared in November to set a club record for the longest unbeaten start to a season, and today they again capitulate obligingly, allowing Villa to experience the flush of victory for the first time in 16-and-a-half hours of football.

The mental scars of such a bleak run do not fade in the space of a single afternoon, however. As if scarcely able to believe their changing luck, Villa remain too ponderous for their control of the game to become a stranglehold until the latter stages.

It is no coincidence that the points are only locked up when Paul Merson comes on in the 56th minute. Having spoken in the build-up to the game of football's role as a release from his off-field problems, Merson graphically illustrates the point with an array of incisive passes that lay the Southampton defence bare and it is his lob over the Saints' back line that sets up Julian Joachim to make the game safe at 2-0 with 65 minutes gone.

It had taken a moment of similar directness to set Villa on their way, ironically supplied by the man Merson replaced. Mark Draper embarks on a looping run from midfield in the 12th minute and takes full advantage of minimal Southampton resistance to hammer home a shot into the far corner from the edge of the penalty area.

It's a settling influence after an opening spell in which Villa's nightmare looked set to continue for another week. Alan Thompson limps off with a hamstring strain after just four minutes and a pass from Matthew Le Tissier catches the home defence flat just a minute later, forcing Mark Bosnich to save with his legs as Egil Østenstad is clean through.

The Norwegian is a willing workhorse for his team but the lack of confidence which he has publicly admitted to this season is apparent and he and Mark Hughes are unable to reward Le Tissier's vision he repeatedly probes the Villa penalty area.

For Villa meanwhile, Draper sees a free-kick that's part cross, part shot, curl towards the far corner after 16 minutes, before Neil Moss, deputising for the injured Paul Jones, tips the ball to safety.

As two mundane sides begin to pick at each other unconvincingly, it takes referee Neale Barry to administer the game's next telling blow, when he decides that an offside may cancel out a Villa attack five minutes before half-time but not the Claus Lundekvam foul on Ian Taylor which follows it.

It's a second yellow card for the defender and a stake through the heart for his depleted team.

The arrival of Merson in the second half merely serves as the last rites. Every telling pass of the final half-hour seems to stem from his boot, save for the cross which Steve Stone provides with two minutes left, enabling Dion Dublin to bury a far post header for his side's third goal.

Jason Dodd and Ken Monkou can only look on as Dion Dublin gets in a powerful header.

Saturday 17th April 1999 • Anfield • 3.00pm

LIVERPOOL 0 ASTON VILLA 1

Half-time 0-1 • Attendance 44,306

Referee Jeff WINTER (Stockton-on-Tees)
Referee's Assistants C. WEBSTER and R. GOULD

Red Shirts, Red Shorts	Goals
1 David JAMES	
4 Rigobert SONG ❑ ‡	
6 Phil BABB	
7 Steve McMANAMAN	
9 Robbie FOWLER	
11 Jamie REDKNAPP	
13 Karlheinz RIEDLE ❑	
17 Paul INCE (c)	
20 Stig Inge BJØRNEBYE †	
21 Dominic MATTEO	
23 Jamie CARRAGHER	
Substitutes	
5 Steve STAUNTON	
8 Øyvind LEONHARDSEN †45	
16 Sean DUNDEE ‡85	
18 Jean Michel FERRI	
19 Brad FRIEDEL (Gk)	

Turquoise Shirts with Black Trim, Black Shorts	Goals
1 Mark BOSNICH ❑	
3 Alan WRIGHT	
4 Gareth SOUTHGATE (c)	
6 Steve WATSON	
7 Ian TAYLOR	33
8 Mark DRAPER	
12 Julian JOACHIM ‡	
14 Dion DUBLIN	
17 Lee HENDRIE †	
26 Steve STONE	
34 Colin CALDERWOOD	
Substitutes	
10 Paul MERSON †69	
13 Michael OAKES (Gk)	
15 Gareth BARRY ‡90	
22 Darius VASSELL	
24 Mark DELANEY	

BEFORE		P	W	D	L	F	A	pts
5	Villa	33	13	10	10	44	39	49
9	Liverpool	31	12	8	11	57	41	44

AFTER		P	W	D	L	F	A	pts
5	Villa	34	14	10	10	45	39	52
9	Liverpool	32	12	8	12	57	42	44

FACTFILE

Villa's first away win since beating Charlton 1-0 on 21st December... Their first back-to-back wins since beating Sheffield Wednesday and Hull City at the turn of the year... Only Villa's second win at Anfield in 20 league visits and their first clean sheet there since September 1981.

Taylor seals rare win at Anfield

Ten years after the Hillsborough disaster, Villa run out at Anfield with an occasion to overcome as much as a football team.

After The Kop recalls the death toll by holding up the number '96' in mosaic, 44,306 people ensure that a minute's silence in memory of the dead is precisely that and Mark Bosnich and Paul Merson receive a standing ovation when they lay flowers in front of the Kop on behalf of their club.

You feel Liverpool must surely be inspired by all this, yet their performance is disjointed and shapeless. Robbie Fowler plays his last game of the season before his six-match ban for taunting both an opponent and fans in a manner that turned crassness into an art form; Steve McManaman will soon be off to Real Madrid; there's nothing left to play for and the hosts do a remarkable impersonation of 11 young men who've only just been introduced. Manager Gerard Houllier needs to work fast, or that famous inscription in the players' tunnel will soon read "This is Anfield. No, really?"

If a most uncharacteristic performance only exacerbates the raw nerves of the home supporters, it's a gift for an opponent which in recent memory has triumphed at Liverpool about as regularly as the Conservative Party.

Even in the game's early stages, when some useful crosses from McManaman pace a promising start by his team, Villa give as good as they get. Bosnich is in the thick of the action in the opening half-hour, sprinting out of his box to stop one attack with his chest, plucking the ball off Fowler's head and then escaping when he fumbles a cross, as the ball remains just out of Paul Ince's reach.

At the other end, however, after Jamie Carragher has already cleared one effort from

Ian Taylor, the Villa midfielder has his revenge in the 33rd minute, although he has the good grace to celebrate with a laugh rather than triumphalism after he finds the net with a completely miscued shot.

No-one in the Villa ranks is laughing seven minutes later, though, when a raised boot belonging to Cameroon defender Rigobert Song takes the ball before thudding into Lee Hendrie's chest. While it's enough to get John Gregory and Liverpool assistant manager Phil Thompson sprinting down the touchline for the purposes of recrimination and damage-assessment, it needs a crunching second-half tackle on Hendrie by German striker Karlheinz Riedle to polish off the young midfielder, who's stretchered off with an ankle injury.

It's a sign of Liverpool's mounting frustration, as Villa's tenacity and the hosts' misfortune combine to prevent an equaliser, even in the face of Liverpool's gathering momentum after the interval.

A nice move between McManaman, Riedle and Fowler leaves the latter free in space between two defenders, only for an offside flag to go up, and McManaman horribly scuffs his 74th minute shot after Øyvind Leonhardsen's cross finds him unmarked just yards from goal.

"The task here is bigger than I thought," says Houllier afterwards. John Gregory's task, on the other hand, grows more pleasant by the week.

Lee Hendrie vies with Steve McManaman.

Saturday 24th April 1999 • Villa Park • 3.00pm

ASTON VILLA 2 NOTTINGHAM FOREST 0

Half-time 1-0 • Attendance 34,492

Referee Paul DURKIN (Portland)

Referee's Assistants G.BEALE and J. PETTITT

Claret and Blue Shirts, White Shorts	Goals
13 Michael OAKES	
3 Alan WRIGHT	
4 Gareth SOUTHGATE (c)	
6 Steve WATSON ‡	
7 Ian TAYLOR	
8 Mark DRAPER	45
10 Paul MERSON	
12 Julian JOACHIM	
14 Dion DUBLIN †	
26 Steve STONE #	
34 Colin CALDERWOOD	
Substitutes	
5 Ugo EHIOGU ‡72	
15 Gareth BARRY †45	57
22 Darius VASSELL	
24 Mark DELANEY #82	
39 Peter ENCKELMAN (Gk)	

White Shirts, Black Shorts	Goals
13 Mark CROSSLEY	
2 Matthieu LOUIS-JEAN	
3 Alan ROGERS	
5 Steve CHETTLE (c)	
6 Jon Olav HJELDE ❏	
10 Andy JOHNSON †	
14 Dougie FREEDMAN #	
22 Des LYTTLE	
25 Jesper MATTSSON	
29 Marlon HAREWOOD	
32 Stale STENSAAS ‡	
Substitutes	
1 Dave BEASANT (Gk)	
9 Neil SHIPPERLEY #74	
11 Chris BART-WILLIAMS †56	
18 Ian WOAN	
40 Pierre VAN HOOIJDONK ‡67	

BEFORE		P	W	D	L	F	A	pts
5	Villa	34	14	10	10	45	39	52
20	Forest	34	4	9	21	30	66	21

AFTER		P	W	D	L	F	A	pts
5	Villa	35	15	10	10	47	39	55
20	Forest	35	4	9	22	30	68	21

FACTFILE

Referee Paul Durkin limped off in first half to be replaced by Mr Pettitt, who in turn, was replaced by L. Hodgson, the fourth official... Forest have now won just one of their last 10 games at Villa Park... Villa notch three straight clean sheets for the fourth time this season, and first since the defeat of Everton in January.

Woeful return for Big Ron

'Never go back', runs the old axiom. Unfortunately, things like Premiership fixture lists make it occasionally inevitable. Thus it is that one of the lowest points of Ron Atkinson's managerial career takes place at the stadium where he was once cheered to the rafters for bringing home the League Cup and guiding Villa to the runners-up spot in the inaugural Premiership.

Within 24 hours of the dismal performance which condemns his Nottingham Forest side to relegation, Atkinson announces his retirement from management with effect from the end of this season.

He is terse and unsmiling; his team were bland, witless and belly-up the moment Mark Draper put them a goal down just seconds before half-time. TS Eliot's line about the world ending not with a bang but a whimper, comes readily to mind.

For all that a win alone is good enough to prolong the visitors' survival, they show little urgency during a scrappy first half in which Villa give the impression that a goal is merely a matter of time.

While the hosts' passing is sloppy, they manufacture enough opportunities to give Paul Merson and Steve Stone shots on goal. The latter is performing like a man possessed against the team for which he played only a month ago and for the sake of the game as a spectacle, it's a shame his crusading spirit doesn't rub off on the rest of his team.

There is finally something for the home crowd to cheer after 49 minutes of a half that was extended when referee Paul Durkin left the game with a knee injury. Draper's head gets a faint touch to an Alan Wright free-kick from the Trinity Road touchline and the ball winds up in the far corner of the net.

When the game resumes after the interval, Forest appear to have decided there's no way back. Their response is condensed into one solitary effort on target, a shot from Alan Rogers two minutes after the restart, that Michael Oakes, in for an injured Mark Bosnich, needs two attempts to gather.

The second-half interest centres more on its details than on the big picture. Gareth Barry replaces Dion Dublin at the interval, the striker having succumbed to a knee injury, and rounds off an enthusiastic performance in midfield by bundling in a cross from Steve Stone after 57 minutes; the youngster's first goal for Villa.

The cheer for Ugo Ehiogu's arrival from the bench 15 minutes later, is if anything, even greater. Defying countless predictions that his season was over, the big central defender returns to the fray, 11 weeks after the eye injury he sustained at St James' Park, and is quickly back into the old routine.

John Gregory takes advantage of a docile contest to give Mark Delaney his debut for the senior side following his recent arrival from Cardiff City. The Welshman makes a solid start, but easily the most eye-catching performance of the second half comes from conga-dancing Forest fans, relieved that their suffering is finally over.

As the final whistle sounds, they aren't the only ones.

Gareth Barry forces home his first Villa goal.

Saturday 1st May 1999 • Old Trafford • 3.00pm

MANCHESTER UNITED 2 ASTON VILLA 1

Half-time 1-1 • *Attendance* 55,189

Referee Keith BURGE (Tonypandy)

Referee's Assistants G. ATKINS and A. WILLIAMS

Red Shirts, White Shorts	Goals	Turquoise Shirts with Black Trim, Black Shorts	Goals
1 Peter SCHMEICHEL (c)		13 Michael OAKES	
2 Gary NEVILLE		3 Alan WRIGHT	
3 Denis IRWIN		4 Gareth SOUTHGATE (c)	
4 David MAY ‡		6 Steve WATSON	19og
5 Ronny JOHNSEN		7 Ian TAYLOR ❏	
7 David BECKHAM	47	8 Mark DRAPER †	
8 Nicky BUTT		10 Paul MERSON	
10 Teddy SHERINGHAM		12 Julian JOACHIM	33
15 Jesper BLOMQVIST †		14 Dion DUBLIN ‡	
18 Paul SCHOLES		26 Steve STONE	
19 Dwight YORKE		34 Colin CALDERWOOD	

Substitutes		*Substitutes*	
12 Phil NEVILLE †63		5 Ugo EHIOGU	
17 Raimond VAN DER GOUW (Gk)		11 Alan THOMPSON †67	
24 Wesley BROWN ‡79		15 Gareth BARRY	
33 Mark WILSON		22 Darius VASSELL ‡75	
34 Jonathan GREENING		39 Peter ENCKELMAN (Gk)	

BEFORE	P	W	D	L	F	A	pts	AFTER	P	W	D	L	F	A	pts
2 United	33	19	11	3	73	33	68	2 United	34	20	11	3	75	34	71
5 Villa	35	15	10	10	47	39	55	5 Villa	36	15	10	11	48	41	55

FACTFILE

Joachim's goal is Villa's first in the league at Old Trafford in five visits... Their unbeaten run ends at five games... There is the small consolation of keeping Dwight Yorke off the scoresheet in both games this season... A minute's silence precedes the game in honour of Sir Alf Ramsey, who died earlier in the week.

'Deadly Spice' does the damage

But for David Beckham, Villa might well have left Old Trafford as delighted as when they departed from Anfield two weeks earlier, for it takes his consummate 30-yard free-kick to divide the teams this afternoon, its timing as wounding as its execution.

When Julian Joachim cancelled out an own goal from Steve Watson with 12 minutes left in the first half, a famous victory looked within Villa's reach against a United team missing Andy Cole, Ryan Giggs, Roy Keane and Jaap Stam.

Yet with most people's half-time refreshment still *en route* to their stomachs, Beckham rejuvenates Old Trafford with a piece of dead-ball expertise that drains the momentum from his opponents. Combining speed and accuracy, his 47th-minute shot couldn't have squeezed more snugly into the top corner had he taken it in his dreams.

It's questionable whether a wall would have stopped him and unquestionable that Gareth Southgate wouldn't. The Villa skipper headed a Beckham free-kick off the line in the first half but later revealed that had he been asked by his goalkeeper to man the line again, he would have stood on the side opposite that attacked by Beckham's strike.

It's minor comfort to Villa that it takes such perfection to beat them. United enjoy much space down the flanks throughout the game, but

Ian Taylor and Colin Calderwood ensure that Dwight Yorke has minimal opportunity to benefit and Villa always threaten to retaliate in equal measure against a Manchester defence that is nothing like as poised as its attack.

Once Watson hurries back to defend in the 19th minute, only to find the ball careering off his body and into the net, Villa fans are entitled to fear the worst after a confident start by the home side, yet theirs is no longer a team that wilts at the first sign of adversity.

With Dion Dublin, facing his former club, and Julian Joachim toiling endlessly, the game is far from over and Watson atones for his own goal when he sends Steve Stone away down the right wing 12 minutes before half-time. Stone whips over a cross and Joachim nips ahead of his marker to tuck the ball home from close-range.

Once United have regained the initiative, the game becomes a tale of two tackles. Mark Draper is impeded by Jesper Blomqvist in the 57th minute, but Villa claims for a penalty merely earn a free-kick for obstruction that Draper hits wide.

United are more successful nine minutes later, when Stone is ruled to have shoved Phil Neville in the Villa box. Penalty taker Denis Irwin slips as he kicks the ball, but Oakes still has to produce a fine save to keep the deficit at one goal.

Villa's best chance of equality departs when Dublin finally surrenders to his various injuries, but to those Villa fans who must have had cold sweats looking ahead to this game in the dark days of February and March, it is still a highly creditable performance.

Steve Watson atoned for his own goal by setting up Villa's reply.

Saturday 8th May 1999 • Villa Park • 3.00pm

ASTON VILLA 3 CHARLTON ATHLETIC 4

Half-time 1-1 • *Attendance* 37,705

Referee Mike RILEY (Leeds)
Referee's Assistants K. HAWKES and A. HOGG

Claret and Blue Shirts, White Shorts		Goals
13	Michael OAKES	
3	Alan WRIGHT	
4	Gareth SOUTHGATE (c)	
6	Steve WATSON ■89	
7	Ian TAYLOR ❑	
8	Mark DRAPER ‡	
10	Paul MERSON	
12	Julian JOACHIM	65,79
15	Gareth BARRY	3og, 7
26	Steve STONE	
34	Colin CALDERWOOD †	
	Substitutes	
5	Ugo EHIOGU †61	
11	Alan THOMPSON	
22	Darius VASSELL ‡61	
31	Jlloyd SAMUEL	
39	Peter ENCKELMAN (Gk)	

Ecru Shirts, Black Shorts		Goals
13	Andy PETTERSON ■79	
2	Danny MILLS ❑	90
3	Chris POWELL	
4	Neil REDFEARN ‡	
5	Richard RUFUS	
8	Mark KINSELLA (c)	
10	Clive MENDONCA #	56
11	John ROBINSON ❑ †	67
19	Steve JONES	
23	Carl TILER	
40	Graham STUART	
	Substitutes	
12	Steve BROWN †80	
14	Mark BOWEN	
27	Scott PARKER	
37	John BARNES ‡84	
39	Martin PRINGLE #84	

BEFORE		P	W	D	L	F	A	pts
5	Villa	36	15	10	11	48	41	55
19	Charlton	36	7	12	17	37	52	33

AFTER		P	W	D	L	F	A	pts
5	Villa	37	15	10	12	51	45	55
18	Charlton	37	8	12	17	41	55	36

FACTFILE

Villa lose their final home game of the season for the first time in three years... They concede own goals in consecutive games for the first time since 8th December 1993... Their first seven-goal game since losing 4-3 at Newcastle United on 30th September 1996... Steve Watson's first ever red card.

Brave Charlton mar home finale

If there are mitigating circumstances for the kind of embarrassment Villa thought they'd put behind them this season, it's that they're not used to teams at death's door behaving like this.

After all, their last two visitors, Southampton and Nottingham Forest, had the courtesy to act like teams staring Division One in the face: flimsy, tentative, and uninspired. Full credit to them for knowing their place.

Not like this Charlton bunch. First they pressure poor young Gareth Barry into heading past his own goalkeeper with three minutes gone and then they ignore not one, but three equalisers by their hosts; three gentle reminders that today is supposed to be about Villa ending their home schedule in style and all but fencing off that precious InterToto Cup spot.

Some people have no respect.

No wonder Charlton boss Alan Curbishley reckons his men are becoming everyone's second-favourite team. They aren't a pretty side but their coolness under fire ultimately wears down a porous Villa defence.

Charlton suffer calamity just four minutes after going 1-0 up, when Richard Rufus, whose own goal separated the sides at The Valley, completes his application for honorary Villa membership when he spurns a straightforward back-pass to his goalkeeper Andy Petterson, in favour of an inexplicable hoof across his penalty area. Hardly daring imagine that redemption might come so soon, Gareth

Barry volleys home his second goal of the game to make it 1-1.

With his team finding few ways to penetrate the Charlton defence, the score is unchanged until 11 minutes after the interval, when Clive Mendonca, in his first game since injuring an ankle at the start of April, pulls away from Gareth Southgate and waits for Michael Oakes to commit himself before shooting his side in front once more.

Julian Joachim cancels it out nine minutes later, with an angled shot from a pass down the left by substitute Darius Vassell, but Villa barely have time to fit their celebrations in, as Southgate is again brushed aside, this time by Steve Jones in the 67th minute. He pulls the ball back for Mendonca's shot to be blocked by Oakes, but only as far as John Robinson, whose looping header Southgate just fails to clear off the line.

When Joachim hooks home yet another equaliser following a 79th minute corner and is felled by Petterson two minutes later, earning the latter a red card, you have to feel Charlton's course is run.

Oh ye of little faith. Well beaten by Martin Pringle with a minute left, Steve Watson hauls him down by the collar and is himself pointed in the direction of the dressing rooms. The free-kick, 20 yards out, is rolled square into the path of Danny Mills, who's arriving like a freight train. Even before he connects, you just know it's the winner.

Devotees of blood and thunder can't say that they haven't had their money's worth.

As for the purists, they were the ones filing out after 70 minutes.

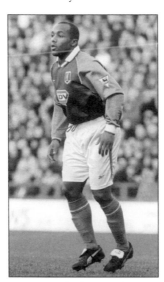

Two-goal Julian Joachim.

Sunday 16th May 1999 • Highbury • 4.00pm

ARSENAL 1 ASTON VILLA 0

Half-time 0-0 • Attendance 38,308

Referee Dermot GALLAGHER (Banbury)

Referee's Assistants P. SHARP and G. TURNER

Red and White Shirts, White Shorts	Goals		Turquoise Shirts with Black Trim, Black Shorts	Goals
1 David SEAMAN		13	Michael OAKES	
2 Lee DIXON		3	Alan WRIGHT	
4 Patrick VIEIRA		4	Gareth SOUTHGATE (c) ❏	
6 Tony ADAMS (c) ❏		5	Ugo EHIOGU	
7 Nelson VIVAS †		6	Steve WATSON ❏ ‡	
9 Nicolas ANELKA ‡		8	Mark DRAPER ❏	
10 Dennis BERGKAMP		10	Paul MERSON	
11 Marc OVERMARS #		12	Julian JOACHIM	
14 Martin KEOWN		16	Simon GRAYSON †	
15 Ray PARLOUR		20	Riccardo SCIMECA ❏	
17 Emmanuel PETIT		34	Colin CALDERWOOD #	
Substitutes			*Substitutes*	
5 Steve BOULD		15	Gareth BARRY	
8 Fredrik LJUNGBERG †14		22	Darius VASSELL †72	
24 John LUKIC (Gk)		24	Mark DELANEY ‡72	
25 Nwankwo KANU ‡61	66	26	Steve STONE #81	
27 Kaba DIAWARA #79		39	Peter ENCKELMAN (Gk)	

BEFORE		P	W	D	L	F	A	pts
2	Arsenal	37	21	12	4	58	17	75
5	Villa	37	15	10	12	51	45	55

AFTER		P	W	D	L	F	A	pts
2	Arsenal	38	22	12	4	59	17	78
6	Villa	38	15	10	13	51	46	55

FACTFILE

Arsenal score same number of points as last year yet fail in the defence of their title, Villa finish a place higher in the Premiership, yet are overtaken by West Ham for the InterToto Cup berth and a last chance at European qualification... Villa lose at Highbury for just the second time in seven Premiership visits.

Quietly into the shadows

Rarely are victors more depressed than the vanquished. If a three game losing run torches Villa's chance of European football next term, at least they haven't just lost the Premiership by a whisker.

After another season where TV demands saw the fixture list manipulated like dough in a baker's, the final day is a traditionalist's dream: 10 games and simultaneous kick-offs. It lends this contest a strange quality, binding it to events 185 miles away and leaving Arsenal fans needing Spurs to play a blinder at Old Trafford, if the Gunners are to take the Championship at Manchester United's expense.

Hell may have icicles the next time the North Bank cheers a Tottenham goal, but when Les Ferdinand puts the visitors ahead against United, Highbury erupts.

It's all Villa need. The only plus to the one-way traffic John Gregory is watching at this stage is that it sends him into the close-season with a crystal-clear vision of the level to which his close-season trading must aspire.

Watching the two sides in attack is like watching the animators of 'The Simpsons' trying to keep pace with Rembrandt. Arsenal surge, Villa plod.

In fairness, Villa's midfield is built more with defence in mind. "The Dogs of War," says one commentator of the addition of Simon Grayson and Riccardo Scimeca to midfield, and to aggravate the problem, the visitors' rare moments of inventiveness are betrayed by their finishing, notably by Scimeca, who puts a great chance wide on the half-hour when found by Julian Joachim, wide open in the box.

Otherwise, Villa's best chances fall to Paul Merson. It's gratifying to discover that some clubs can still extend a generous reception to those who once served them well and Merson responds to the applause by running onto a pass on the turn from Joachim before stabbing the ball past David Seaman's right hand post in the 79th minute.

Joachim is denied a promising chance when he does Tony Adams for pace late in the game. The Arsenal captain's response is to wrestle the striker to the floor with the goal looming large.

Steve Watson walked for a similar example of caveman football only eight days previously, yet Adams escapes with a yellow card, the same sanction Watson himself inexplicably received in the first half, following an accidental clash of feet with an Arsenal player who was actually behind him at the time. This is not referee Gallagher's finest hour.

For the most part, however, the momentum is red and white, Arsenal's pace and assuredness the moment their midfield finds the ball at its feet, setting up a string of shots from the edge of Michael Oakes' penalty area. Nwankwo Kanu touches home a corner from close range for the game's only goal after 66 minutes and but for a magnificent defensive performance by his opponents, it may well have been five.

After United's comeback win, though, not even ten would have made any difference. It may be end of term for two teams at Highbury, but the party is elsewhere.

Riccardo Scimeca made an impressive return to the side.

Wednesday 22nd July 1998 • The Bush • 7.45pm

PELSALL VILLA 0 ASTON VILLA 7

Half-time 0-3 • Attendance 2,060

Referee K. TOWNSEND

Referee's Assistants P. SLATER and S. TAYLOR

Red and Black Halved Shirts, Black Shorts	Goals		Sky Blue and White Shirts with Claret Band, Blue Shorts	Goals
1 Scott TURBOTT ††		1	Matthew GHENT	
2 Sean HOOPER †		2	Ben PETTY §§	
3 John BIRT ‡		3	Tommy JASZCZUN †	
4 Ian TURNBULL		4	David HUGHES	
5 Adrian HORNE		5	Aaron LESCOTT #	
6 Tom BAYLEY		6	Reuben HAZELL ## §§70	
7 Steve PEMBERTON		7	Darius VASSELL ≠	10
8 Steve HURFORD		8	Lee COLLINS ‡	
9 Tony DIXON		9	Richard WALKER †† ≠80	25
10 John HANSON #		10	Darren MIDDLETON § 15pen	
11 Simon HUGHES §		11	Fabio FERRARESI ‡‡	
Substitutes			*Substitutes*	
12 Jimmy TUFF †25		12	Martin RIDLEY †45	90
13 Paul MADDERS (Gk) ††35		13	Jlloyd SAMUEL ‡45	65,80
14 Simon LYONS ‡25		14	Michael STANDING #45	
15 Neil HOLMES #25		15	Gavin MELAUGH §45	
16 Gareth PALMER §25		16	Alan LEE ††45	73
		17	Andy SAMBROOK ‡‡45	
		18	David CURTOLO ##45	

Villa dominated a one-sided game from start to finish, although to their credit Pelsall never gave up trying, right up to the final whistle. The fact that Villa made use of all seven substitutes at half-time, including trialist Andy Sambrook, made no difference to the pattern of the game in the second half and they added another four goals, with defender Jlloyd Samuel helping himself to a brace as Villa took full advantage of their superior fitness.

FACTFILE

Friday 24th July 1998 • Rockingham Road • 7.45pm

CORBY TOWN 2 ASTON VILLA 1

Half-time 1-1

Referee Barry MALE

Referee's Assistants P. BRAND and G. CAPPS

Black and White Halved Shirts, Black Shorts	Goals	Sky Blue and White Shirts with Claret Band, White Shorts	Goals
1 Danny LIQUORISH		1 Matthew GHENT	
2 Andy COLEMAN		2 Martin RIDLEY ‡‡	
3 Paul TIFFNEY ‡		3 Jlloyd SAMUEL ††	
4 Scott JAMES		4 David HUGHES	
5 Rich TUFFEY		5 Lee COLLINS †	
6 Kevin MacDONALD †		6 Ben PETTY	
7 Tyronne MINTUS	77	7 Fabio FERRARESI §	
8 David HOLLIS		8 Aaron LESCOTT	
9 Danum RUSSELL		9 Darren BYFIELD ‡	10pen
10 Ossie MINTUS	21pen	10 Darius VASSELL #	
11 Danny POULTNEY		11 Michael STANDING	
Substitutes		*Substitutes*	
12 Danny KITCHEN †59		12 Reuben HAZELL †23	
14 Nicky FINNEY ‡82		13 Richard WALKER ‡45	
		14 Darren MIDDLETON #45	
		15 David CURTOLO §45	
		16 Tommy JASZCZUN ††45	
		17 Alan LEE ‡‡45	

Darren Byfield – put Villa ahead from the penalty spot.

FACTFILE

Corby took the honours in this open and entertaining game, which was evenly contested throughout. A host of changes at half-time did not dull the exchanges and the second half was end-to-end stuff, Town taking the honours with a goal 23 minutes from time.

Tuesday 28th July 1998 • Adams Park • 7.45pm

WYCOMBE WANDERERS 0 ASTON VILLA 3

Half-time 0-2 • Attendance 4,245

Referee Paul REJER (Tipton)

Referee's Assistants S. HEAD and B. CAPEL

Yellow and Dark Blue Quartered Shirts, Yellow Shorts	Goals	Claret and Blue Shirts, White Shorts	Goals
1 Martin TAYLOR		1 Mark BOSNICH ‡	
2 Jason KAVANAGH		2 Simon GRAYSON	
3 Alan BEETON ††		3 Alan WRIGHT	
4 Keith RYAN ‡		4 Gareth SOUTHGATE §	
5 Jason COUSINS		5 Ugo EHIOGU §§	
6 Nicky MOHAN		6 David UNSWORTH #	
7 Dave CARROLL §		7 Ian TAYLOR ††	
8 John CORNFORTH †		8 Mark DRAPER †	
9 Paul READ #		9 Stan COLLYMORE ##	30
10 Mark STALLARD ‡‡		10 Lee HENDRIE ≠	
11 Maurice HARKIN		11 Julian JOACHIM ‡‡	28,60
Substitutes		*Substitutes*	
12 Steve BROWN †45		12 David HUGHES §§81	
14 Paul McCARTHY ‡57		13 Michael OAKES (Gk) ‡63	
SIMPSON §65		14 Gareth BARRY #63	
PATTON ††80		15 Fabio FERRARESI ††73	
BULMAN ‡‡80		16 Alan THOMPSON †55	
BAIRD #57		17 Riccardo SCIMECA §68	
		18 Russel LATAPY ≠81	
		19 Darren BYFIELD ‡‡76	
		20 Darius VASSELL ##76	

Dwight Yorke out with minor injury... Trinidadian trialist Russel Latapy makes brief appearance... Stan Collymore in top form, makes one and scores one... David Unsworth, making his one and only appearance for Villa, concedes 38th minute penalty which Mark Bosnich saves brilliantly.

FACTFILE

Saturday 1st August 1998 • Red Lion Ground • 3.00pm

BLAKENALL 1 ASTON VILLA 7

Half-time 0-1

Referee Terry KETTLE (Shrewsbury)

Referee's Assistants P.A. HARDMAN and D. RODEN

Blue and White Halved Shirts, Blue Shorts		Goals	Claret and Blue Shirts, White Shorts		Goals
1	Matthew LOWE		1	Adam RACHEL	
2	Darren SIMKIN §		2	Martin RIDLEY ‡‡	
3	Steve McGINTY #		4	Richard WALKER †† ≠≠75	
4	Mark CLIFTON		6	Ben PETTY ≠	
5	Malcolm HAZELWOOD ‡‡		8	Michael BLACKWOOD ##	
6	David READ	og60	9	Graham EVANS ‡ †††80	85
7	Peter HOWLES †		10	Darren BYFIELD # ##64	5
8	Peter DUCKETT ††		12	Reuben HAZELL §§	
9	Richard DANDY		14	Russell LATAPY § §§70	90
10	Jason RHODES		16	Aaron LESCOTT † ≠75	
11	Mark HURST ‡		17	Jlloyd SAMUEL ≠≠	
	Substitutes			*Substitutes*	
12	J. MINTON ‡‡48		3	Darren MIDDLETON ‡45	
13	Mick WILLIAMS †45		7	Darius VASSELL #45	
14	Les PALMER ‡45		13	Alan LEE ‡‡64	
15	Andrew DODDS #45		18	Gavin MELAUGH §45	50,55
16	John HUMPHRIES §45		19	Michael STANDING †32 †††	
17	Michael HARRISON ††45	88	20	David CURTOLO ††45	89

A young Villa side proved too strong for a game Blakenall side, who held out well in the first half, despite going behind as early as the fifth minute to a Darren Byfield goal. However, in the second half, after both teams had made changes, a brace of goals from midfielder Gavin Melaugh within ten minutes of the resumption opened the floodgates and there was no stopping Villa as Blakenall tired. Mike Harrison did pull one back for the home side in the 88th minute, but Villa went to the other end and added a couple more before the final whistle.

Wednesday 5th August 1998 • Victoria Ground • 7.30pm

BROMSGROVE ROVERS 0 ASTON VILLA 1

Founded 1885

Half-time 0-0 • Attendance 730

Referee Eddie WALSH

Referee's Assistants J. HARRIS and R. JANSSENS

Green and White Striped Shirts, Black Shorts	Goals	Claret and Blue Shirts, White Shorts	Goals
1 Derek DUDLEY †		1 Adam RACHEL	
2 Kevin ASHLEY §		2 Jlloyd SAMUEL §	
3 Matt PENDLETON		3 David CURTOLO	
4 Ian COOPER ‡ ††78		4 David HUGHES	
5 Matt McALLUM		5 Ben PETTY	
6 Steve ULFIG		6 Reuben HAZELL #	
7 Lee JUKES		7 Aaron LESCOTT ‡	
8 Tom DAVIES #		8 Michael STANDING ‡‡	
9 Paul ROBINSON		9 Richard WALKER † ##84	
10 Stuart PAYNE		10 Darius VASSELL	
11 Peter SUTTON ††		11 Darren BYFIELD †† ‡‡69 ##	
Substitutes		*Substitutes*	
12 John NESBITT #78		12 Alan LEE †45	
13 Nore GABBINDON (Gk) †45		13 Gavin MELAUGH ‡45	
14 Matt SOUTHWICK ‡45		14 Lee COLLINS #45	60
16 Russell PHILPOTT §78		15 Darren MIDDLETON §45	
		16 Michael BLACKWOOD ††45	

Lee Collins.

FACTFILE

This match turned out to be a tough examination for Villa's youngsters, as Rovers competed well for the full 90 minutes. Just one goal separated the sides, scored on the hour by central defender Lee Collins, who had come as a substitute at half time.

Friday 7th August 1998 • Estadio Municipal de La Linea • 10.00pm

SEVILLA FC 1 ASTON VILLA 2

Half-time 0-2 • *Attendance* 6,000

Referee Juan MARMOLEJO

Referee's Assistants H. RODRIGUEZ and R. REYES

White Shirts, White Shorts	Goals	Claret and Blue Shirts, White Shorts	Goals
1 Paco LEAL		1 Mark BOSNICH §	
2 Juan VELASCO		2 Gary CHARLES	
3 Fernando Martinez 'NANDO'		3 Alan WRIGHT ❏ #	
4 Sebastián CORONA		4 Gareth SOUTHGATE	
5 David CORDON ❏		5 Riccardo SCIMECA †	
6 Jose Maria QUEVEDO		6 Gareth BARRY	
7 Mirolad RATKOVIC †		7 Ian TAYLOR	
8 Dejan VUKECEVIC #		8 Lee HENDRIE ††	
9 Igor GLUSCEVIK 86pen		9 Julian JOACHIM ‡	34
10 Vassilis TSARTAS §		10 Dwight YORKE	
11 Dominguez CARLOS ‡		11 Alan THOMPSON ❏	14
Substitutes		*Substitutes*	
12 Santaelena Aguado 'ALFREDO' §83		12 Fabio FERRARESI ††90	
13 José Antonio LUQUE		13 Michael OAKES (Gk) §87	
14 Carlos Gabriel CORRER #78		14 Russel LATAPY ‡62	
15 Ivan JURIC †61		15 Ugo EHIOGU †18	
16 Rashid ROKKI ‡76		16 Simon GRAYSON #84	
17 GAUTEZ		17 Mark DRAPER	

FACTFILE

Villa travel to the Spanish border with Gibraltar for their final pre-season fixture... they defeat Spanish second division side Seville to win the La Linea Trophy after an often stormy encounter on a poor playing surface... Ugo Ehiogu has to replace Riccardo Scimeca after 18 minutes, when the latter takes an elbow in the shoulder from Gluscevik... Alan Thompson scores from a 25-yard free-kick with 14 minutes gone... Julian Joachim makes it 2-0 20 minutes later, to cap a first half dominated by the English side... with Carlos giving Villa problems after the break, however, an 86th-minute Seville penalty reduces the arrears, making for a tense finish, but Villa hold on.

Saturday 8th August 1998 • The Pilot Field • 3.00pm

HASTINGS TOWN 1 ASTON VILLA 2

Half-time 1-2 • Attendance 412

Referee Keith STILLWELL (St. Leonards)

Referee's Assistants G. SMITH and G. CROFT

White Shirts, White Shorts	Goals	Claret and Blue Shirts, White Shorts	Goals
1 Tony KESSELLS		1 Adam RACHEL	
2 Steve SMITH		2 Alan LEE † ‡‡45	10
3 Spence MINTRIM †		3 Richard WALKER ‡‡ §§70 ≠	
4 Stuart PLATFORD		4 David HUGHES	
5 Mark MORRIS		5 Jlloyd SAMUEL	
6 Stuart MYALL §		6 Ben PETTY §	
7 Steve TATES ‡		7 David CURTOLO ††	
8 Steve SERGENT		8 Michael STANDING ##	
9 Simon FOX ††	11	9 Darius VASSELL ‡ ≠80	
10 Lee McROBERT ‡‡		10 Darren BYFIELD §§	45
11 Paul TUPPENEY #		11 Michael BLACKWOOD # ##60	
Substitutes		*Substitutes*	
12 Danny SIMMONS †26		12 Darren MIDDLETON #45	
14 Dunlan JONES ††84		13 Martin RIDLEY †35	
15 Graham MORRIS ‡‡84		14 Reuben HAZELL §45	
16 Owen BALL ‡60		15 Gavin MELAUGH ††45	
17 Adam DAY #75		16 Aaron LESCOTT ‡39	
19 Dean SMITH §75			

FACTFILE

Villa kicked off this game with an adventurous line-up, with strikers Alan Lee and Richard Walker in the wing-back positions and Darius Vassell and Darren Byfield playing up front. Lee got forward to open the scoring in the tenth minute, but Hastings were level within a minute, when centre forward Simon Fox got the better of Adam Rachel. After a first-half of end-to-end attacking football, it was the visitors who took the lead, when Darren Byfield shot past Kessells in the Town goal. There was no further scoring as both sides made changes in the second half.

Tuesday 11th August 1998 • The Lamb • 7.30pm

TAMWORTH 1 ASTON VILLA 6

Half-time 0-3 • Attendance 1,775

Referee P. BARROW (Tamworth)

Referee's Assistants S. BARROW and E. WHITEHOUSE

Red Shirts, Red Shorts		Goals	Claret and Blue Shirts, White Shorts		Goals
1	Tony ROWE		1 Adam RACHEL		
2	Rob WARNER		2 Ben PETTY		7
3	Darren SHAW		4 David HUGHES		
4	David FOY		5 Fabio FERRARESI		
5	John HOWARD		6 Jlloyd SAMUEL #		
6	Simon BURGER		7 Aaron LESCOTT		
7	Nick COLLEY		8 Michael STANDING ††		
8	Ian BENNETT §		9 Richard WALKER §		
9	Gary SMITH ‡		10 Darren BYFIELD † §72		5,33,75,90
10	Michael GRAY #		11 Michael BLACKWOOD ‡ ††75		
11	Warren HOUGHTON †		14 Ugo EHIOGU		

Substitutes			Substitutes		
13	John PRICE ‡65		3 Darius VASSELL †45		48
14	Leon MICHELL #65		12 Tommy JASZCZUN ‡45		
14	James WOODS §65	68	15 Reuben HAZELL #45		
15	Martin RUDDOCK				
	Paul HADEN †50				
	Dennis MULLHOLLAND				

FACTFILE

Ugo Ehiogu played the full 90 minutes as Villa ran out easy winners, thanks to a four-goal blast from striker Darren Byfield. And try as they might, Tamworth could make no impression on a strong visitors' defence.

Ben Petty.

Tuesday 11th August 1998 • Recreation Ground • 7.30pm

TOTAL NETWORK SOLUTIONS 3 ASTON VILLA 2

Half-time 1-1 • Attendance 262

Referee Neil CARPENTER (Oswestry)

Referee's Assistants M. WILLIAMS and T. THOMAS

Green Shirts, White Shorts		Goals	Claret and Blue Shirts, White Shorts		Goals
1	Andy MULLINER		1	Matthew GHENT †	
2	Dewi PARRY		2	Martin RIDLEY	
3	Robert MORRIS		3	Darren MIDDLETON	
4	Mick GALLAGHER †		4	Stuart THORNLEY ‡	
5	Tim EDWARDS		5	Jamie KEARNS	
6	Gary EVANS		6	Brian MULHOLLAND ††	
7	Gareth WILSON	45,61	7	David HARDING §	
8	Neil MARSH		8	Gavin MELAUGH	
9	Frankie MOTTRAM	78	9	Alan LEE	55
10	Riki EVANS ‡		10	Graham EVANS #	18
11	Darren RYAN		11	Luke PRINCE	

Substitutes			*Substitutes*	
	Gary POWELL †20		12	Stephen EVANS #72
	John WHELAN ‡63		13	Michael PRICE (Gk) †45
	Ian LANCASTER		14	Jay SMITH §76
	James WATKINS		15	Gary McSEVERNEY ††76
	Craig TAIT		16	Liam FOLDS ‡45
	Damion CURRIER			

Total Network Solutions (previously known as Llansantffraid), are a team who compete in the League of Wales, their base being just across the border with England. A Villa Youth side put up a strong performance and looked set for a share of the spoils after twice taking the lead with goals from Graham Evans and Alan Lee, until striker Frankie Mottram beat Matthew Ghent with the winner 12 minutes from time; a spirited assault on the home goal in the final ten minutes failing to produce an equaliser.

FACTFILE

Saturday 15th August 1998 • Manor Park • 3.00pm

NUNEATON BOROUGH 1 ASTON VILLA 3

Half-time 1-2 • Attendance 841

Referee M.E. CALLOW

Referee's Assistants J. THIRLAWAY and M. MADELEY

Blue and White Striped Shirts, Blue Shorts		Goals	Claret and Blue Shirts, White Shorts		Goals
1	Richard WILLIAMS		1	Adam RACHEL	
2	Leigh EVERITT ‡		2	Martin RIDLEY ‡	
3	Steve PRINDIVILLE	og14	3	Tommy JASZCZUN	
4	Gary STATHAM		4	David HUGHES ■50	
5	Barry WILLIAMS		5	Reuben HAZELL	
6	David CROWLEY		6	Lee COLLINS	
7	Shaun WRAY ††		7	Jlloyd SAMUEL	
8	Nicky ANDERSEN ❏ †		8	Gavin MELAUGH †	
9	Anton THOMAS #		9	Alan LEE	27,90
10	Malcolm CHRISTIE §		10	David CURTOLO	
11	Richie GARDNER	43	11	Graham EVANS	
	Substitutes			*Substitutes*	
12	Terry ANGUS #65		12	Stephen EVANS	
14	Kevin WILKIN †60		14	Stuart THORNLEY	
15	Rob STRAW §75		15	Michael BLACKWOOD †45	
16	Peter BARRY ‡60		16	Matthew GHENT (Gk)	
17	Brett HEALY ††80		17	Richard WALKER	
18	Martin ROUNDTREE		18	Darren MIDDLETON ‡45	
	Lee CRAIN (Gk)				

FACTFILE

Steve Prindiville set Villa on the way to a hard-earned win when he sliced an attempted clearance into his own net. Striker Alan Lee added to the tally before half-time; but Villa were reduced to ten men five minutes into the second-half when David Hughes was sent off for a bad tackle. Villa held on gamely for the rest of the game, with Lee adding another on the break on the stroke of time.

Tuesday 8th September 1998 • Masons Road • 7.30pm

STRATFORD TOWN 1 ASTON VILLA 3

Half-time 0-1 • *Attendance 163*

Referee John SMART

Referee's Assistants R. CRADDOCK and D. WAITE

Tangerine Shirts, Black Shorts		Goals	Claret and Blue Shirts, Blue Shorts		Goals
1	Marcus TOWNSEND		1	Adam RACHEL	
2	Dave ROBERTS		2	Martin RIDLEY	
3	Andy BEECHEY		3	Michael BLACKWOOD	
4	Carl BANNISTER		4	Reuben HAZELL	
5	Colin GRINHAM		5	Lee COLLINS §	
6	Gary JOYNES		6	Jamie KEARNS	
7	Leon WOODLEY		7	David HARDING #	
8	Mark SHAW ‡		8	Aaron LESCOTT	
9	Sammy PERCIVAL #		9	Alan LEE ‡	
10	Adrian DUFF		10	Darren MIDDLETON	65
11	Martin BISHOP †		11	Graham EVANS †	25
	Substitutes			*Substitutes*	
11	James SMITH #45		12	Richard WALKER †63	66
12	O. TROUDLE †45		13	Jlloyd SAMUEL §76	
14	Michael CLEAVER ‡45	77	14	Stephen EVANS ‡74	
			15	Brian MULHOLLAND #74	

<table>
</table>

For the first hour this was an evenly contested game, with both keepers seeing plenty of action. But two goals in as many minutes from midfielder Darren Middleton and striker Richard Walker, put Villa in full command and they ran out good winners despite a late consolation goal from Town substitute, Michael Cleaver.

FACTFILE

Darren Middleton.

Monday 5th October 1998 • Keys Park • 7.45pm

HEDNESFORD TOWN 0 ASTON VILLA 4

Half-time 0-1 • Attendance 1,922

Referee J. HUBBARD

Referee's Assistants K. FRIEND and M. HEAVER

Black and White Striped Shirts, Black Shorts	Goals	Turquoise Shirts with Black Trim, Black Shorts	Goals
1 Scott COOKSEY		1 Michael OAKES ‡‡	
2 Gary FITZPATRICK		2 Simon GRAYSON ≠	
3 Kevin COLLINS ††		3 Alan WRIGHT ‡	
4 Russell BRADLEY #		4 Riccardo SCIMECA §§	
5 Chris BRINDLEY		5 Ugo EHIOGU ##	
6 Jake SEDGEMORE † ‡‡85		6 Jlloyd SAMUEL	
7 Paul WARE		7 Ian TAYLOR †	
8 Jimmy KELLY		8 Mark DRAPER ≠≠	
9 Neil DAVIS ‡‡		9 Stan COLLYMORE (c) §	4
10 Robbie DENNISON ‡		10 Julian JOACHIM ††	60
11 Joe O'CONNOR §		11 Alan THOMPSON #	

Substitutes		*Substitutes*	
12 Ged KIMMINS		12 Darius VASSELL ††60	77
14 Andy COMYN †45		13 Adam RACHEL (Gk) ‡‡62	
16 Lee COLLIN ‡45		14 Darren BYFIELD §57	
17 Leon JACKSON #62		15 Fabio FERRARESI †45	
18 Mark RICHARDS §68		16 Ben PETTY ##62	
19 Dale ANDERSON ††72		17 Tommy JASZCZUN ‡45	
		18 Aaron LESCOTT #45	55
		19 Reuben HAZELL §§67	
		20 Darren MIDDLETON ≠72	
		20 Steve HARRISON ≠≠85	

FACTFILE

Stan Collymore headed Villa in front after four minutes from a cross by Alan Wright. Only stout defending by the Pitmen kept Villa out until the second half, but the visitors' extra class eventually told and they ran out clear winners.

Wednesday 11th November 1998 • Vale Stadium • 7.30pm

PAGET RANGERS 0 ASTON VILLA 6

Half-time 0-4 • Attendance 693

Referee T. JOHNSON

Referee's Assistants P. EDWARDS and M. HOWLES

Yellow Shirts, Black Shorts	Goals	Claret and Blue Shirts, White Shorts	Goals
1 Peter ENCKELMAN		1 Gary PRICE	
2 Richard FIELD ‡‡		2 Ben PETTY	
3 Stuart CLARK †† ‡‡62		3 Tommy JASZCZUN	
4 Richard BROWN		4 Reuben HAZELL	
5 Stuart RANDLE #		5 Martin RIDLEY †	
6 Gary KNIGHT		6 David HUGHES	
7 John HUNT		7 Darren MIDDLETON	37pen
8 Keith CASSON †		8 Aaron LESCOTT	
9 Trevor BURROUGHS § ##75		9 Richard WALKER	45
10 Rasheed ANIFOWOSE ##		10 Alan LEE	28,43,63,85
11 Danny ANSTICE		11 Alan THOMPSON	
Substitutes		*Substitutes*	
12 S. MERCHANT †45		12 Jlloyd SAMUEL	
13 Marcus HAHNEMANN (Gk) ‡45		14 Fabio FERRARESI	
14 Mark PHILLIPS #45		15 Michael STANDING	
15 Steve WALKER §45		16 Gordon COWANS †45	
16 D. CAMPBELL ††45			

A Villa side dominated by under-21 reserve team players went to Vale Stadium for the Official opening of Paget's new Vale Stadium. Included in the squad were Alan Thompson, who requested a game after being on the first team subs' bench for a couple of games; and youth team coach, Gordon Cowans, who paraded his skills again for the claret and blue. A four-goal haul was just reward for a wholehearted performance from Alan Lee. Darren Middleton from the penalty spot and Richard Walker were the other scorers in a one-sided contest. Two keepers on trial with Villa shared the duties in goal for Paget to give them a chance to show their worth, whilst the Rangers' keeper went between the sticks for Villa.

CHRIS PRICE TESTIMONIAL

Tuesday 15th December 1998 • Edgar Street • 7.30pm

HEREFORD UNITED 0 ASTON VILLA 2

Half-time 0-2 • Attendance 3,394

Referee M.A. WILLIAMS

Referee's Assistants M. FORDER and S. MOGGS

White Shirts with Black Trim, Black Shorts	Goals	Claret and Blue Shirts, White Shorts	Goals
1 Andy QUY		1 Michael OAKES ‡	
2 John SHIRKEY		3 Alan WRIGHT ≠≠	
3 Matthew CROSS		5 Ugo EHIOGU ≠	
4 John SNAPE †		6 Steve WATSON §	
5 Ian WRIGHT		7 Ian TAYLOR ##	
6 Stuart EVANS		8 Lee HENDRIE §§	
7 Mark DRUCE		9 Stan COLLYMORE (c) ††	
8 Wayne DYER		11 Alan THOMPSON #	45
9 Richard LEADBEATER		12 Julian JOACHIM ‡‡	17
10 Gavin WILLIAMS		15 Gareth BARRY †††	
11 Paul PARRY		17 Lee COLLINS †	

Substitutes		*Substitutes*	
12 John HILL		2 Gary CHARLES §50	
13 Mark JONES		4 Simon GRAYSON ≠52	
14 Gordon COWANS †45		10 Reuben HAZELL †34	
		13 Peter ENCKELMAN (Gk) ‡45	
		14 Fabio FERRARESI #45 ‡‡‡	
		16 Aaron LESCOTT ≠≠80	
		18 David HARDING §§70	
		18 Darius VASSELL †††80	
		19 Graham EVANS ‡‡‡85	
		19 Andy MARFELL ##67	
		20 Darren MIDDLETON ††58	
		20 Stephen EVANS ‡‡65	

FACTFILE

Only Gareth Southgate and Dion Dublin are missing from the starting line-up which beat Arsenal the previous weekend. Julian Joachim opened the scoring, hitting home the rebound after Quy had parried his shot. Thompson threaded his way through the United defence to score the second on the stroke of half-time. Villa continued to dominate after the break, Darren Middleton missing a 75th minute penalty. Gordon Cowans guested for United.

Tuesday 11th May 1999 • Ninian Park • 7.30pm

CARDIFF CITY 1 ASTON VILLA 3

Half-time 0-3 • Attendance 3,515

Referee KEITH COOPER

Referee's Assistants M. SANSOM and M. IQBAL

Blue and White Shirts, White Shorts	Goals
1 Seamus KELLY #	
2 Wayne O'SULLIVAN	
3 Andy LEGG ‡	
4 Jeff ECKHAARDT	
5 Mike FORD	
6 Mark BONNER †	
7 Danny HILL	
8 Lee PHILLIPS	
9 Jason BOWEN	
10 Dai THOMAS	
11 Craig MIDDLETON	
Substitutes	
12 Nathan CADDETTE ‡31 §	
13 Ian LOVELACE (Gk) #31	
16 Jason FOWLER †20	
1 Neville SOUTHALL* (Gk)	
2 Derek BRAZIL*	
3 Damon SEARLE*	
4 Roger GIBBINS* §68	
5 Jason PERRY*	
6 Nathan WIGG*	
7 Rob EARNSHAW*	
8 Chris ROBERTS*	
9 Chris PIKE*	
10 Carl DALE*	90pen
11 Cohen GRIFFITH*	

Claret and Blue Shirts, Blue Shorts	Goals
1 Peter ENCKELMAN ††	
2 Mark DELANEY ≠	
3 Jlloyd SAMUEL †	
4 Gareth SOUTHGATE (c) ‡‡	
5 Colin CALDERWOOD ‡	
6 Angel DOMINGUEZ ¶ **	
7 Steve STONE #	9
8 Darius VASSELL §§	
9 Julian JOACHIM ##	17
10 Paul MERSON	41
11 Alan THOMPSON §	
Substitutes	
1 Michael OAKES (Gk) ††45 ≠≠	
3 Alan WRIGHT †45	
4 Gareth BARRY ‡‡45	
5 Ugo EHIOGU ‡45	
6 Steve HARRISON ¶72	
7 Steve WATSON #45	
9 Riccardo SCIMECA ##45	
11 Ian TAYLOR §45 †††	
14 Simon GRAYSON ≠55	
16 Michael STANDING †††72	
20 Mark DRAPER §§55	
Paul BARRON (Gk) ≠≠72	

* The whole Cardiff team changed at half-time.

** Paraguayan trialist.

Aston Villa First Team Squad, start of 98-99 season. Back row, left to right: Darren Byfield, Fabio Ferraresi, Gary Charles (now Benfica), Alan Lee, Ugo Ehiogu, David Hughes, David Unsworth (now Everton), Lee Collins (now Stoke City), Ben Petty (now Stoke City), Richard Walker, Darius Vassell. Middle row: Jim Walker (physio), Simon Grayson, Riccardo Scimeca, Ian Taylor, Matthew Ghent, Michael Oakes, Mark Bosnich, Adam Rachel, Gareth Southgate, Alan Thompson, Gareth Barry, Gordon Cowans (coach). Front row: Kevin MacDonald (coach), Lee Hendrie, Mark Draper, Stan Collymore, Paul Barron (goalkeeping coach), John Gregory (manager), Steve Harrison (first team coach), Dwight Yorke (now Man. Utd), Julian Joachim, Alan Wright, Malcolm Beard (reserve team manager).

After the upheaval that inevitably accompanies a change of manager, Aston Villa were able to enjoy a season of comparative calm and continuity in their team behind the team.

If their labours only bore fruit for half of the season, Manager John Gregory, who took over from his predecessor Brian Little last term, can console himself with the knowledge that he has now just about seen it all.

After the run of success that followed his arrival from Wycombe Wanderers (which might well have been good enough to lift the Premiership title had the season run from February to December!), he had a good long look at the other side of the coin when his team hit their flat spot in the first quarter of this year.

Those who wondered if the easy-going lord of the one-liner might degenerate into Victor Meldrew mode the moment the going got tough, had to hand it to Gregory. While the pain of the lean times was occasionally etched on his face, his public mood steered an even keel through good days and bad, and if his occasional penchant for delegating post-game press conference duties to coach Steve Harrison wasn't always well received, he always faced the music in person if the scoreline was a bad one.

His plain-speaking was a double-edged sword, sometimes whipping up storms that a more politic approach might have avoided, yet also cutting refreshingly through the twaddle surrounding a sport that is expected to produce far more headlines than it's capable of. One practical example of this

JOHN GREGORY   STEVE HARRISON

is his willingness to allow the public to watch training sessions at Bodymoor. Some managers of the cloak-and-dagger school would be appalled, yet to Gregory it is a harmless exercise in good public relations. For the public, it also means free entertainment, particularly if first-team coach Steve Harrison is in form and not drowned out by one of Bodymoor's Arctic gales.

Ask any Villa player about the good spirit in the camp, even during the losing run, and the conversation soon comes round to Harrison, who manages to combine the job of a Premiership coach with a thriving, if unpaid, career as morale booster and possibly one of the funniest men you'll meet in the game.

The son of a professional comedian, he walks the same tightrope that confronts anyone of a similar disposition; being himself, yet still being taken seriously.

An hour spent listening to him talk about

MALCOLM BEARD   KEVIN MacDONALD   GORDON COWANS   PAUL BARRON

his job dispels any doubts on that score. Let Harrison tell you how he works with players, his coaching methods and what he looks for on the training ground. He'll fill every inch of tape in your recorder; all fascinating stuff and not a punchline anywhere.

Or watch him suffering on the touchlines when all is not well with his beloved defence. The best thing about being 3-0 up against Nottingham Forest, he said, was being able to sit back for the last five minutes for once and just enjoy the game...

Paul Barron again filled the role of goal-keeping coach this season and found his cup overflowing, with not only Mark Bosnich but also Michael Oakes and Adam Rachel seeing first team action this season, and Peter Enckelman arriving from Finland.

A key addition to the back-room staff was 36-year-old Ross MacLaren, the former reserve team coach at Swindon Town. Ross joked that if you wanted to know what his precise job description was, you'd have to ask John Gregory, but in the latter's eyes he fulfilled an invaluable function, not only on the coaching side but also in instigating a major over-haul of the club's scouting system.

For all his pride in fielding a predominantly English team this season, Gregory is by no means averse to looking to foreign shores for the right player and in that respect, Ross MacLaren is likely to be kept very busy.

Villa were delighted to welcome Gordon Cowans back for the third time in his career, to coach the youth sides along with ex-Liverpool player Kevin MacDonald. Malcolm

Beard continued in charge of the Reserve team until his departure in June 1999.

Looking after the walking wounded, physio-therapist Jim Walker's dedication to his work takes him to Loughborough University one day a week, to study for a degree in Sports Science, a term that embraces nutrition, bio-mechanics, psychology and physiology. "I'm what's known as a very mature student!" says the 51-year-old.

Assisting Jim and acting as physio to the Villa Youth Academy, is Terry Standring, who in April also acted as physio to the England team which took part in the World Under-20 Championship in Nigeria.

Looking out for the Villa players of tomor-row is the club's Football Academy Director, Bryan Jones, who has guided the Academy through its first season, assisted by his Assistant Director Steve Burns and Youth Development Officer, Alan Miller.

The purpose of the Academy is to provide young football talent an environment in which players can be nurtured and their ability developed without them being played to exhaustion by the demands of school, district and county sides.

Whereas some youngsters would be playing 75 games a season a year or two ago, they play something like 30 under the auspices of the Academy, where they enjoy good-quality coaching in top-class facilities.

It's only the first rung of a very long ladder but as Lee Hendrie, Gareth Barry and Darius Vassell illustrate, if you're good enough, you'll soon be old enough in the eyes of Aston Villa.

ROSS MacLAREN   JIM WALKER   TERRY STANDRING   BRYAN JONES

GARETH BARRY

Born Hastings, 23rd February 1981. *Joined Villa* on YTS terms in 1997, signed professional forms 23/2/98. *Villa debut* as sub v Sheffield Wednesday, Lge (a) 2/5/98.

Villa's *Young Player of the Year* award had Gareth Barry's name on it from about October onwards, in a season which confirmed what had been hinted at in his two outings at the end of 1997-98: that Villa have one of the best prospects in the country on their books.

The Sussex youngster turned 18 in mid-season and promptly signed up to a five-year contract with Villa, the reward for a season in which his calmness in defence, coupled with his enterprise whenever pressing forward, continued to impress.

Occasionally caught trying to be constructive when circumstances called for the hoof to Row Z, he made his mistakes, as any player of his tender years would, and injuries elsewhere may have led to him having to play more often than was ideal, but the pluses greatly outweigh the minuses and he was rewarded with his first senior goals at the end of the season.

Career Record:

Season	Club	League		Cups	
		Apps	Gls	Apps	Gls
97-98	Aston Villa	1 (1)	-	-	-
98-99	Aston Villa	27 (5)	2	5	-
TOTAL		28 (6)	2	5	-

★ *England Under-18 (1 cap) and Under-21 International (3 caps).*

● Striker Julian Joachim signed a new five year contract with the club in July 1998. In the same month defender Riccardo Scimeca pledged his future to Villa by signing a four year contract.

MARK BOSNICH

Born Fairfield, Australia, 13th January 1972. *Joined Villa* February 1992 from Sydney Croatia. *Villa debut* v Luton Town, Lge (a) 25/4/92.

With endless speculation as to where he was going next season, Mark Bosnich's final term at Villa Park was, ironically, a year in which his career stood still. On duty, his game remained as sharp as ever. Getting on duty, though, was the problem. A shoulder injury ruined his season, then a foot injury and his manager's growing impatience with the Australian's reluctance to show his hand for 1999-2000, removed him from the lineup for the last few games. The rumour mill finally shut down when he completed a free transfer to Manchester United under the Bosman ruling, on 2nd June.

Career Record:

Season	Club	League		Cups	
		Apps	Gls Ag	Apps	Gls Ag
89-90	Man. United	1	-	-	-
90-91	Man. United	2	2	-	-
91-92	Aston Villa	1	1	-	-
92-93	Aston Villa	17	12	1	-
93-94	Aston Villa	28	28	12 (1)	11
94-95	Aston Villa	30	44	4	5
95-96	Aston Villa	38	35	13	7
96-97	Aston Villa	20	16	4	4
97-98	Aston Villa	30	35	12	9
98-99	Aston Villa	15	10	2	2
Villa record		*179*	*181*	*48 (1)*	*38*
TOTAL		182	183	48 (1)	38

★ *Australian international*

● NOTE: *Career records of goalkeepers Mark Bosnich (above) and Michael Oakes and Adam Rachel (p123) list number of goals conceded in the goals columns.*

● NOTE: *All international records are up to the end of the English domestic season (16th May 1999).*

DARREN BYFIELD

Born Birmingham, 29th September 1976. *Joined Villa* on Associate Schoolboy forms in 1991, turned pro in 1994. *Villa debut* v Leeds Utd, Lge (a) 28/12/97.

1998-99 proved a frustrating experience for Darren Byfield, who was aiming to build on the handful of first team appearances he made at the end of last season. His only two first team starts were painful affairs in more ways than one, however. Against Strømsgodset, he laboured in vain for a goal before making way for Darius Vassell, who promptly scored two, and then his Worthington Cup appearance at Stamford Bridge saw him on the end of a horrible challenge by Dennis Wise.

On loan at Preston North End during the season, Byfield was in talks with John Gregory as summer approached, with a view to a transfer to another club and more regular first-team football.

Career Record:

| Season | Club | League | | Cups | |
		Apps	Gls	Apps	Gls
97-98	Aston Villa	1 (6)	-	- (1)	-
98-99	Aston Villa	-	-	2	-
(loan)	Preston N.E.	4 (2)	1	-	-
Villa record		*1 (6)*	-	*2 (1)*	-
TOTAL		5 (8)	1	2 (1)	-

● Gordon Cowans rejoined the club as a coach in June 1998. Gordon, who was with Villa for three spells as a player, is now involved with the Youth Academy.

Gordon came back to Villa Park in the wake of youth team coach, Tony McAndrew's departure to join former manager Brian Little in a similar position at Stoke City.

COLIN CALDERWOOD

Born Glasgow, 20th January 1965. *Joined Villa* March 1999 from Tottenham Hotspur, £225,000. *Villa debut* v West Ham United, Lge (h) 2/3/99.

When 34-year-old Colin Calderwood arrived from White Hart Lane, it had the look of stop-gap cosmetic surgery to the Villa roster. Just weeks later, however, John Gregory was talking of a more long-term role for the Scotland World Cup player, a testimony to the steadying effect of Calderwood's arrival in the back line.

Career Record:

| Season | Club | League | | Cups | |
		Apps	Gls	Apps	Gls
81-82	Mansfield T.	1	-	-	-
82-83	Mansfield T.	28	-	3	-
83-84	Mansfield T.	27 (3)	1	4	1
84-85	Mansfield T.	41	-	10	-
85-86	Swindon T.	46	2	10	-
86-87	Swindon T.	46	1	13	-
87-88	Swindon T.	33 (1)	1	13	-
88-89	Swindon T.	43	4	7	-
89-90	Swindon T.	46	3	12	-
90-91	Swindon T.	22 (1)	2	-	-
91-92	Swindon T.	46	5	11	1
92-93	Swindon T.	46	2	6	-
93-94	Tottenham H.	26	-	8	-
94-95	Tottenham H.	35 (1)	2	7	-
95-96	Tottenham H.	26 (3)	1	7	-
96-97	Tottenham H.	33 (1)	-	5	-
97-98	Tottenham H.	21 (5)	4	2 (2)	1
98-99	Tottenham H.	11 (1)	-	5	-
98-99	Aston Villa	8	-	-	-
TOTAL		585 (16)	28	123 (2)	3

● *At Swindon also appeared in four Play-Offs, making 13 appearances.*

★ *Full Scotland international (34 caps, 1 goal).*

GARY CHARLES

Born London,
13th April 1970.
Joined Villa January 1995
from Derby County, £1m.
Villa debut as sub v
Nottingham Forest,
Lge (a) 21/1/95.

Despite two important goals in his first six games this season, Gary Charles was fighting for his place once Steve Watson arrived from Newcastle and he had to make do with two appearances from the subs' bench once the Geordie took over at right wing-back for the visit of Spurs.

A brief appearance as substitute in the FA Cup game with Hull City proved to be Charles' swansong in a Villa shirt and Graeme Souness signed him for Portuguese side Benfica.

Career Record:

Season	Club	League		Cups	
		Apps	Gls	Apps	Gls
87-88	Nottingham F.	-	-	-	-
88-89	Nottingham F.	1	-	1	-
(loan)	Leicester City	5 (3)	-	-	-
89-90	Nottingham F.	- (1)	-	- (2)	-
90-91	Nottingham F.	9 (1)	-	7	1
91-92	Nottingham F.	30	1	12 (2)	-
92-93	Nottingham F.	14	-	1	-
93-94	Derby County	43	1	8 (1)	-
94-95	Derby County*	18	2	7	-
	Aston Villa	14 (2)	-	-	-
95-96	Aston Villa	34	1	13	-
96-97	Aston Villa	-	-	-	-
97-98	Aston Villa	14 (4)	1	2 (5)	-
98-99	Aston Villa	10 (1)	1	5 (1)	1
Villa record		72 (7)	3	20 (6)	1
TOTAL		192 (12)	7	56 (11)	2

* N.B. Cup figures for Derby Co. 94-95 include only Anglo-Italian and Coca-Cola Cup competitions

★ *Full England international (2 caps).*
Also capped at Under-21 level.

STAN COLLYMORE

Born Stone, Staffordshire,
22nd January 1971.
Joined Villa May 1997
from Liverpool, £7m.
Villa debut v Leicester
City, Lge (a) 9/8/97.

Just when it seemed that Stan was getting to grips with life at Villa, clinical depression intervened and he was eventually given leave of absence to receive full-time treatment, thus ending his season.

While injuries prevented him getting fully into stride in the first half of the schedule, Collymore at least appeared to be getting his professional life back on track and provided his many fans with signs that their refusal to give up on him would be vindicated.

He looked to have a renewed appetite for the game and for a while he and Dion Dublin seemed poised to become Villa's 'Dream Team'. Then the inner gremlins struck and while he tried to dovetail his treatment with his football commitments, it proved unsuccessful.

Career Record:

Season	Club	League		Cups	
		Apps	Gls	Apps	Gls
90-91	Crystal Palace	- (6)	-	-	-
91-92	Crystal Palace	4 (8)	1	1 (2)	1
92-93	Crystal Palace	- (2)	-	1 (1)	-
92-93	Southend Utd	30	15	3	3
93-94	Nottingham F.	27 (1)	18	5	6
94-95	Nottingham F.	37	23	6	3
95-96	Liverpool	30 (1)	14	10 (3)	5
96-97	Liverpool	25 (5)	12	6 (1)	4
97-98	Aston Villa	23 (2)	6	11 (1)	2
98-99	Aston Villa	11 (9)	1	4	6
Villa Record		34 (11)	7	15 (1)	8
TOTAL		187 (34)	90	47 (8)	30

★ *Full England international (3 caps).*

MARK DELANEY

Born Haverfordwest, 13th May 1976.
Joined Villa March 1999 from Cardiff C., £500,000.
Villa debut as sub v Nottingham Forest, Lge (h) 24/4/99.

Mark Delaney will probably spend the summer pinching himself, after completing a move to Aston Villa from Cardiff just a year after playing League of Wales football with Carmarthen.

The wing-back was originally scheduled to spend the rest of this season acclimatising in the Reserves, but Villa's stroll against Nottingham Forest in the season's closing weeks persuaded John Gregory to introduce him from the bench for a spell late in the game.

A good passer and tackler, his progress in 1999-2000 will be keenly followed.

Career Record:

Season	Club	League Apps	Gls	Cups Apps	Gls
98-99	Cardiff City	28	-	10 (2)	1
98-99	Aston Villa	- (2)	-	-	-
TOTAL		28 (2)	-	10 (2)	1

★ *Wales Under-21 international.*

● Villa's defeat at Arsenal on the final day of the season, coupled with West Ham United's 4-0 defeat of Middlesbrough, meant Villa missed out on their final chance of European football next season. The Hammers pipped them to fifth place in the Premiership, booking the solitary InterToto Cup place open to English clubs.

The three teams who come through the InterToto competition receive places in the 1999-00 UEFA Cup, although it would have meant an early start to competitive football for Villa, had they finished above West Ham, with the InterToto games scheduled to begin in mid-July.

MARK DRAPER

Born Derby, 11th November 1970.
Joined Villa July 1995 from Leicester City, £3.25m.
Villa debut v Manchester Utd, Lge (h) 19/8/95.

One of several players whose season was held back somewhat by injury, Mark Draper still showed enough when fit to indicate that he has much to offer Aston Villa.

A nagging ankle injury caused by a build-up of debris around the bone meant that the midfielder had a stop-start first half of the season, although he scored Villa's only Worthington Cup goal of the season and showed his game has as much grit as guile, with a tenacious performance at Celta Vigo.

Once mid-season surgery largely corrected his injury, Draper enjoyed his most extended run of the season in April and May and celebrated with goals against Southampton and Nottingham Forest.

Career Record:

Season	Club	League Apps	Gls	Cups Apps	Gls
88-89	Notts County	16 (4)	3	3 (1)	-
89-90	Notts County	29 (5)	3	6	1
90-91	Notts County	41 (4)	9	12 (1)	1
91-92	Notts County	32 (3)	1	4 (1)	2
92-93	Notts County	44	11	5	1
93-94	Notts County	44	13	15	4
94-95	Leicester City	39	5	4	-
95-96	Aston Villa	36	2	13	3
96-97	Aston Villa	28 (1)	-	3 (1)	-
97-98	Aston Villa	31	3	12	-
98-99	Aston Villa	13 (10)	2	5 (1)	1
Villa record		*108 (11)*	*7*	*33 (2)*	*4*
TOTAL		353 (27)	52	82 (5)	13

★ *England Under-21 international.*

DION DUBLIN

Born Leicester, 22nd April, 1969. *Joined Villa* November 1998 from Coventry City, £5.75m. *Villa debut* v Tottenham, Lge (h) 7/11/98.

Had Villa's £5.75m signing from Coventry finished his first season with Villa as he began it, who knows how much rosier the year might have been?

Seven goals in his first three games was a dream start for the striker, while his 6-1 stature gave Villa a genuine target man for the first time this season.

Unfortunately, he couldn't escape the post-Christmas malaise that blighted his team: a hernia and latterly a knee injury reduced his effectiveness, yet his willingness to play on was admirable and few things should give Villa greater cause for optimism than the prospect of a fully-fit Dublin returning to action.

Career Record:

Season	Club	League Apps	Gls	Cups Apps	Gls
88-89	Cambridge U.	12 (9)	6	1 (1)	1
89-90	Cambridge U.	37 (9)	15	14 (2)	6
90-91	Cambridge U.	44 (2)	16	13	7
91-92	Cambridge U.	40 (3)	15	9	4
92-93	Manchester U.	3 (4)	1	-	-
93-94	Manchester U.	1 (4)	1	2 (3)	1
94-95	Manchester U.	-	-	-	-
94-95	Coventry City	31	13	7	3
95-96	Coventry City	34	14	4 (1)	2
96-97	Coventry City	33 (1)	13	4 (1)	-
97-98	Coventry City	36	18	7	5
98-99	Coventry City	10	3	2	-
	Aston Villa	24	11	-	-
TOTAL		305 (32)	126	63 (8)	29

● *At Cambridge also appeared in two Play-Offs, making 5 appearances, 2 goals.*

★ *England international (4 caps).*

UGO EHIOGU

Born Hackney, London, 3rd November 1972. *Joined Villa* July 1991 from West Bromwich Albion, £40,000. *Villa debut* v Arsenal, Lge (h) 24/8/91.

It was when a collision with the boot of Alan Shearer deprived us of Ugo's presence in the team for 11 games that his value became apparent. As Villa's defensive resources became too thinly spread, the 6-2 stopper could only watch in frustration from the sidelines.

The immediate priority, of course, was the sight in the eye which had borne the brunt of the contact with the Newcastle striker. This was briefly in the balance and intricate surgery was needed to rebuild the socket. It was no great surprise when Ugo got the biggest cheer of the day when he returned as substitute against Nottingham Forest in April.

Quietly effective in defence and scorer of two points-saving goals, against Leicester and Sheffield Wednesday, Ugo appears to have come through his return without any adverse consequences.

Career Record:

Season	Club	League Apps	Gls	Cups Apps	Gls
90-91	W.B.A.	- (2)	-	-	-
91-92	Aston Villa	4 (4)	-	1 (1)	-
92-93	Aston Villa	1 (3)	-	1	-
93-94	Aston Villa	14 (3)	-	- (2)	-
94-95	Aston Villa	38 (1)	3	9	1
95-96	Aston Villa	36	1	13	1
96-97	Aston Villa	38	3	7	1
97-98	Aston Villa	37	2	11	-
98-99	Aston Villa	23 (2)	2	6	-
Villa record		191 (13)	11	48 (3)	3
TOTAL		191 (15)	11	48 (3)	3

★ *England international at Full (1 cap) and Under-21 levels.*

FABIO FERRARESI

Born Fano, Italy,
24th May 1979.
Joined Villa June 1998
from Cesena, on a Free
Transfer.
Villa debut as sub v
Strømsgodset, UEFA
Cup (a) 29/9/98.

One half of Villa's unfashionably tiny
foreign legion this season, Italian
midfielder Fabio Ferraresi joined Villa
from Cesena as a long-term prospect, but
with just a brief substitute's outing in
the UEFA Cup second leg against
Strømsgodset to show for his efforts, the
youngster's English excursion was ended
when he returned to Italy in the close
season.

Career Record:

Season	Club	League Apps	Gls	Cups Apps	Gls
98-99	Aston Villa	-	-	- (1)	-

★ *Italian Under-18 international.*

● It wasn't the first time a player had left
a club because he felt he was going
nowhere, but in David Unsworth's case,
the circumstances were slightly different.
He had been a Villa player for less than a
week and his concern was that he was
going nowhere whenever he tried to go
home.

Only after he signed for Villa from
West Ham in July, did Unsworth realise
that negotiating the M6 between
Birmingham and his Merseyside home
twice a day was no picnic. With his wife
unwilling to relocate, he was looking for
a new employer with the ink barely dry
on his contract.

Everton stepped in and one of the
shortest Villa careers on record was over,
with Villa receiving only a pre-season
friendly at Wycombe and a solitary run-
out in the Reserves in return for their £3m.

SIMON GRAYSON

Born Ripon, Yorkshire,
16th December 1969
Joined Villa June 1997
from Leicester City,
£1.35m.
Villa debut v Blackburn
Rovers, Lge (h) 13/8/97.

Utility player Simon Grayson saw more
of the bench than a High Court judge
this season, yet went uncomplainingly
about his work.

After a string of sub appearances early
in the season, no-one could criticise him
for looking a gift horse in the mouth
when he made three starts in four games
in February. At a time when his team's
crumbling form might have persuaded
lesser men to find somewhere to hide,
'Larry' was a man possessed in defence
and midfield.

Such determination deserved better
reward than the ankle injury which
knocked him out of the reckoning late in
the season, just when he was enjoying a
run in the side.

Career Record:

Season	Club	League Apps	Gls	Cups Apps	Gls
87-88	Leeds United	2	-	1	-
88-89	Leeds United	-	-	-	-
89-90	Leeds United	-	-	-	-
90-91	Leeds United	-	-	-	-
91-92	Leeds United	-	-	- (1)	-
91-92	Leicester City	13	-	3	-
92-93	Leicester City	14 (10)	1	3 (2)	-
93-94	Leicester City	39 (1)	1	9	-
94-95	Leicester City	34	-	5	-
95-96	Leicester City	39 (2)	2	8 (1)	-
96-97	Leicester City	36	-	10	2
97-98	Aston Villa	28 (5)	-	8 (3)	2
98-99	Aston Villa	4 (11)	-	3 (2)	-
Villa record		32 (16)	-	11 (5)	2
TOTAL		209 (29)	4	50 (9)	4

LEE HENDRIE

Born Birmingham, 18th May 1977. *Joined Villa* July 1993 as YTS trainee. July 1994 on professional forms. *Villa debut* As sub v Queens Park Rangers, Lge (a) 23/12/95.

It was something of a frustrating season for Lee Hendrie, who was keen to build on the breakthrough into regular first-team football he made last term.

In the first half of the season, he could do little wrong and was on cloud nine when making his full England debut against the Czech Republic.

As the season wore on however, he was one of several Villa players dragged down by the team's general lack of form.

Occasionally a peripheral figure when the formation left him isolated on the wing, his slight figure was also prey for opponents well aware of his reputation. He admitted to being exhausted by club and country commitments and two blood-curdling challenges on him at Anfield ended his season.

While he needs to learn to walk away from potential flash points in this card-crazy era, Hendrie remains one of Villa's best providers of the telling pass into the penalty area. His overhead scoop to set up Julian Joachim's goal against Middlesbrough was one of the cameos of the season.

Career Record:

Season	Club	League Apps	Gls	Cups Apps	Gls
94-95	Aston Villa	-	-	-	-
95-96	Aston Villa	2 (1)	-	-	-
96-97	Aston Villa	- (4)	-	1 (2)	-
97-98	Aston Villa	13 (4)	3	4 (3)	-
98-99	Aston Villa	31 (1)	3	5	-
TOTAL		46 (10)	6	10 (5)	-

★ *England Under-21 (7 caps, 2 goals); 'B' (1 cap) and Full international (1 cap).*

DAVID HUGHES

Born Wrexham, 1st February 1978. *Joined Villa* as associate schoolboy April 94; full professional 1st July 96. *Villa debut* as sub v Liverpool, Lge (h) 2/3/97.

There has been no joy for the Welsh U21 international since he made four first team appearances in 1996-97.

Returning from a loan spell at Carlisle, he made the subs' bench on a handful of occasions but as last season, none of them resulted in him getting onto the field.

The central defender is a victim of Villa's strength in that department, with Ugo Ehiogu, Colin Calderwood, the two Gareths and Riccardo Scimeca all fighting for a place.

Career Record:

Season	Club	League Apps	Gls	Cups Apps	Gls
96-97	Aston Villa	4 (2)	-	-	-
97-98	Aston Villa	-	-	-	-
(loan)	Carlisle Utd	1	-	-	-
98-99	Aston Villa	-	-	-	-
Villa record		4 (2)	-	-	-
TOTAL		5 (2)	-	-	-

★ *Welsh Under-21 international.*

● Reserve team striker Alan Lee did not feature in the first team during the season, but went out on loan on two occasions during the season.
On 5th November 1998 he went to Torquay United where his record was:
League - 7(1) appearances, 2 goals.
Cup - 1 appearance, 1 goal.
On 2nd March 1999 Alan went to Port Vale, where he stayed until the end of the season, he record read:
League - 3(1) appearances, 2 goals.

TOMMY JASZCZUN

Born Kettering,
19th September 1977.
Joined Villa July 1994 as
YTS trainee. July 1996
on professional forms.
Villa debut as sub v
Chelsea, League Cup (a)
28/10/98.

He was a regular in the Reserves, but there was just the one first team appearance for this 21-year-old defender. It was not one he'll forget in a hurry, however, coming on for the tempestuous last 15 minutes of the Worthington Cup game at Chelsea.

He was back on the bench for the next game, at home to Celta Vigo, but that was his last first-team involvement for the season.

Career Record:

Season	Club	League Apps	Gls	Cups Apps	Gls
98-99	Aston Villa	-	-	- (1)	-

● Villa chairman Doug Ellis turned author early in the season when his autobiography *Deadly!* was launched.

The chairman played an ace at the official launch when he was joined in front of the media by the first manager he hired at Villa Park, Tommy Docherty.

After that, there began a whistle-stop round of book signing appearances at bookstores in the region, as copies of *Deadly!* began to sell like hot cakes.

In conjunction with football writer Dennis Shaw and published by Sports Projects, the book was written over a six month period, but Mr Ellis was quick to point out that its publication should not be taken as a sign that his days at the Villa helm will soon be over.

"I'm not retiring; I don't believe in it," he explained. "Although perhaps if we won the Champions' League..."

JULIAN JOACHIM

Born Peterborough,
12th September 1974
Joined Villa February
1996 from Leicester City,
£1.5m.
Villa debut as sub v
Wimbledon, Lge (a)
24/2/96.

Whatever Villa's form in this up and down season, Julian Joachim was one of its dependable constants. Play him alongside Stan Collymore, put him next to Dion Dublin, bring him off the bench: this refreshingly uncomplicated individual could be always be counted on to torment defences with his pace and maintain a regular supply of goals.

His previous tendency to run out of steam was firmly put behind him and far from pouting when he was left out earlier in the season, when Villa had three strikers chasing two places, he simply responded in the best possible way; scoring the winner at Vigo and then salvaging points for his team with two goals at Nottingham Forest and the equaliser at home to Manchester United.

Achieving a career-best 16 goals for the season, 'JJ' showed signs of building up a good understanding with Dion Dublin.

Career Record:

Season	Club	League Apps	Gls	Cups Apps	Gls
92-93	Leicester City	25 (1)	10	5 (1)	4
93-94	Leicester City	27 (9)	11	5 (2)	1
94-95	Leicester City	11 (4)	3	2	-
95-96	Leicester City	12	2	2	-
	Aston Villa	4 (7)	1	-	-
96-97	Aston Villa	3 (12)	3	2	-
97-98	Aston Villa	16 (10)	8	2 (2)	-
98-99	Aston Villa	29 (7)	14	7	2
Villa record		52 (36)	26	11 (2)	2
TOTAL		127 (50)	52	25 (5)	7

★ *England Youth and Under-21 International (8 caps).*

AARON LESCOTT

Born Birmingham,
2nd December, 1978.
Joined Villa July 1995 as
YTS trainee. July 1996 on
professional forms.
Villa debut as sub v
Hull City, FA Cup (h)
2/1/99.

Local lad Aaron Lescott was on substitute
duty for four games this season but one
of them became that all-important first
team debut when John Gregory threw
him into a won FA Cup game against
Hull City.

A regular in the Reserves, the 20-year-
old midfielder will look to make a bigger
impact on the senior side next season.

Career Record:

Season	Club	League Apps	Gls	Cups Apps	Gls
98-99	Aston Villa	-	-	- (1)	-

JUST THE TICKET

● Among various alterations to Villa Park
before and during the season, one in
particular was well-received by supporters.

A spacious new ticket office, located in
Villa Village, makes exposure to the
elements for ticket queues a thing of the
past. Replacing the North Stand ticket
office, the new office features a generous
amount of space for queuing indoors,
together with an outdoor canopy to
protect those forced to wait outside, at
times when demand for tickets is
particularly high.

In the North Stand, meanwhile, the
first-floor banqueting suite was
refurbished together with the Centenary
Suite and Executive Suite on the second
floor, while the third floor saw the
installation of nine new hospitality
suites for corporate use.

continued on page 123

PAUL MERSON

Born Northolt, Middle-
sex, 20th March 1968.
Joined Villa September
1998 from Middles-
brough, £6.75m.
Villa debut v Wimbledon,
Lge (h) 12/9/98.

It was a curate's egg season for Villa's
purchase from Middlesbrough. A lengthy
back injury in mid-season took the
steam out of what had been a promising
start to his Villa career.

Against this, his vision and distribution
when on song took his team to a new
dimension.

His half-hour substitute's appearance
against Nottingham Forest at Villa Park
became an object lesson in the art of
dismantling an opponent and his 25-
yard strike at Newcastle was one of
Villa's goals of the season.

Career Record:

Season	Club	League Apps	Gls	Cups Apps	Gls
86-87	Arsenal	5 (2)	3	-	-
(loan)	Brentford	6 (1)	-	1 (1)	-
87-88	Arsenal	7 (8)	5	1 (1)	-
88-89	Arsenal	29 (8)	10	7 (1)	4
89-90	Arsenal	21 (8)	7	4 (3)	-
90-91	Arsenal	36 (1)	13	12	3
91-92	Arsenal	41 (1)	12	9	1
92-93	Arsenal	32 (1)	6	17	2
93-94	Arsenal	24 (9)	7	15 (1)	5
94-95	Arsenal	24	4	11 (1)	3
95-96	Arsenal	38	5	9	-
96-97	Arsenal	32	6	8	3
97-98	Middlesbrough	45	12	10	4
98-99	Middlesbrough	3	-	-	-
98-99	Aston Villa	21 (5)	5	1	-
TOTAL		364 (44)	95	105 (8)	25

★ *England Youth International; Under-21 (4 caps);*
'B' (4 caps); Full International (21 caps, 2 goals).

MICHAEL OAKES

Born Northwich, 30th October 1973. *Joined Villa* July 1991 as a non-contract player, February 1992 on professional forms *Villa debut* v Wigan Ath., CCC (a) 5/10/94.

Stepping into Mark Bosnich's shoes for much of the season was possibly the most thankless task on offer in the Villa ranks and it is to Michael Oakes' credit that he not only dealt with the pressure so stoically but also grew noticeably into the job as his tenure between the posts progressed.

In one season, the 25-year-old played almost as many games as he had throughout his previous four seasons on Villa's books.

He was desperately unlucky to be sent off for a handball offence against Blackburn Rovers, but referee Dermot Gallagher thankfully realised his error upon viewing the replay after the match and was big enough to rescind the sending-off.

Career Record:

| Season | Club | League | | | Cups | |
		Apps	Gls Ag		Apps	Gls Ag
91-92	Aston Villa	-	-		-	-
92-93	Aston Villa	-	-		-	-
93-94	Aston Villa	-	-		-	-
(loan)	Scarborough	2	*		-	-
(loan)	Tranmere	-	-		-	-
94-95	Aston Villa	-	-		1	-
95-96	Aston Villa	-	-		-	-
96-97	Aston Villa	18 (2)	18		3	2
97-98	Aston Villa	8	13		1	2
98-99	Aston Villa	23	35		5	9
Villa record		49 (2)	66		10	13
TOTAL		51 (2)	66		10	13

★ *England Under-21 international.*

* Goals conceded whilst on loan at Scarborough not known.

ADAM RACHEL

Born Birmingham, 10th December, 1976. *Joined Villa* July 1993 as YTS trainee. Later on professional forms. *Villa debut* as sub v Blackburn Rovers, Lge (a) 26/12/98.

Adam made his first team debut in unexpected circumstances, coming on for Michael Oakes after the latter was sent off at Blackburn. With Villa channelling their indignation at the red card into a stirring second half performance, Rachel looked set for a quiet night's work until Tim Sherwood scored a late winner for the hosts.

Adam played understudy for most of Oakes' run as the starting 'keeper, before making way for the Finn, Peter Enckelman.

Career Record:

| Season | Club | League | | Cups | |
		Apps	Gls	Apps	Gls
98-99	Aston Villa	- (1)	1	-	-

continued from page 122

In what was previously empty space in the Doug Ellis Stand, a magnificent new suite, christened the David Targett Club, in honour of the former Villa director, was built to run almost the length of the stand, while 'The Strikers Club' was a brand new membership area on the site of a former concourse in the Holte End.

Finally, commercial staff relocated from the North Stand to new offices in the Villa Village complex. This was done partly to accommodate Villa's expanding commercial operation and also to house the Commercial and Conference & Banqueting Departments in close proximity to each other, as they had previously been situated on different floors in the North Stand.

RICCARDO SCIMECA   GARETH SOUTHGATE

Born Leamington Spa, 13th June 1975.
Joined Villa July 1991 as YTS trainee. July 1993 on professional forms.
Villa debut As sub v Manchester United, Lge (h) 19/8/95.

Had Riccardo Scimeca taken over from Michael Oakes when the latter was red-carded at Blackburn, he could have created a little bit of history by playing in every sector of the field in a single season.

The central defender began the campaign by reverting to his old position of striker while Villa sought to plug the gap left by the departure of Dwight Yorke.

Against Celta Vigo in the first leg of the UEFA Cup second round tie, he filled in as a midfielder when suspension accounted for Alan Thompson and Ian Taylor, then finally, it was back to his first-choice role at the heart of the defence following Ugo Ehiogu's eye injury.

Throw in a couple of goals - his first recorded for the senior side - and it turned into quite a busy campaign for a man who reluctantly submitted a transfer request earlier in the season in a bid to find more regular first team football.

Career Record:

Season	Club	League		Cups	
		Apps	Gls	Apps	Gls
93-94	Aston Villa	-	-	-	-
94-95	Aston Villa	-	-	-	-
95-96	Aston Villa	7 (10)	-	3 (2)	-
96-97	Aston Villa	11 (6)	-	4 (1)	-
97-98	Aston Villa	16 (5)	-	7 (1)	-
98-99	Aston Villa	16 (2)	2	4 (2)	-
TOTAL		50 (23)	2	18 (6)	-

★ *England Under-21 international. (5 caps).*

Born Watford, 3rd September 1970.
Joined Villa June 1995 from Crystal Palace, £2.5m.
Villa debut v Manchester United, Lge (h) 19/8/95.

Considering that World Cup commitments made him a year-round player, Villa's captain displayed remarkable stamina as he played a key role in his club's water-tight defence over the first half of the season.

In tandem with Ugo Ehiogu, he kept the best strikers in the Premiership in check. When Ehiogu was forced out of the side for a lengthy period, however, Southgate was left looking after two young central defenders alongside him, in Gareth Barry and Riccardo Scimeca.

Something had to give and it was concern that Gareth was having to spread himself too thinly that persuaded John Gregory to bring in Colin Calderwood, marking a return to form of the defensive unit.

Career Record:

Season	Club	League		Cups	
		Apps	Gls	Apps	Gls
88-89	Crystal Palace	-	-	-	-
89-90	Crystal Palace	-	-	-	-
90-91	Crystal Palace	1	-	1 (1)	-
91-92	Crystal Palace	26 (4)	-	9	-
92-93	Crystal Palace	33	3	6	2
93-94	Crystal Palace	46	9	7	3
94-95	Crystal Palace	42	3	15	2
95-96	Aston Villa	31	1	12	1
96-97	Aston Villa	28	1	6	-
97-98	Aston Villa	32	-	11	-
98-99	Aston Villa	38	-	6	-
Villa record		129	2	35	1
TOTAL		277 (4)	17	73 (1)	8

★ *Full England international (30 caps, 1 goal).*

STEVE STONE

Born Gateshead, 20th August 1971. *Joined Villa* March 1999 from Nottingham Forest for £5.5m. *Villa debut* v Tottenham Hotspur, Lge (a) 13/3/99.

A move to Aston Villa must have looked like a move from fire to frying pan when Steve Stone swapped relegation-bound Nottingham Forest for Villa in March. The colour of his shirt may have changed but his team was still wondering where the next win was coming from.

As Villa fortunes improved, however, we began to see what £6m had bought. Crosses had been a weakness in the Villa gameplan all season yet suddenly the bustling Geordie was landing the ball on a sixpence from the right flank to order.

Two such efforts brought goals for Gareth Barry and Julian Joachim against Nottingham Forest and Manchester United respectively.

The likable north-easterner is now with only his second club in a seven-year professional career. If he becomes as popular a fixture at Villa as he was at the City Ground, £6m will be a bargain.

Career Record:

Season	Club	League Apps	Gls	Cups Apps	Gls
91-92	Nottingham F.	- (1)	-	-	-
92-93	Nottingham F.	11 (1)	1	- (1)	-
93-94	Nottingham F.	45	5	9	-
94-95	Nottingham F.	41	5	6	-
95-96	Nottingham F.	34	7	16	2
96-97	Nottingham F.	5	-	-	-
97-98	Nottingham F.	27 (2)	2	-	-
98-99	Nottingham F.	26	3	4	2
	Aston Villa	9 (1)	-	-	-
TOTAL		198 (5)	23	35 (1)	4

★ *Full England international (9 caps, 2 goals).*

IAN TAYLOR

Born Birmingham, 4th June 1968. *Joined Villa* December 1994 in straight swop deal with Guy Whittingham from Sheffield Wed. *Villa debut* v Arsenal, Lge (a) 26/12/94.

Not helped by playing through injury on various occasions during the year, Ian Taylor struggled against the odds to make his usual impact this season.

The popular midfielder's ambition had been to reach double figures in the scoring charts, having fallen just one short last term.

After three goals in his first seven starts this season, including two at Coventry City, the 31-year-old looked well on his way to that target but it would be Anfield in mid April before he added to his total.

A virtual deck of yellow cards stands as testimony to his unwavering commitment to the cause, exemplified by the key part he played in frustrating former team-mate Dwight Yorke when Villa travelled to Old Trafford.

Career Record:

Season	Club	League Apps	Gls	Cups Apps	Gls
92-93	Port Vale	41	15	15	4
93-94	Port Vale	42	13	8	3
94-95	Sheff. Wed.	9 (5)	1	2 (2)	1
	Aston Villa	21	1	2	-
95-96	Aston Villa	24 (1)	3	7 (2)	2
96-97	Aston Villa	29 (5)	2	3	1
97-98	Aston Villa	30 (2)	6	12	3
98-99	Aston Villa	31 (2)	4	4 (1)	-
Villa record		*135 (10)*	*16*	*28 (3)*	*6*
TOTAL		227 (15)	45	53 (5)	14

ALAN THOMPSON

Born Newcastle,
22nd November 1973.
Joined Villa June 1998
from Bolton Wanderers,
£4.5m.
Villa debut v Everton,
Lge (a) 15/8/98.

Brought in last summer from Bolton for £4.5m to give Villa a presence and some goals from the left side of midfield, Thompson will be disappointed with a return of only two goals, compared to the 10 goals he registered in Bolton's unsuccessful battle against relegation last season.

His famed left footed free-kicks, launched with blistering ferocity from around the box yielded just goal, during the home win against Middlesbrough, and he'll be keen to get the gyroscopes re-aligned for next season.

He chose the toughest fixture of all to show his potential, dominating midfield at home to Manchester United, showing Roy Keane who's boss and hitting the post to boot.

The popular Geordie's honesty and commitment to his task never wavered and were apparent to the Villa Park faithful, who quickly christened him 'Super Al'.

Career Record:

Season	Club	League Apps	Gls	Cups Apps	Gls
91-92	Newcastle U.	12 (2)	-	1	-
92-93	Newcastle U.	1 (1)	-	3	-
93-94	Bolton W.	19 (8)	6	10 (2)	2
94-95	Bolton W.	34 (3)	7	11 (1)	2
95-96	Bolton W.	23 (3)	1	6	1
96-97	Bolton W.	34	11	5 (1)	2
97-98	Bolton W.	33	9	5	1
98-99	Aston Villa	20 (5)	2	3 (1)	-
TOTAL		176 (22)	36	44 (5)	8

★ *English Youth International; Under-21 (2 caps).*

DARIUS VASSELL

Born Birmingham,
30th June 1980.
Joined Villa July 1996 as YTS trainee. March 1998 on professional forms.
Villa debut as sub v Middlesbrough, Lge (h) 23/8/98/.

First team debuts don't come much better than Darius Vassell's sensational arrival at home to Strømsgodset. With his team on the brink of a sensational 2-1 upset by the Norwegians, Vassell observed to the letter coach Steve Harrison's instruction to "Get yourself out there, score a couple of goals and win us the game."

It was merely a continuation of the goalscoring form that saw the local striker score nine goals for Villa at Reserve and U19 level and represent his country at U18 and U21 level.

He had to make do with several substitute appearances for the first team and will obviously look to build on that in 1999-00.

Career Record:

Season	Club	League Apps	Gls	Cups Apps	Gls
98-99	Aston Villa	- (6)	-	- (5)	2

★ *England Under-18 International (5 caps, 5 goals), Under-21 international (1 cap).*

● In August 1998 midfielder Mark Draper and full-back Gary Charles both signed four year contracts with the club, Charles, however, left to join Benfica in January 1999.

In the same month, midfield player, Lee Hendrie also signed a new contract, this time for five years.

In October 1998 captain Gareth Southgate also pledged his long-term future to the club by signing a five year contract.

RICHARD WALKER

Born Birmingham,
8th November, 1977.
Joined Villa on YTS terms
in 1993 at the age of 16,
now full time profes-
sional.
Villa debut as sub v Leeds
Utd, Lge (a) 28/12/97.

The Birmingham-born striker built on
the solitary substitute's appearance he
made for Villa last season, but it was
with another team.

Walker was given the chance for more
regular first team action when he went
on loan to Cambridge United in
November 1998 for the remainder of the
season, playing a part in the Us
promotion from Division Three.

Career Record:

Season	Club	League Apps	Gls	Cups Apps	Gls
97-98	Aston Villa	- (1)	-	-	-
98-99	Aston Villa	-	-	-	-
loan	Cambridge U.	7 (13)	3	1 (2)	1
TOTAL		7 (14)	3	1 (2)	1

● A new pre-match feature at Villa Park
this season was the occasional display of
a giant Villa shirt that adorned the pitch.

Measuring 70 square metres, the shirt
was passed above the heads of spectators
in the Holte End immediately prior to
kick off, reminiscent of similar displays
seen in Italian football. It took a game or
two to get the hang of it but eventually
it made for a stunning effect prior to the
arrival of the teams.

A more subtle alteration to the
standard Villa attire was called for when
the team played in the UEFA Cup. The
word 'Vans' had to be removed from the
LDV Vans logo on the shirt, in order to
avoid confusion in countries where the
word has a different meaning.

STEVE WATSON

Born North Shields,
1st April 1974
Joined Villa October 1998
from Newcastle United,
£3.5m.
Villa debut as sub v
Leicester C., Lge (h)
24/10/98

It was a season of transition for the
former Newcastle United player, who,
like fellow Geordie Steve Stone, left the
only club he'd ever known to join Aston
Villa.

Informed by Newcastle boss Ruud
Gullit that his days in the black and
white stripes were over last October, and
having to move 200 miles from his
home town, Watson could have been
forgiven had he taken a while to settle in
his new surroundings.

Instead, the £4m signing brought new
respectability to the term 'utility player'.
Settling in at the right wing-back slot he
assumed from Gary Charles, Watson put
a string of poised performances together
and allied some nifty footwork going
forward with some hard tackling when
called to defend.

Career Record:

Season	Club	League Apps	Gls	Cups Apps	Gls
90-91	Newcastle Utd	22 (2)	-	4	-
91-92	Newcastle Utd	23 (5)	1	2	-
92-93	Newcastle Utd	1 (1)	-	2 (1)	-
93-94	Newcastle Utd	29 (3)	2	5 (1)	-
94-95	Newcastle Utd	22 (5)	4	4 (4)	1
95-96	Newcastle Utd	15 (8)	3	3 (3)	1
96-97	Newcastle Utd	33 (3)	1	7 (3)	-
97-98	Newcastle Utd	27 (2)	1	13 (2)	-
98-99	Newcastle Utd	7	-	1	-
98-99	Aston Villa	26 (1)	-	3	-
TOTAL		205 (30)	12	44 (14)	2

★ *England Youth; England Under-21 (12 caps);
England 'B' (1 cap).*

ALAN WRIGHT

Born Ashton-under-Lyme, 28th September 1971.
Joined Villa March 1995 from Blackburn Rovers, £900,000.
Villa debut v West Ham Utd, Lge (h) 18/3/95.

Villa's only ever-present of the season (see separate feature), Alan Wright's resilience in an alternating defensive formation was as much mental as physical, never hiding from his tactical responsibilities as either an attacking wing-back or a deeper lying traditional full-back.

Always available as the outlet pass for a team-mate in difficulty; always willing to get involved in the thick of the action, he was a team player *par excellence* and was showing some of his best form just as the season came to a climax.

Career Record:

Season	Club	League Apps	Gls	Cups Apps	Gls
87-88	Blackpool	- (1)	-	-	-
88-90	Blackpool	14 (2)	-	3 (1)	-
89-90	Blackpool	20 (4)	-	9 (3)	-
90-91	Blackpool	45	-	12	-
91-92	Blackpool	12	-	5	-
	Blackburn R.	32 (1)	1	5	-
92-93	Blackburn R.	24	-	9	-
93-94	Blackburn R.	7 (5)	-	2	-
94-95	Blackburn R.	4 (1)	-	- (1)	-
	Aston Villa	8	-	-	-
95-96	Aston Villa	38	2	13	-
96-97	Aston Villa	38	1	7	-
97-98	Aston Villa	35 (2)	-	13	-
98-99	Aston Villa	38	-	7	-
Villa record		157 (2)	3	40	-
TOTAL		315 (16)	4	85 (5)	-

★ *England Under-21 International.*

DWIGHT YORKE

Born Canaan, Tobago, 3rd November 1971.
Joined Villa December 1989 from Signal Hill in Tobago, £120,000.
Villa debut v C.Palace, Lge (a) 24/3/90.

After a glittering career in claret and blue, it was a shame Dwight Yorke's final performance for the club had to be such an anonymous affair at Everton in the opening game of the season.

His much publicised desire to join Manchester United ate up the column inches in the ever news-hungry national press, culminating in his eventual £12.6m move to Old Trafford.

His lasting epitaph to Villa fans will be the 98 goals he scored over ten seasons for the club.

Career Record:

Season	Club	League Apps	Gls	Cups Apps	Gls
89-90	Aston Villa	- (2)	-	-	-
90-91	Aston Villa	8 (10)	2	3	-
91-92	Aston Villa	27 (5)	11	8	6
92-93	Aston Villa	22 (5)	6	6 (2)	1
93-94	Aston Villa	2 (10)	2	- (2)	1
94-95	Aston Villa	33 (4)	6	6	2
95-96	Aston Villa	35	17	13	8
96-97	Aston Villa	37	17	6	3
97-98	Aston Villa	30	12	10	4
98-99	Aston Villa	1	-	-	-
TOTAL		195 (36)	73	52 (4)	25

★ *Full international with Trinidad & Tobago.*

● Defender/midfield player Gareth Barry, who has made such an explosive impression on the Premiership this season, celebrated his 18th birthday on 23rd February 1999 by signing a five year contract with the club.

FINAL TABLE

			Home					Away					Total					
		Pl	W	D	L	F	A	W	D	L	F	A	W	D	L	F	A	Pts
1	Manchester United	38	14	4	1	45	18	8	9	2	35	19	22	13	3	80	37	79
2	Arsenal	38	14	5	0	34	5	8	7	4	25	12	22	12	4	59	17	78
3	Chelsea	38	12	6	1	29	13	8	9	2	28	17	20	15	3	57	30	75
4	Leeds United	38	12	5	2	32	9	6	8	5	30	25	18	13	7	62	34	67
5	West Ham United	38	11	3	5	32	26	5	6	8	14	27	16	9	13	46	53	57
6	**Aston Villa**	38	10	3	6	33	28	5	7	7	18	18	15	10	13	51	46	55
7	Liverpool	38	10	5	4	44	24	5	4	10	24	25	15	9	14	68	49	54
8	Derby County	38	8	7	4	22	19	5	6	8	18	26	13	13	12	40	45	52
9	Middlesbrough	38	7	9	3	25	18	5	6	8	23	36	12	15	11	48	54	51
10	Leicester City	38	7	6	6	25	25	5	7	7	15	21	12	13	13	40	46	49
11	Tottenham Hotspur	38	7	7	5	28	26	4	7	8	19	24	11	14	13	47	50	47
12	Sheffield Wednesday	38	7	5	7	20	15	6	2	11	21	27	13	7	18	41	42	46
13	Newcastle United	38	7	6	6	26	25	4	7	8	22	29	11	13	14	48	54	46
14	Everton	38	6	8	5	22	12	5	2	12	20	35	11	10	17	42	47	43
15	Coventry City	38	8	6	5	26	21	3	3	13	13	30	11	9	18	39	51	42
16	Wimbledon	38	7	7	5	22	21	3	5	11	18	42	10	12	16	40	63	42
17	Southampton	38	9	4	6	29	26	2	4	13	8	38	11	8	19	37	64	41
18	Charlton Athletic	38	4	7	8	20	20	4	5	10	21	36	8	12	18	41	56	36
19	Blackburn Rovers	38	6	5	8	21	24	1	9	9	17	28	7	14	17	38	52	35
20	Nottingham Forest	38	3	7	9	18	31	4	2	13	17	38	7	9	22	35	69	30

ROLL OF HONOUR

Champions: Manchester United
Runners-up: Arsenal
UEFA Cup Qualifiers: Leeds United, Newcastle United, Tottenham Hotspur
Relegated: Charlton Athletic, Blackburn Rovers, Nottingham Forest
FA Cup winners: Manchester United
Worthington Cup winners: Tottenham Hotspur

FACTS & FIGURES

Of the 380 games played in the Premiership, 169 resulted in home wins, 97 in away wins and 114 draws. A total of 965 goals were scored at an average of 2.52 per game, with 551 being scored by the home clubs and 405 by the visitors

Most goals scored: 80, Manchester United
Most home goals: 45, Manchester United
Most away goals: 35, Manchester United
Least goals scored: 35, Nottingham Forest
Least home goals: 18, Nottingham Forest
Least away goals: 8, Southampton
Least goals conceded: 17, Arsenal

Least home goals conceded: 5, Arsenal
Least away goals conceded: 12, Arsenal
Most goals conceded: 69, Nottingham Forest
Most home goals conceded: 31, Nottingham F.
Most away goals conceded: 42, Wimbledon

Highest goals aggregate: 117, Manchester United and Liverpool
Lowest goals aggregate: 76, Arsenal

Best home record: 47 pts, Arsenal
Best away record: 33 pts, Manchester United and Chelsea
Worst home record: 16 pts, Nottingham Forest
Worst away record: 10 pts, Southampton

Highest home score:
Liverpool 7 Southampton 1, 16.1.99

Highest away score:
Nottingham F. 1 Manchester Utd 8, 6.2.99

Penalties scored: 46
Hat-tricks: 11
Own goals: 16
Yellow cards: 1,384
Red Cards: 72
Bookings per game: 3.83

LEADING SCORERS

(Including Cup & European games)

29 Dwight Yorke (Manchester United)
24 Andy Cole (Manchester United)
23 Michael Owen (Liverpool)
21 Alan Shearer (Newcastle United)
20 Jimmy Floyd Hasselbaink (Leeds United)
19 Nicolas Anelka (Arsenal)
18 Robbie Fowler (Liverpool)
18 Hamilton Ricard (Middlesbrough)
17 Ole Gunnar Solskjaer (Manchester United)
16 Dennis Bergkamp (Arsenal)
16 Tony Cottee (Leicester City)
16 Julian Joachim (Aston Villa)
15 Dion Dublin* (Aston Villa)
15 Gianfranco Zola (Chelsea)
14 Gustavo Poyet (Chelsea)
13 Tore Andre Flo (Chelsea)
13 Steffen Iversen (Tottenham Hotspur)
13 Noel Whelan (Coventry City)
12 Chris Armstrong (Tottenham Hotspur)
12 Deon Burton (Derby County)
12 Darren Huckerby (Coventry City)
12 Dougie Freedman (Nottingham Forest)
11 Marcus Gayle (Wimbledon)
11 Marc Overmars (Arsenal)
10 Jason Euell (Wimbledon)
10 Ryan Giggs (Manchester United)
10 Jamie Redknapp (Liverpool)
10 Paul Scholes (Manchester United)
10 Gianluca Vialli (Chelsea)
10 Paulo Wanchope (Derby County)

* *Includes goals for other Premiership clubs.*

JOINT GOLDEN BOOT WINNERS

(Premiership games only)

18 Jimmy Floyd Hasselbaink, Michael Owen
    and Dwight Yorke

QUICK OFF THE MARK

Villa's fastest goal of the season was scored in the Premiership by Lee Hendrie against Leicester City in a 2-2 draw at Filbert Street on 6th April 1999. The goal was timed at 79 seconds.

THE GATE LEAGUE

	Total	Best	Lowest	Average
Manchester Utd	1,048,580	55,316	55,052	55,188
Liverpool	823,105	44,852	36,019	43,321
Arsenal	722,445	38,303	37,323	38,023
Aston Villa	701,795	39,241	29,559	36,937
Newcastle Utd	696,631	36,783	36,352	36,665
Everton	687,856	40,185	30,357	36,203
Leeds United	681,056	40,255	30,012	35,845
Chelsea	660,273	35,016	34,382	34,751
Middlesbrough	653,393	34,687	33,387	34,389
Tottenham	650,307	36,878	28,338	34,227
Derby County	554,725	32,913	25,747	29,196
Sheffield Wed	508,161	39,475	19,321	26,745
Blackburn Rovers	489,459	30,436	21,754	25,761
West Ham Utd	487,996	26,044	23,153	25,684
Nottingham Forest	463,894	30,025	20,480	24,415
Coventry City	395,137	23,098	16,006	20,797
Leicester City	388,910	22,091	17,725	20,469
Charlton Athletic	376,637	20,046	16,488	19,823
Wimbledon	346,468	26,121	11,717	18,235
Southampton	287,653	15,255	14,354	15,140

Highest attendance:
55,316, Manchester Utd v Southampton, 27.2.99

Lowest attendance:
11,717, Wimbledon v Coventry City, 5.12.98

Four goals in a game:
Michael Owen (Liverpool) v N. Forest 24.10.98
Ole Gunnar Solskjaer (Man U.) v N. Forest 6.2.99

Three goals in a game:
Clive Mendonca (Charlton) v Southampton 22.8.98
Michael Owen (Liverpool) v Newcastle 30.8.98
Dion Dublin (Villa) v Southampton 14.11.98
Robbie Fowler (Liverpool) v Villa 21.11.98
Chris Armstrong (Tottenham) v Everton 28.12.98
Darren Huckerby (Coventry) v N. Forest 9.1.99
Robbie Fowler (Liverpool) v Southampton 16.1.99
Dwight Yorke (Man U.) v Leicester 16.1.99
Nicolas Anelka (Arsenal) v Leicester 20.2.99
Kevin Campbell (Everton) v West Ham U. 8.5.99

PREMIERSHIP STATISTICS

PREMIERSHIP ALL-TIME TABLE 1992-99

		P	W	D	L	F	A	Pts	1993	1994	1995	1996	1997	1998	1999
1	Manchester United	278	168	73	37	526	239	577	1st	1st	2nd	1st	1st	2nd	1st
2	Arsenal	278	127	84	67	383	229	465	10th	4th	12th	5th	3rd	1st	2nd
3	Liverpool	278	126	73	79	454	309	451	6th	8th	4th	3rd	4th	3rd	7th
4	Blackburn Rovers	278	122	74	82	409	315	440	4th	2nd	1st	7th	13th	6th	19th
5	**Aston Villa**	278	114	73	91	353	309	415	2nd	10th	18th	4th	5th	7th	6th
6	Leeds United	278	108	85	85	368	314	409	17th	5th	5th	13th	11th	5th	4th
7	Chelsea	278	108	84	86	382	334	408	11th	14th	11th,	11th	6th	4th	3rd
8	Newcastle United	236	108	61	67	371	263	385	-	3rd	6th	2nd	2nd	13th	13th
9	Tottenham Hotspur	278	94	82	102	365	378	364	8th	15th	7th	8th	10th	14th	11th
10	Sheffield Wednesday	278	93	82	103	371	383	361	7th	7th	13th	15th	7th	16th	12th
11	Wimbledon	278	92	82	104	338	398	358	12th	6th	9th	14th	8th	15th	16th
12	Everton	278	85	78	115	330	373	333	13th	17th	15th	6th	15th	17th	14th
13	Coventry City	278	79	94	105	304	373	331	15th	11th	16th	16th	17th	11th	15th
14	Southampton	278	81	72	125	335	417	315	18th	18th	10th	17th	16th	12th	17th
15	West Ham United	236	82	62	92	275	316	308	-	13th	14th	10th	14th	8th	5th
16	Nottingham Forest	198	60	59	79	229	287	239	22nd	-	3rd	9th	20th	-	20th
17	QPR	164	59	39	66	224	232	216	5th	9th	8th	19th	-	-	-
18	Manchester City	164	45	54	65	180	222	189	9th	16th	17th	18th	-	-	-
19	Leicester City	156	43	49	64	182	221	178	-	-	21st	-	9th	10th	10th
20	Middlesbrough	156	44	48	64	188	239	177*	21st	-	-	12th	19th	-	9th
21	Norwich City	126	43	39	44	163	180	168	3rd,	12th	20th	-	-	-	-
22	Derby County	114	40	33	41	137	152	153	-	-	-	-	12th	9th	8th
23	Crystal Palace	122	30	37	55	119	181	127	20th	-	19th	-	-	20th	-
24	Ipswich Town	126	28	38	60	121	206	122	16th,	19th	22nd	-	-	-	-
25	Sheffield United	84	22	28	34	96	113	94	14th	20th	-	-	-	-	-
26	Oldham Athletic	84	22	23	39	105	142	89	19th	21st	-	-	-	-	-
27	Bolton Wanderers	76	17	18	41	80	132	69		-	-	20th	-	18th	-
28	Sunderland	38	10	10	18	35	53	40	-	-	-	-	18th	-	-
29	Charlton Athletic	38	8	12	18	41	56	36	-	-	-	-	-	-	18th
30	Barnsley	38	10	5	23	37	82	35	-	-	-	-	-	19th	-
31	Swindon Town	42	5	15	22	47	100	30	-	22nd	-	-	-	-	-
	Totals	2906	2073	833	2073	7548	7548	7882 (7885)							

Middlesbrough deducted 3 points in 96/97 season for failing to fulfil a fixture at Blackburn on 21.12.96. Final total of 6857 points takes this into account.
Italised positions denote relegated teams.

FIRST TEAM APPEARANCES & GOALSCORERS

	LEAGUE		FA CUP		LGE CUP		UEFA CUP		TOTAL	
	Apps	Gls	Apps	Gls	Apps	Gls	Apps	Gls	Apps	Gls
Gareth BARRY	27 (5)	2	2	-	-	-	3	-	32 (5)	2
Mark BOSNICH	15	-	-	-	-	-	2	-	17	-
Darren BYFIELD	-	-	-	-	1	-	1	-	2	-
Colin CALDERWOOD	8	-	-	-	-	-	-	-	8	-
Gary CHARLES	10 (1)	1	- (1)	-	1	-	4	1	15 (2)	2
Stan COLLYMORE	11 (9)	1	1	2	-	-	3	4	15 (9)	7
Mark DELANEY	- (2)	-	-	-	-	-	-	-	- (2)	-
Mark DRAPER	13 (10)	2	1	-	1	1	3 (1)	-	18 (11)	3
Dion DUBLIN	24	11	-	-	-	-	-	-	24	11
Ugo EHIOGU	23 (2)	2	2	-	1	-	3	-	29 (2)	2
Fabio FERRARESI	-	-	-	-	-	-	- (1)	-	- (1)	-
Simon GRAYSON	4 (11)	-	- (1)	-	1	-	2 (1)	-	7 (13)	-
Lee HENDRIE	31 (1)	3	2	-	-	-	3	-	36 (1)	3
Tommy JASZCZUN	-	-	-	-	- (1)	-	-	-	- (1)	-
Julian JOACHIM	29 (7)	14	2	1	1	-	4	1	36 (7)	16
Aaron LESCOTT	-	-	- (1)	-	-	-	-	-	- (1)	-
Paul MERSON	21 (5)	5	1	-	-	-	-	-	22 (5)	5
Michael OAKES	23	-	2	-	1	-	2	-	28	-
Adam RACHEL	- (1)	-	-	-	-	-	-	-	- (1)	-
Riccardo SCIMECA	16 (2)	2	2	-	1	-	1 (2)	-	20 (4)	2
Gareth SOUTHGATE	38	1	2	-	-	-	4	-	44	1
Steve STONE	9 (1)	-	-	-	-	-	-	-	9 (1)	-
Ian TAYLOR	31 (2)	4	1	-	1	-	2 (1)	-	35 (3)	4
Alan THOMPSON	20 (5)	2	-	-	- (1)	-	3	-	23 (6)	2
Darius VASSELL	- (6)	-	- (1)	-	- (1)	-	- (3)	2	- (11)	2
Steve WATSON	26 (1)	-	2	-	1	-	-	-	29 (1)	-
Alan WRIGHT	38	-	2	-	1	-	4	-	45	-
Dwight YORKE	1	-	-	-	-	-	-	-	-	-
Own goals		1		-		-		-		-

Unused Substitutes: (figures in brackets refer to cup matches)
Michael Oakes 15(2), Darius Vassell 15(2), Simon Grayson 13(2), Adam Rachel 12(5), Jlloyd Samuel 8(1), Peter Enckelman 6, Mark Draper 6, Gary Charles 5, Fabio Ferraresi 5(3), Gareth Barry 4, Riccardo Scimeca 4, Alan Thompson 4, Mark Delaney 3, Aaron Lescott 3, Mark Bosnich 2, Matthew Ghent 2, David Hughes 2, Julian Joachim 2, Stan Collymore 1, Ugo Ehiogu 1, Alan Lee 1, Paul Merson 1, Ben Petty 1, Michael Standing 1, Steve Watson 1, Lee Hendrie (1), Tommy Jaszczun (1).

Goalscorers in friendly games:
Alan Lee 9; Darren Byfield 7; Julian Joachim 6; Graham Evans 3, Darren Middleton 3, Darius Vassell 3; Stan Collymore 2, Gavin Melaugh 2, Jlloyd Samuel 2, Alan Thompson 2, Richard Walker 2; Martin Ridley 1, David Curtolo 1, Russel Latapy 1, Lee Collins 1, Ben Petty 1, Brian Mulholland 1, Aaron Lescott 1, Steve Stone 1, Paul Merson 1; own goals 2.

HIGHEST AND LOWEST

Highest home attendance: 39,241 (5 times)
v Newcastle United 9.9.98, v Leicester City
24.10.98, v Tottenham Hotspur 7.11.98,
v Liverpool 21.11.98, v Manchester United
5.12.98.

(There were a further four full houses at
Villa Park during the season, the capacity
having been reduced to 39,217.)

Lowest home attendance: 28,893
v Strømsgodset (UEFA Cup 1/1) 15.9.98

Highest away attendance: 55,189
v Manchester United 1.5.99

Lowest away attendance: 4,835
v Strømsgodset (UEFA Cup 1/2) 29.9.98

Biggest victory:
4-1 v Southampton (a) 14.11.98;
3-0 v Strømsgodset (a) 29.9.98, v Hull City
(h) 2.1.99, v Everton (h) 18.1.99 and v
Southampton (h) 10.4.99.

Heaviest defeat:
1-4 v Chelsea (a) 28.10.98, Coventry City (h)
27.2.99

Most goals in a match:
3 - Stan Collymore v Strømsgodset (a)
(UEFA 1/2) 29.9.98 and
Dion Dublin v Southampton (a) 14.11.98.

Most goals against:
3 - Robbie Fowler (Liverpool) (h) 21.11.98

Clean Sheets: 18
Failed to score in: 10
Villa scored first: 19
Scored first and won: 17
Scored first and drew: 1
Scored first and lost: 1
Opponents scored first: 20
Lost after opponents scored first: 15
Drew after opponents scored first: 3
Won after opponents scored first: 2
Highest League position: 1st
Lowest League position: 6th

SEQUENCE RECORDS

Most matches undefeated:
13, Aug 15 - Oct 28
Most home matches undefeated:
6, Aug 23 - Oct 24
Most away matches undefeated:
7, Aug 15 - Oct 20
Most wins in succession:
5, Aug 23 - Sept 15

Most home wins in succession:
5, Aug 23 - Sept 26
Most away wins in succession:
2, Sept 29 - Oct 3
Longest run without a win:
11, Jan 23 - Apr 6
Longest run without a home win:
6, Jan 23 - Apr 2
Longest run without an away win:
7, Dec 26 - Apr 6
Most defeats in succession:
4, Jan 23 - Feb 17 and Feb 27 - Mar 21
Goals for in successive matches:
15, Oct 20 - Jan 2
Goals against in successive matches:
10, Oct 24 - Dec 12
Longest run without scoring:
318 minutes, Mar 10 - Apr 6
Longest run without conceding a goal:
408 minutes, Sept 15 - Oct 3
Most consecutive appearances:
45 - Alan Wright, Aug 15 - May 16
Ever Presents: Alan Wright; Gareth Southgate
was an ever-present in the Premiership, but
missed one cup game.

DEBUTANTS

Twelve players made their Villa debuts this
season, they were:
Alan Thompson v Everton (a),
Darius Vassell v Middlesbrough as sub (h),
Paul Merson v Wimbledon (h),
Fabio Ferraresi v Strømsgodset as sub (UEFA)
(a), Steve Watson v Leicester City (h),
Tommy Jaszczun v Chelsea as sub (WC) (a),
Dion Dublin v Tottenham Hotspur (h),
Adam Rachel v Blackburn Rovers as sub (a),
Aaron Lescott v Hull City as sub (FAC) (h),
Steve Stone v Tottenham Hotspur (a),
Colin Calderwood v West Ham United (h)
Mark Delaney v Nottingham Forest as sub (h).

PENALTIES

Villa were awarded seven penalties during the
season, three were converted and four were
missed.

Scored: Lee Hendrie v Newcastle Utd
(9.9.98) Holte End. Stan Collymore v Celta
Vego (UEFA Cup) (3.11.98) Witton End. Dion
Dublin v Coventry City (27.2.99) Holte End.
Missed: Alan Thompson v Middlesbrough
(23.8.98) Witton End. Alan Thompson v

Wimbledon (12.9.98) Holte End. Paul Merson v Wimbledon (12.9.98) Witton End (scored from rebound). Dion Dublin v Liverpool (21.11.98) Holte End.

Penalties conceded were: John Collins for Everton (a) (15.8.98) Mark Bosnich saved. Darren Anderton for Spurs (7.11.98) Holte End, scored. Denis Irwin for Manchester Utd (a) (1.5.99) Michael Oakes saved.

RED CARDS

Stan Collymore against Liverpool at Villa Park for two bookable offenses; Michael Oakes v Blackburn Rovers at Ewood Park for a professional foul; later rescinded by referee, no suspension served; Steve Watson against Charlton Athletic at Villa Park for a professional foul, were the three Villa players sent of during the season.

Seven opposing players were sent off in games against Villa:
Carl Leaburn (Wimbledon) 12/9/98 at Villa Park (professional foul). Dennis Wise (Chelsea) (LC) 28/10/98 at Stamford Bridge (bad tackle). Rafeal Berges (Celta Vigo) (UEFA) 3/11/98 at Villa Park (2 bookable offences). Dejan Stefanovic (Sheff Wed) 28/12/98 at Villa Park (2 bookable offences). Alex Cleland (Everton) 18/1/99 at Villa Park (2 bookable offences). Claus Lundekvam (Southampton) 10/4/99 at Villa Park (2 bookable offences). Andy Petterson (Charlton Athletic) 8/5/99 at Villa Park (profesional foul).

HOLTE END v WITTON END

Of the 75 goals scored at Villa Park in all competitions during the season, 42 were scored at the Holte End (27 for Villa and 15 against) and 33 at the Witton End (13 for Villa and 20 against).

ARRIVALS

Alan Thompson 5.6.98 from Bolton W. for £4.5m. Fabio Ferraresi 23.6.98 from Cesena (Italy) Free. David Unsworth 24.7.98 from West Ham Utd for £3m. Paul Merson 8.9.98 from Middlesbrough for £6.75m. Steve Watson from Newcastle Utd for £3.5m. Dion Dublin 5.11.98 from Coventry City for £5.75m. Peter Enckelman 3.2.99 from Turku (Finland) for £200,000. Mark Delaney 9.3.99 from Cardiff City for £350,000 rising to

£500,000. Steve Stone 11.3.99 from Nottingham Forest for £5.5m. Colin Calderwood 23.3.99 from Tottenham Hotspur for £225,000. Neil Tarrant 27.4.99 from Ross County for £150,000 rising to £250,000.

DEPARTURES

Fernando Nelson 9.7.98 to Porto (Portugal) for £1.1m. Dwight Yorke 20.8.98 to Manchester Utd for £12.6m. David Unsworth 20.8.98 to Everton for £3m. Ben Petty 27.11.98 to Stoke City, Free. Gary Charles 14.1.99 to Benfica (Portugal) for £1.5m. Lee Collins 19.2.99 to Stoke City, Free. Mark Bosnich 2.6.99 to Manchester United, Free.

EVER READY WRIGHT

Yet again, Villa wing-back Alan Wright came through the winter without so much as a chipped fingernail, appearing in Villa's starting lineup for all 45 games of the season.

It means he has now started every Premiership game in three of the last four seasons, having failed to start only three of them last term.

The former Blackpool and Blackburn Rovers player has no maintenance tips to hand on to more vulnerable souls but merely puts his remarkable run down to luck.

He had two hernia ops while at Ewood Park but has since then stayed sound in body and spirit, giving John Gregory one of his easier tasks when it comes to filling in the team-sheet.

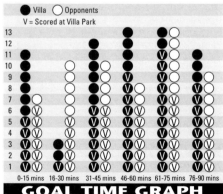

GOAL TIME GRAPH

GROUND IMPROVEMENTS

After a long-running debate between the club, the council and the local residents, Villa and Birmingham City Council Planning Department finally reached agreement on how Villa Park and its environs can best be developed to achieve the club's dream of a 50,000 seat stadium.

In May, city planners formally approved the latest set of plans submitted by the club, and it is now hoped that the advent of the new Millennium will be marked by the commencement of work on the Trinity Road Stand, followed in 2001 by redevelopment of the North Stand.

The latest plans incorporate all Villa's efforts to take the local community into account when the revamp of Villa Park begins.

The development 'package' also includes a transportation plan for the area, designed to minimise matchday congestion and open up additional car parking sites; a local shopping plaza and industrial units; a 144-bedroom hotel on the site of the old Holte Hotel and a sports college to be used by nine Aston schools.

ATTENDANCES ON THE UP

Villa Park's average league attendance rose again in 1998-99, for the third successive season.

The average turn-out of 36,937 was an improvement of 800 spectators per game on last season's figure, while the 1996-97 average was 36,027.

The capacity attendance of 39,241 was achieved against Newcastle United, Leicester City, Tottenham Hotspur, Liverpool, and Manchester United.

Ironically, the lowest home attendance in the league was for the very first game of the season, when 29,559 watched the 3-1 defeat of Middlesbrough.

NEW SPONSORS

Aston Villa welcomed new club sponsors when the season began, in the shape of Birmingham van-maker LDV.

A two-year, seven-figure deal saw the company take its first major plunge into sports sponsorship, having previously tested the water with no less than boxer Evander Holyfield, who featured along with snooker's Ronnie O'Sullivan in a 'Famous Vans' campaign, the success of which prompted LDV to take the next step in its brand development programme.

LDV had supplied Villa with vans and minibuses for some years before striking the deal, and is the largest British-owned vehicle maker in the country, exporting all over the Continent, as well as to South Africa, Singapore and New Zealand.

SOUTHGATE STAYS

Villa were delighted to agree a new contract with club captain Gareth Southgate in October. The 28-year-old England international defender put his name to a five-year contract which should effectively keep him at Villa Park for the rest of his career.

Southgate joined Aston Villa in 1995 and made his 100th Premiership appearance for the team this season

A WOMAN'S PLACE...

The home game with Chelsea won't be remembered for the result but it made a little piece of history for Aston Villa, as it was the first game at Villa Park which saw a woman running the line.

Wendy Toms was one of the two assistant referees on duty and with most Villa fans' attention focused on their team's plight in a 3-0 defeat by the Londoners, she had the benefit of a comparatively uneventful game!

VILLA'S SUPER START

Going 12 games unbeaten at the start of their Premiership game represented a new club record for Aston Villa.

Not since 1932-33 had the club made such an impressive start to their league campaign. That season, Villa had beaten their previous record of seven games, set just two years earlier, and had the bonus of notching an

11th game unbeaten against arch-rivals Birmingham City, whom they defeated 1-0 at Villa Park on 22nd October 1932.

The run ended at The Hawthorns a week later, however, and was finally bettered 66 years later when Villa beat Southampton 4-1 at The Dell on 14th November 1998, before losing their very next game, at home to Liverpool.

NEW SEASON, NEW LOOK

Two amendments to the Villa image were announced late in the season.

Firstly, subtle changes have been made to the Aston Villa 'Rampant Lion' crest. This is designed to give more sharpness to the famous lion, whose features are portrayed in greater detail.

The number of claret and blue stripes behind the lion has also been increased from six to seven, to give a more balanced background, and while the club motto, 'Prepared', has been retained, it is now incorporated in the 'shield' instead of on a scroll underneath it.

The new crest is now a registered trade mark of Aston Villa.

Secondly, Villa will have two new kits for next season, while retaining the existing 'away' kit as a third choice.

The design for the new home kit was still to be announced as we went to press, but like the new away kit, with its claret and blue diagonal stripe across a white shirt, it will feature a distinctive new look as well as the new club crest.

GARETH AND JULIAN TAKE THE HONOURS

The club's Player and Young Player of the Year were named as Julian Joachim and Gareth Barry respectively at the annual Gala Night in the Holte Suite on 8th May.

Joachim was one of the team's most consistent performers during the season, and appeared either as a starter or on the subs' bench in every game. His 16 goals in all competitions made him leading scorer.

Gareth Barry's award came on the back of a season of remarkable maturity in which the 18-year-old frequently played like a veteran. He enhanced his growing reputation when being called up to the England Under-21 squad as well as finding the scoresheet for his club late in the season.

VILLA PARK HOSTS LAST EVER CUP FINAL

Villa Park added another distinction to its roll-call of famous events when it was chosen to host the final of the last-ever European Cup Winners' Cup competition on 19th May.

Italian giants Lazio emerged victorious, beating Spanish side Real Mallorca 2-1 in a closely fought game.

It was fitting that the game should be played on British soil, as with 10 winners of the competition over the years, Britain has claimed the trophy on more occasions than any other country.

The only other final to have been played at Villa Park was the replay of the 1981 League Cup Final, when Liverpool beat West Ham 2-1, although the stadium has hosted more FA Cup semi-finals than any other English venue (48 after this season), as well as 12 full internationals.

A SMALL MATTER OF 30 YEARS' SERVICE

Aston Villa bade farewell to its Stadium Manager of 30 years, this season, when Ted Small announced his retirement.

Some 200 guests turned up at a special retirement to say 'goodbye' to the man who has overseen numerous redevelopment projects at Villa Park since taking up the job shortly after the arrival of chairman Doug Ellis in 1968.

Among those invited to Ted's send-off were former management duo Brian Little and Alan Evans, ex-captain Leighton Phillips, Ted's wife Mary and their four grandchildren. Written tributes were also received from the likes of Graham Taylor, Ron Saunders, Dr Jo Venglos and Charlie Aitken.

JUSTICE FOR JOHN

John Gregory finally received official recognition of the sterling work he has done since his arrival at Villa, when he collected the Carling Manager of the Month award for September, the club's first such award since Brian Little won it in January 1995.

FOUR MORE LIKELY LADS

The signings this season of Alan Thompson, Steve Watson, Steve Stone and Neil Tarrant continued a remarkable link between Aston Villa and the north-east. Tynesiders Stone, Thompson and Watson and Darlington-born Tarrant arrived to follow in the footsteps of men such as Brian Little, Gordon Cowans, Kevin Richardson, Johnny Dixon, Tommy Ball and Bob Chatt, who were all born between the Tyne and the Tees.

VILLA PROVIDE THREE MORE LIONS

England's 2-0 defeat of the Czech Republic on 18th November was an especially proud night for Aston Villa, as it was the first time in 69 years that three Villa players took part in an England international.

Dion Dublin, Paul Merson and substitute Lee Hendrie all appeared for their country, echoing the achievement of their predecessors from the 1930-31 season, Eric Houghton, Joe Tate and Pongo Waring. For good measure, Merson managed to score one of the two goals in England's win.

PROFITS UP AS TURNOVER SOARS

The surge in Villa's form following the arrival of John Gregory, and decent runs in the FA and UEFA Cups, were reflected in the Aston Villa accounts for the year ending 31st May 1998.

Turnover rose by 44% on the previous year's figure to £31.77m, 65% of which came from the club's commercial activities.

Pre-tax profits rose to a record £11.74m from a loss of nearly £4m in 1996-97, after taking player transfers into account.

GEORGE BEESON

Former Villa player George Beeson died during the season at the age of 90.

Acquired from Sheffield Wednesday, the full-back made 71 league and cup appearances for the club following his arrival at Villa Park in 1934. It was an eventful period for the club, who had seen their League Championship challenge in the early 1930s thwarted by the dominant Arsenal side of the era.

George left Villa in 1937, to join Walsall.

BOB MACKAY

Former Aston Villa Director, Bob Mackay died in April at the age of 75, having been in poor health for a number of years.

Bob was part of the new Board of Directors which gave the club a fresh lease of life in 1968 following the arrival of current chairman Doug Ellis, and he played a major role in the acquisition of the Bodymoor Heath training ground.

The results were formally reported to shareholders at the AGM on 20th August, held in the Holte Suite, the opening of which had helped catering turnover rise by £1m for the year.

Other points covered in the Annual Report included:

- Payroll costs increased by almost 25%, a rise of £2.3m
- Broadcasting revenue increased by £3.3m to £9.3m
- Merchandising rose by £1.6m to £5.7m
- Gate receipts improved from £7.3m to £9.9m.

RESERVE TEAM RESULTS & SCORERS 1998-99

PONTIN'S LEAGUE – PREMIER DIVISION

Aug	17	A	Leicester City	1-1	Walker
Aug	26	**H**	**Stoke City**	4-1	Draper, Walker, Grayson, Byfield (pen)
Sept	2	A	Manchester United	0-4	
Sept	17	**H**	**Nottingham Forest**	3-2	og, Lee, Samuel
Sept	22	A	Blackburn Rovers	1-2	Byfield
Oct	1	**H**	**Leeds United**	3-0	Byfield, Vassell 2
Oct	14	**H**	**Sunderland**	0-1	
Nov	2	A	Preston North End	0-1	
Nov	18	**H**	**Birmingham City**	4-0	Thompson, Joachim 2, Vassell
Dec	1	A	Liverpool	0-3	
Dec	8	A	Everton	0-0	
Dec	16	**H**	**Leicester City**	1-1	Blackwood
Jan	6	**H**	**Manchester United**	1-5	Vassell
Jan	13	**H**	**Derby County**	2-3	Collymore, Grayson
Feb	3	A	Nottingham Forest	0-2	
Mar	15	A	Sunderland	1-1	Byfield
Mar	24	**H**	**Preston North End**	0-1	
Mar	30	A	Derby County	3-1	Byfield 2, Vassell
Apr	7	A	Leeds United	4-3	Merson, Delaney, Vassell 2
Apr	14	A	Birmingham City	3-1	Byfield 2, Barry (pen)
Apr	22	A	Stoke City	1-2	Marfell
Apr	26	**H**	**Liverpool**	0-1	
Apr	28	**H**	**Everton**	3-0	Thompson (pen), Delaney, Blackwood
May	4	**H**	**Blackburn Rovers**	1-1	Marfell

Rollercoaster ride for youngsters

There were mixed fortunes for the reserve and youth teams in a season of inconsistency at both levels. The reserves started and ended the campaign well but, in the four months around the turn of the year, they failed to win a single match in eight attempts. The youth team did well to reach the quarter finals of the FA Youth Cup, but in the newly constituted FA Academy League neither the Under-19s nor Under-17s could produce a run of consistently good results.

The explanation for the rollercoaster campaign lay in the changeable make-up of reserve and youth team line-ups, which were rarely the same in successive matches due to injuries (several long term), calls from higher-level sides within the club and, on occasions, the inclusion of senior players in the second team when they were returning from injury.

The most obvious example of younger players whisked off to higher levels was central defender Gareth Barry, who was still eligible for the youth team but played most of the season in the Premiership. Barry and his youth team striker colleague Darius Vassell, another regular in the

first team squad, also won their first England Under-21 caps during a season of fine individual achievement by both players.

Other youth team members to earn elevation to the first team squad (though not, as yet, making appearances at Premiership level) were midfielder Michael Standing, defender Jlloyd Samuel and goalkeeper Matthew Ghent. Lower down the age scale in the club's youth section, first year trainees Danny Haynes (defender), Jay Smith (midfielder) and Andy Marfell (striker) broke into the reserve team, while associate schoolboys Leon Hylton and Jonathan Bewers (both defenders) won England Under-16 caps to add their names to Villa's roster of internationals.

PREMIER ACADEMY LEAGUE - UNDER-19

	P	W	D	L	F	A	Pts
Everton	22	12	4	6	39	25	40
Manchester Utd	22	12	4	6	38	25	40
Crewe Alexandra	22	11	6	5	30	20	39
Blackburn Rovers	22	11	3	8	46	29	36
Liverpool	22	9	9	4	33	17	36
Aston Villa	22	7	4	11	34	44	25
Manchester City	22	4	3	15	20	50	15
Bolton Wanderers	22	3	3	16	28	63	12

PREMIER ACADEMY LEAGUE - UNDER-17

	P	W	D	L	F	A	Pts
Manchester Utd	22	14	7	1	66	20	49
Blackburn Rovers	22	14	5	3	56	23	47
Liverpool	22	9	10	3	47	36	37
Everton	22	10	5	7	44	33	35
Manchester City	22	9	6	7	49	42	33
Crewe Alexandra	22	6	8	8	30	31	26
Aston Villa	22	7	3	12	27	54	24

PONTIN'S PREMIER LEAGUE TABLE

	P	W	D	L	F	A	Pts
Sunderland	24	14	7	3	46	18	49
Liverpool	24	13	7	4	28	15	46
Manchester Utd	24	13	4	7	48	28	43
Nottingham F.	24	11	6	7	38	26	39
Everton	24	11	5	8	34	28	38
Blackburn Rovers	24	8	7	9	31	26	31
Leeds United	24	9	3	12	40	43	30
Leicester City	24	8	6	10	30	41	30
Aston Villa	24	8	5	11	36	37	29
Stoke City	24	7	7	10	24	32	28
Preston N.E.	24	7	5	12	20	42	26
Birmingham City	24	5	9	10	24	33	24
Derby County	24	3	7	14	26	52	16

FA YOUTH CUP

Dec	22	**H**	**Hull City** (Rd 3)	5-1	Marfell, Smith J, Standing (pen), Bewers, McSeveney
Jan	26	**H**	**Huddersfield T.** (Rd 4)	4-1	Marfell (2), Smith J, Evans S.
Mar	9	**H**	**Watford** (Rd 5)	2-0	Marfell, Smith J
Mar	23	A	Everton (Rd 6)	0-1	

YOUTH ACADEMY (UNDER-19)

Sep	4	H	**Norwich City**	1-0	Standing
Sep	12	A	Sheffield Wednesday	2-4	Kearns, Evans S.
Sep	19	A	Arsenal	0-2	
Sep	26	H	**Charlton Athletic**	3-4	Standing, Melaugh, Kearns
Oct	3	A	Crystal Palace	4-3	Ridley, Curtolo, Standing, Blackwood
Oct	17	H	**Blackburn Rovers**	4-2	Evans G., Evans S. (2), Harding
Oct	24	A	Crewe Alexandra	2-2	Evans S. (2)
Oct	31	H	**Bolton Wanderers**	3-3	Nkubi, Standing (p), Samuel
Nov	7	A	Liverpool	2-3	Vassell, Samuel
Nov	14	H	**Manchester City**	5-0	Evans G. (2), Evans S. (2), Ridley
Nov	21	A	Manchester Utd	0-4	
Nov	28	H	**Everton**	1-0	Harding
Dec	12	A	Blackburn Rovers	0-0	
Jan	16	A	Bolton Wanderers	1-2	Samuel
Jan	22	A	Crewe Alexandra	0-3	
Feb	13	A	Manchester City	2-0	Nkubi, Vassell
Feb	20	H	**Manchester United**	0-2	
Mar	5	H	**Fulham**	0-4	
Mar	13	A	Everton	0-1	
Mar	17	H	**Liverpool**	2-1	Jay Smith, og
Mar	20	A	Wimbledon	0-2	
Mar	27	H	**Sunderland**	2-2	Jay Smith, Marfell
			Play-Offs		
Apr	17	A	Watford (1st Rd)	1-3	Standing

Goalscorers:
Stephen Evans 7;
Michael Standing 5;
Graham Evans 3; Jlloyd Samuel 3;
David Harding 2;
Jamie Kearns 2; Isaac Nkubi 2; Martin Ridley 2; Jay Smith 2; Darius Vassell 2;
Michael Blackwood 1; David Curtolo 1; Andrew Marfell 1; Gavin Melaugh 1; own goal 1.

YOUTH ACADEMY (UNDER-17)

Sep	5	H	Leeds United	1-1	Berks
Sep	12	H	Sheffield Wednesday	3-2	Marfell, Smith A., Walters
Sep	19	H	Arsenal	0-2	
Sep	26	H	Charlton Athletic	1-0	Smith A.
Oct	3	H	Crystal Palace	0-1	
Oct	17	H	Blackburn Rovers	3-2	Marfell, Hylton, Edwards J.
Oct	24	A	Crewe Alexandra	3-0	Debolla, Richards, Jay Smith
Oct	31	H	West Ham United	0-2	
Nov	7	A	Liverpool	1-4	Marfell
Nov	14	H	Manchester City	2-1	Debolla (2)
Nov	21	A	Manchester United	0-5	
Nov	28	H	Everton	1-3	Folds
Dec	19	A	Crewe Alexandra	1-0	Marfell
Jan	16	A	Coventry City	4-0	Marfell 3, Smith A.
Jan	23	A	Blackburn Rovers	0-4	
Feb	13	A	Manchester City	0-8	
Feb	20	H	Manchester United	1-5	Marfell
Mar	5	H	Fulham	1-2	Moore
Mar	13	H	Everton	1-1	Hylton
Mar	17	H	Liverpool	0-5	
Mar	20	A	Wimbledon	2-4	McGuire, Husbands
Mar	27	H	Sunderland	2-2	Smith A, Debolla
		Play-Offs			
Apr	10	A	West Ham United (1st Rd)	3-2	Marfell, Jay Smith, Moore
Apr	17	H	Sunderland (2nd Rd)	1-7	Debolla

Goalscorers:
Andrew Marfell 9;
Mark Debolla 5; Adam Smith 4; Leon Hylton 2; Stefan Moore 2; Jay Smith 2;
David Berks 1; Jamie Edwards 1; Liam Folds 1; Michael Husbands 1; Lee McGuire 1; Mark Richards 1;
Greg Walters 1.

RESERVE & YOUTH TEAM APPEARANCES

	CENTRAL LGE		YTH ACC. U19		YTH ACC. U17		FA YTH CUP	
	Apps	Gls	Apps	Gls	Apps	Gls	Apps	Gls
Ryan Amoo	- (-)	-	- (2)	-	2 (-)	-	- (-)	-
David Andrewarthur	- (-)	-	- (1)	-	4 (2)	-	1 (1)	-
Neil Barnes	- (-)	-	- (-)	-	1 (-)	-	- (-)	-
Gareth Barry	5 (-)	1	- (1)	-	- (-)	-	- (-)	-
Liam Bell	- (-)	-	- (-)	-	1 (-)	-	- (-)	-
David Berks	- (-)	-	- (-)	-	6 (-)	1	- (-)	-
Jonathan Bewers	- (-)	-	- (-)	-	2 (-)	-	3 (1)	1
Michael Blackwood	10 (7)	2	18 (2)	1	- (-)	-	- (-)	-
Matthew Brooker	- (-)	-	- (-)	-	1 (3)	-	- (-)	-
Darren Byfield	14 (2)	8	- (-)	-	- (-)	-	- (-)	-
Colin Calderwood	1 (-)	-	- (-)	-	- (-)	-	- (-)	-
Dudley Campbell*	- (-)	-	1 (-)	-	1 (-)	-	- (-)	-
Gary Charles	1 (-)	-	- (-)	-	- (-)	-	- (-)	-
Lee Collins	7 (-)	-	- (-)	-	- (-)	-	- (-)	-
Stan Collymore	1 (-)	1	- (-)	-	- (-)	-	- (-)	-
Danny Cox*	- (-)	-	- (-)	-	1 (-)	-	- (-)	-
Jamie Cunnington	- (-)	-	- (1)	-	1 (1)	-	- (-)	-
David Curtolo	7 (2)	-	16 (1)	1	- (-)	-	2 (-)	-
Callum Davenport	- (-)	-	- (-)	-	- (1)	-	- (-)	-
Gary Davies	- (-)	-	- (-)	-	- (3)	-	- (-)	-
Mark Delaney	8 (-)	2	- (-)	-	- (-)	-	- (-)	-
Mark Debolla	- (-)	-	- (1)	-	13 (4)	5	- (-)	-
Mark Draper	4 (-)	1	- (-)	-	- (-)	-	- (-)	-
Jamie Edwards	- (-)	-	- (-)	-	3 (6)	1	- (-)	-
Robert Edwards	- (-)	-	- (-)	-	3 (1)	-	- (-)	-
Ugo Ehiogu	2 (-)	-	- (-)	-	- (-)	-	- (-)	-
Peter Enckelman	7 (-)	-	1 (-)	-	- (-)	-	- (-)	-
Graham Evans	- (-)	-	12 (6)	3	- (-)	-	- (-)	-
Stephen Evans	- (1)	-	15 (5)	7	- (-)	-	4 (-)	1
Neil Fairhurst*	- (-)	-	- (-)	-	1 (1)	-	- (-)	-
Fabio Ferraresi	12 (-)	-	- (-)	-	- (-)	-	- (-)	-
Liam Folds	- (-)	-	- (1)	-	13 (-)	1	- (-)	-
Matthew Ghent	3 (-)	-	20 (-)	-	- (-)	-	4 (-)	-
Simon Grayson	9 (-)	2	- (-)	-	- (-)	-	- (-)	-
David Harding	- (-)	-	21 (2)	2	- (-)	-	1 (-)	-
Danny Haynes	4 (-)	-	3 (2)	-	19 (-)	-	3 (1)	-
Reuben Hazell	17 (1)	-	- (-)	-	- (-)	-	- (-)	-
David Hughes	13 (-)	-	- (-)	-	- (-)	-	- (-)	-
Michael Husbands	- (-)	-	- (-)	-	1 (2)	1	- (-)	-
Leon Hylton	- (-)	-	1 (-)	-	18 (-)	2	3 (-)	-
Danny Jackman	- (-)	-	- (2)	-	2 (1)	-	- (-)	-
Ben Jackson	- (-)	-	- (-)	-	3 (-)	-	- (-)	-
Karl Johnson	- (-)	-	- (-)	-	21 (-)	-	- (-)	-
Julian Joachim	3 (-)	2	- (-)	-	- (-)	-	- (-)	-
Tommy Jaszczun	12 (-)	-	- (-)	-	- (-)	-	- (-)	-
Jamie Kearns	- (1)	-	22 (-)	2	- (-)	-	1 (-)	-
Russel Latapy*	1 (-)	-	- (-)	-	- (-)	-	- (-)	-
Alan Lee	3 (-)	1	- (-)	-	- (-)	-	- (-)	-

RESERVE & YOUTH TEAM APPEARANCES (cont.)

	CENTRAL LGE		YTH ACC. U19		YTH ACC. U17		FA YTH CUP	
	Apps	Gls	Apps	Gls	Apps	Gls	Apps	Gls
Aaron Lescott	16 (1)	-	- (-)	-	- (-)	-	- (-)	-
Andrew Marfell	2 (1)	2	3 (1)	1	20 (-)	9	4 (-)	4
Adam Marsh*	- (-)	-	- (-)	-	1 (1)	-	- (-)	-
Declan McArthy*	- (-)	-	- (-)	-	1 (-)	-	- (-)	-
Craig McCarthy*	- (-)	-	1 (-)	-	- (-)	-	- (-)	-
Peter McConnell	- (-)	-	- (-)	-	4 (1)	-	- (-)	-
Lee McGuire	- (-)	-	- (-)	-	2 (1)	1	- (-)	-
Gary McSeveney	- (-)	-	2 (-)	-	22 (-)	-	1 (-)	1
Wesley Meecham	- (-)	-	- (-)	-	- (1)	-	- (-)	-
Gavin Melaugh	7 (2)	-	20 (1)	1	- (-)	-	4 (-)	-
Paul Merson	3 (-)	1	- (-)	-	- (-)	-	- (-)	-
Darren Middleton	4 (2)	-	- (-)	-	- (-)	-	- (-)	-
Stefan Moore	- (-)	-	- (1)	-	6 (4)	2	- (2)	-
Brian Mulholland	- (-)	-	8 (4)	-	10 (-)	-	- (1)	-
Boaz Myhill	- (-)	-	1 (-)	-	19 (-)	-	- (-)	-
Alex Nicholas	- (-)	-	- (-)	-	5 (-)	-	- (-)	-
Isaac Nkubi	1 (1)	-	9 (5)	2	- (-)	-	- (2)	-
Michael Oakes	9 (-)	-	- (-)	-	- (-)	-	- (-)	-
Jamie Pawley	- (-)	-	- (1)	-	- (1)	-	- (-)	-
Ben Petty	7 (-)	-	- (-)	-	- (-)	-	- (-)	-
Michael Price	- (-)	-	1 (-)	-	1 (-)	-	- (-)	-
Luke Prince	- (-)	-	15 (2)	-	- (-)	-	1 (-)	-
Adam Rachel	5 (-)	-	- (-)	-	- (-)	-	- (-)	-
Jonathan Rhule	- (-)	-	- (-)	-	- (1)	-	- (-)	-
Mark Richards	- (-)	-	- (-)	-	3 (-)	1	- (-)	-
Liam Ridgewell*	- (-)	-	- (-)	-	1 (2)	-	- (-)	-
Martin Ridley	3 (5)	-	19 (-)	2	- (-)	-	- (-)	-
Matthew Roberts	- (-)	-	- (-)	-	1 (-)	-	- (-)	-
Jlloyd Samuel	18 (2)	1	16 (3)	3	- (-)	-	4 (-)	-
Riccardo Scimeca	5 (-)	-	- (-)	-	- (-)	-	- (-)	-
Lawrence Shannon	- (-)	-	- (-)	-	- (1)	-	- (-)	-
Adam Smith	- (-)	-	- (-)	-	13 (3)	4	- (-)	-
Dean Smith	- (-)	-	- (-)	-	6 (2)	-	- (-)	-
James Smith*	- (-)	-	- (1)	-	- (-)	-	- (-)	-
Jay Smith	- (-)	-	5 (-)	2	19 (-)	2	4 (-)	3
Michael Standing	12 (1)	-	17 (2)	5	- (-)	-	4 (-)	1
Neil Tarrant	2 (-)	-	- (-)	-	- (-)	-	- (-)	-
Alan Thompson	3 (-)	2	- (-)	-	- (-)	-	- (-)	-
David Unsworth	1 (-)	-	- (-)	-	- (-)	-	- (-)	-
Darius Vassell	16 (1)	7	6 (2)	2	- (-)	-	- (-)	-
Richard Walker	5 (1)	2	- (-)	-	- (-)	-	- (-)	-
Greg Walters	- (-)	-	- (1)	-	11 (1)	1	- (-)	-
Steve Watson	1 (-)	-	- (-)	-	- (-)	-	- (-)	-
Andrew Wells	- (-)	-	- (-)	-	2 (3)	-	- (-)	-
Own Goals	- (-)	1	- (-)	1	- (-)	-	- (-)	-

Triallist.

Aston Villa Youth Squad, start of 98-99 season. Back row, left to right: Kevin MacDonald (coach), Greg Walters, Stephen Evans, Brian Mulholland, Stuart Thornley, David Berks, Danny Haynes, David Curtolo, Terry Standring (physio). Middle row: Malcolm Beard (coach), Liam Folds, Jlloyd Samuel, Matthew Ghent, Gareth Barry, Michael Price, Gary McSeveney, Jamie Kearns, Gordon Cowans (coach). Front row: David Harding, Karl Johnson, Gavin Melaugh, Alan Miller (youth development officer), Bryan Jones (youth development officer), Steve Burns (assistant director of Academy), Luke Prince, Jay Smith, Michael Standing.

COMPLETE PREMIERSHIP APPEARANCES & SCORERS

	LEAGUE		FA CUP		LGE CUP		UEFA CUP		TOTAL	
	Apps	Gls	Apps	Gls	Apps	Gls	Apps	Gls	Apps	Gls
Dalian ATKINSON	68 (5)	22	3	-	14	11	7	2	92 (5)	35
(Seasons played: 92/93, 93/94, 94/95)										
Earl BARRETT	105 (1)	1	9	-	15	1	7	-	136 (1)	2
(Seasons played: 92/93, 93/94, 94/95)										
Gareth BARRY	28 (6)	2	2	-	-	-	3	-	33 (6)	2
(Seasons played: 97/98, 98/99)										
Stefan BEINLICH	7 (7)	1	-	-	-	-	-	-	7 (7)	1
(Seasons played: 92/93, 93/94)										
Mark BLAKE	- (1)	-	-	-	-	-	-	-	- (1)	-
(Seasons played: 92/93)										
Chris BODEN	- (1)	-	-	-	-	-	-	-	- (1)	-
(Seasons played: 94/95)										
Mark BOSNICH	178	-	17	-	20 (1)	-	11	-	226 (1)	-
(Seasons played: 92/93, 93/94, 94/95, 95/96, 96/97, 97/98, 98/99)										
Matthias BREITKREUTZ	3 (2)	-	-	-	- (1)	-	-	-	3 (3)	-
(Seasons played: 92/93, 93/94)										
Paul BROWNE	2	-	-	-	-	-	-	-	2	-
(Seasons played: 95/96)										
Darren BYFIELD	1 (6)	-	- (1)	-	1	-	1	-	3 (7)	-
(Seasons played: 97/98, 98/99)										
Colin CALDERWOOD	8	-	-	-	-	-	-	-	8	-
(Seasons played: 98/99)										
Franz CARR	1 (2)	-	1	1	-	-	-	-	2 (2)	1
(Seasons played: 94/95, 95/96)										
Martin CARRUTHERS	- (1)	-	-	-	-	-	-	-	- (1)	-
(Seasons played: 92/93)										
Gary CHARLES	72 (7)	2	5 (2)	-	9 (1)	-	6 (3)	1	92 (13)	3
(Seasons played: 94/95, 95/96, 97/98, 98/99)										
Stan COLLYMORE	34 (11)	7	5	3	1	-	9 (1)	5	49 (12)	15
(Seasons played: 97/98, 98/99)										
Gordon COWANS	9 (2)	-	-	-	2	-	4	-	15 (2)	-
(Seasons played: 93/94)										
Neil COX	22 (13)	3	4 (2)	1	5 (2)	-	1	-	32 (17)	4
(Seasons played: 92/93, 93/94)										
Sasa CURCIC	20 (9)	-	2	1	1 (1)	-	- (1)	-	23 (11)	1
(Seasons played: 96/97, 97/98)										
Tony DALEY	27 (13)	3	2	-	5 (1)	-	2	-	36 (14)	3
(Seasons played: 92/93, 93/94)										
Neil DAVIS	- (2)	-	- (1)	-	-	-	-	-	- (3)	-
(Seasons played: 95/96)										
Mark DELANEY	- (2)	-	-	-	-	-	-	-	- (2)	-
(Seasons played: 98/99)										
Mark DRAPER	108 (11)	7	12	2	11 (1)	2	10 (1)	-	141 (13)	11
(Seasons played: 95/96, 96/97, 97/98, 98/99)										
Dion DUBLIN	24	11	-	-	-	-	-	-	24	11
(Seasons played: 98/99)										
Ugo EHIOGU	187 (9)	11	16 (1)	1	16 (1)	1	15	1	234 (11)	14
(Seasons played: 92/93, 93/94, 94/95, 95/96, 96/97, 97/98, 98/99)										
Dave FARRELL	5 (1)	-	-	-	2	-	-	-	7 (1)	-
(Seasons played: 92/93, 93/94, 94/95)										
Gareth FARRELLY	2 (6)	-	-	-	- (1)	-	-	-	2 (7)	-
(Seasons played: 95/96, 96/97)										
John FASHANU	11 (2)	3	2	-	-	-	1	-	14 (2)	3
(Seasons played: 94/95)										
Graham FENTON	16 (16)	3	-	-	2 (5)	-	-	-	18 (21)	3
(Seasons played: 93/94, 94/95, 95/96)										

COMPLETE PREMIERSHIP APPEARANCES & SCORERS

	LEAGUE		FA CUP		LGE CUP		UEFA CUP		TOTAL	
	Apps	Gls	Apps	Gls	Apps	Gls	Apps	Gls	Apps	Gls
Fabio FERRARESI *(Seasons played: 98/99)*	-	-	-	-	-	-	- (1)	-	- (1)	-
Steve FROGGATT *(Seasons played: 92/93, 93/94)*	24 (2)	2	3 (1)	-	1 (1)	-	-	-	28 (4)	2
Simon GRAYSON *(Seasons played: 97/98, 98/99)*	32 (16)	-	4 (1)	2	1 (1)	-	6 (3)	-	43 (21)	2
Lee HENDRIE *(Seasons played: 95/96, 96/97, 97/98, 98/99)*	46 (10)	6	5 (4)	-	-	-	5 (1)	-	56 (15)	6
Ray HOUGHTON *(Seasons played: 92/93, 93/94, 94/95)*	83 (12)	6	7	2	11 (2)	2	4 (2)	1	105 (16)	11
David HUGHES *(Seasons played: 96/97)*	4 (3)	-	-	-	-	-	-	-	4 (3)	-
Tommy JASZCZUN *(Seasons played: 98/99)*	-	-	-	-	- (1)	-	-	-	- (1)	-
Julian JOACHIM *(Seasons played: 95/96, 96/97, 97/98, 98/99)*	52 (36)	26	4 (1)	1	2	-	5 (1)	1	63 (38)	28
Tommy JOHNSON *(Seasons played: 94/95, 95/96, 96/97)*	38 (19)	13	5 (2)	1	5	2	1 (1)	1	49 (22)	17
Phil KING *(Seasons played: 94/95)*	13 (3)	-	-	-	3	-	4	-	20 (3)	-
Dariusz KUBICKI *(Seasons played: 92/93, 93/94)*	1 (1)	-	-	-	1	-	-	-	2 (1)	-
Nii LAMPTEY* *(Seasons played: 94/95)*	1 (5)	-	-	-	2 (1)	3	-	-	3 (6)	3
Aaron LESCOTT *(Seasons played: 98/99)*	-	-	- (1)	-	-	-	-	-	- (1)	-
Frank McAVENNIE † *(Seasons played: 92/93)*	3	-	-	-	-	-	-	-	3	-
Paul McGRATH *(Seasons played: 92/93, 93/94, 94/95, 95/96, 96/97)*	137 (5)	6	11 (1)	-	20 (1)	1	8 (1)	-	176 (8)	7
Paul MERSON *(Seasons played: 98/99)*	21 (5)	5	1	-	-	-	-	-	22 (5)	5
Savo MILOSEVIC *(Seasons played: 95/96, 96/97, 97/98)*	84 (6)	28	10	2	8 (1)	1	8	2	110 (7)	33
Scott MURRAY *(Seasons played: 95/96, 96/97)*	4	-	-	-	-	-	-	-	4	-
Fernando NELSON *(Seasons played: 96/97, 97/98)*	54 (5)	-	1 (1)	-	3	-	7 (2)	-	65 (8)	-
Michael OAKES *(Seasons played: 94/95, 95/96, 96/97, 97/98, 98/99)*	49 (2)	-	2	-	3	-	5	-	59 (2)	-
Garry PARKER *(Seasons played: 92/93, 93/94, 94/95)*	66 (4)	12	5	-	12	-	- (2)	-	83 (6)	12
Adam RACHEL *(Seasons played: 98/99)*	- (1)	-	-	-	-	-	-	-	- (1)	-
Cyrille REGIS *(Seasons played: 92/93)*	7 (6)	1	- (2)	-	1 (1)	-	-	-	8 (9)	1
Kevin RICHARDSON *(Seasons played: 92/93, 93/94, 94/95)*	100 (1)	7	7	-	13	3	8	-	128 (1)	10
Dean SAUNDERS *(Seasons played: 92/93, 93/94, 94/95)*	111 (1)	38	9	4	15	7	8	1	143 (1)	50
Riccardo SCIMECA *(Seasons played: 95/96, 96/97, 97/98, 98/99)*	50 (23)	2	9 (1)	-	4 (3)	-	5 (2)	-	68 (29)	2
Bryan SMALL *(Seasons played: 92/93, 93/94, 94/95)*	23 (5)	-	-	-	2	-	2	-	27 (5)	-
Gareth SOUTHGATE *(Seasons played: 95/96, 96/97, 97/98, 98/99)*	129	3	12	-	10	1	13	-	164	4

	LEAGUE		FA CUP		LGE CUP		UEFA CUP		TOTAL	
	Apps	Gls	Apps	Gls	Apps	Gls	Apps	Gls	Apps	Gls
Nigel SPINK	51 (4)	-	4	-	6	-	6	-	67 (4)	-
(Seasons played: 92/93, 93/94, 94/95, 95/96)										
Steve STAUNTON	168 (3)	13	15 (1)	1	15 (2)	1	15 (1)	-	213 (7)	15
(Seasons played: 92/93, 93/94, 94/95, 95/96, 96/97, 97/98)										
Steve STONE	9 (1)	-	-	-	-	-	-	-	9 (1)	-
(Seasons played: 98/99)										
Ian TAYLOR	135 (10)	16	8 (1)	1	9 (1)	2	11 (1)	3	163 (13)	22
(Seasons played: 94/95, 95/96, 96/97, 97/98, 98/99)										
Shaun TEALE	104 (1)	2	8	-	13	2	4	-	129 (1)	4
(Seasons played: 92/93, 93/94, 94/95)										
Alan THOMPSON	20 (5)	2	-	-	- (1)	-	3	-	23 (6)	2
(Seasons played: 98/99)										
Carl TILER	10 (2)	1	2	-	1	-	-	-	13 (2)	1
(Seasons played: 92/93, 93/94, 94/95, 95/96, 96/97)										
Andy TOWNSEND	133 (1)	8	12	-	20	2	10	1	175 (1)	11
(Seasons played: 92/93, 93/94, 94/95, 95/96, 96/97, 97/98)										
Darius VASSELL	- (6)	-	- (1)	-	- (1)	-	- (2)	2	- (11)	2
(Seasons played: 97/98, 98/99)										
Richard WALKER	- (1)	-	-	-	-	-	-	-	- (1)	-
(Seasons played: , 97/98, 98/99)										
Steve WATSON	26 (1)	-	2	-	1	-	-	-	29 (1)	-
(Seasons played: 98/99)										
Guy WHITTINGHAM	17 (8)	5	-	-	4 (1)	1	2 (1)	-	23 (10)	6
(Seasons played: 93/94, 94/95)										
Alan WRIGHT	157 (2)	3	14	-	12	-	14	-	197 (2)	3
(Seasons played: 94/95, 95/96, 96/97, 97/98, 98/99)										
Dwight YORKE	160 (19)	60	15 (2)	9	16 (2)	8	10	2	201 (23)	79
(Seasons played: 92/93, 93/94, 94/95, 95/96, 96/97, 97/98, 98/99)										
Own Goals	-	11	-	-	-	1	-	-	-	12

* On loan.   † On trial.

FANS ROLL CALL FOR 2000

If you wish to have your name, or that of a family member or friend, recorded in the next edition of the Aston Villa Review (2000), then simply write to Sports Projects Ltd. at the address below, with your name, address, telephone number and name to be included in the Fans' Roll Call.

Closing date for the 2000 edition is Friday 26th May 2000

Sports Projects Ltd. 188 Lightwoods Hill, Smethwick, Warley, West Midlands B67 5EH

Telephone: 0121-632 5518   Fax: 0121-633 4628

email: info@sportproject.u-net.com

web site: http://www.sportsprojects.com

VILLA'S ALL-TIME LEAGUE RECORD – CLUB BY CLUB

	P	W	D	L	F	A	W	D	L	F	A
			Home						Away		
Accrington	10	4	0	1	26	12	1	2	2	9	10
Arsenal	140	38	15	17	140	98	20	15	35	80	114
Barnsley	12	3	2	1	9	3	5	1	0	16	2
Birmingham City	96	23	13	12	82	60	16	12	20	68	74
Blackburn Rovers	134	35	17	15	139	90	18	12	37	90	144
Blackpool	62	16	9	6	65	39	10	7	14	44	51
Bolton Wanderers	130	35	15	15	139	84	17	13	35	67	126
Bournemouth	4	1	1	0	3	2	1	0	1	2	4
Bradford Park Avenue	10	4	0	1	12	4	1	2	2	8	16
Bradford City	28	9	2	3	32	12	4	4	6	17	23
Brentford	6	2	1	0	12	4	3	0	0	8	3
Brighton & Hove Albion	16	6	2	0	16	4	3	2	3	8	7
Bristol City	32	10	3	3	27	19	5	6	5	18	14
Bristol Rovers	8	3	1	0	8	3	2	1	1	4	4
Burnley	94	28	12	7	109	47	11	8	28	71	113
Bury	52	17	6	3	59	31	10	6	10	39	39
Cardiff City	44	14	3	5	39	20	8	2	12	23	30
Carlisle United	10	4	1	0	5	1	2	2	1	6	6
Charlton Athletic	40	10	6	4	44	22	6	6	8	23	33
Chelsea	104	27	12	13	104	75	17	10	25	64	77
Chesterfield	8	2	1	1	7	4	3	0	1	8	3
Coventry City	50	14	10	1	40	16	13	6	6	37	29
Crystal Palace	24	8	2	2	22	9	2	6	4	6	10
Darwen	4	2	0	0	16	0	1	1	0	6	2
Derby County	110	36	10	9	135	59	18	11	26	74	94
Doncaster Rovers	4	1	1	0	4	3	0	0	2	1	3
Everton	168	41	19	24	158	114	22	21	41	103	151
Fulham	34	8	5	4	30	22	2	5	10	20	34
Gillingham	2	1	0	0	2	1	0	1	0	0	0
Glossop	2	1	0	0	9	0	0	0	1	0	1
Grimsby Town	20	5	3	2	29	19	5	1	4	16	20
Halifax Town	4	1	1	0	2	1	1	0	1	2	2
Huddersfield Town	64	20	9	3	74	31	7	10	15	32	51
Hull City	16	4	3	1	21	8	2	2	4	7	12
Ipswich Town	40	11	6	3	40	17	5	4	11	20	30
Leeds United	70	17	10	8	59	42	6	13	16	32	57
Leicester City	74	17	8	12	76	57	6	10	23	50	89
Leyton Orient	10	4	1	0	8	3	1	2	2	3	6
Lincoln City	2	0	1	0	1	1	0	1	0	0	0
Liverpool	148	37	16	21	152	97	13	14	47	79	169
Luton Town	32	10	1	5	29	15	1	3	12	8	24
Manchester City	124	32	19	11	114	67	14	15	33	79	118

TO THE END OF SEASON 1998 - 99

	P	W	D	L	F	A	W	D	L	F	A
			Home						Away		
Manchester United	132	32	17	17	135	96	10	15	41	62	135
Mansfield Town	4	0	0	2	0	2	0	1	1	1	3
Middlesbrough	108	31	10	13	124	60	18	15	21	70	81
Millwall	18	4	4	1	14	8	3	2	4	9	12
Newcastle United	122	32	14	15	118	66	12	9	40	79	136
Northampton Town	2	0	0	1	1	2	0	0	1	1	2
Norwich City	46	14	6	3	42	25	4	7	12	28	41
Nottingham Forest	108	34	10	10	110	53	16	17	21	76	99
Notts County	66	23	7	3	83	29	12	8	13	49	52
Oldham Athletic	30	9	3	3	34	8	7	6	2	29	17
Oxford United	14	4	2	1	9	3	1	3	3	8	11
Plymouth Argyle	14	5	1	1	19	9	2	2	3	12	12
Portsmouth	60	19	7	4	73	39	8	7	15	42	65
Port Vale	4	2	0	0	3	0	0	1	1	4	6
Preston North End	98	37	3	9	108	44	13	11	25	64	90
Queen's Park Rangers	38	8	4	7	32	26	3	3	13	14	29
Reading	4	2	0	0	4	2	2	0	0	7	3
Rochdale	4	2	0	0	3	0	0	1	1	1	2
Rotherham United	8	3	0	1	8	3	2	1	1	6	3
Scunthorpe United	2	1	0	0	5	0	1	0	0	2	1
Sheffield United	120	40	12	8	145	55	17	16	27	85	111
Sheffield Wednesday	126	44	9	10	157	66	17	8	38	88	132
Shrewsbury Town	6	3	0	0	6	0	1	1	1	4	4
Southampton	48	13	8	3	41	17	6	7	11	25	40
Stockport County	2	1	0	0	7	1	1	0	0	3	1
Stoke City	88	31	7	6	108	36	13	13	18	54	66
Sunderland	140	46	11	13	144	88	14	21	35	88	135
Swansea City	14	7	0	0	19	0	4	0	3	12	10
Swindon Town	10	3	1	1	10	5	2	2	1	6	4
Torquay United	4	1	0	1	5	2	0	1	1	2	3
Tottenham Hotspur	112	25	14	17	90	78	18	9	29	88	112
Tranmere Rovers	4	2	0	0	3	0	1	1	0	2	1
Walsall	4	0	2	0	0	0	0	1	1	1	4
Watford	12	3	2	1	11	6	0	2	4	9	16
West Bromwich Albion	124	39	8	15	118	74	19	15	28	86	99
West Ham United	72	19	7	10	71	45	6	11	19	45	79
Wimbledon	24	6	1	5	21	11	3	4	5	18	19
Wolverhampton Wan.	96	26	10	12	109	64	15	12	21	67	86
Wrexham	4	1	0	1	5	4	2	0	0	5	2
York City	4	2	0	0	5	0	1	1	0	2	1
TOTALS	3938	1135	427	407	4098	2243	536	471	962	2502	3522

VILLA'S ALL-TIME LEAGUE RECORD – SEASON BY SEASON

Season	Div	Teams	Pos	P	W	D	L	F	A	W	D	L	F	A	Pts	Cup Honours
1888-89	1	12	2nd	22	10	0	1	44	16	2	5	4	17	27	29	*(FAC Winners in 1886-87)*
1889-90	1	12	8th	22	6	2	3	30	15	1	3	7	13	36	19	
1890-91	1	12	9th	22	5	4	2	29	18	2	0	9	16	40	18	
1891-92	1	14	4th	26	10	0	3	63	23	5	0	8	26	33	30	*FAC Runners-up*
1892-93	1	16	4th	30	12	1	2	50	24	4	2	9	23	38	35	
1893-94	**1**	**16**	**1st**	**30**	**12**	**2**	**1**	**49**	**13**	**7**	**4**	**4**	**35**	**29**	**44**	
1894-95	1	16	3rd	30	12	2	1	51	12	5	3	7	31	31	39	**FAC Winners**
1895-96	**1**	**16**	**1st**	**30**	**14**	**1**	**0**	**47**	**17**	**6**	**4**	**5**	**31**	**28**	**45**	
1896-97	**1**	**16**	**1st**	**30**	**10**	**3**	**2**	**36**	**16**	**11**	**2**	**2**	**37**	**22**	**47**	**FAC Winners**
1897-98	1	16	6th	30	12	1	2	47	21	2	4	9	14	30	33	
1898-99	**1**	**18**	**1st**	**34**	**15**	**2**	**0**	**58**	**13**	**4**	**5**	**8**	**18**	**27**	**45**	
1899-00	**1**	**18**	**1st**	**34**	**12**	**4**	**1**	**45**	**18**	**10**	**2**	**5**	**32**	**17**	**50**	
1900-01	1	18	15th	34	8	5	4	32	18	2	5	10	13	33	30	*FAC Semi-finalists*
1901-02	1	18	8th	34	9	5	3	27	13	4	3	10	15	27	34	
1902-03	1	18	2nd	34	11	3	3	43	18	8	0	9	18	22	41	*FAC Semi-finalists*
1903-04	1	18	5th	34	13	1	3	41	16	4	6	7	29	32	41	
1904-05	1	18	4th	34	11	2	4	32	15	8	2	7	31	28	42	**FAC Winners**
1905-06	1	20	8th	38	13	2	4	51	19	4	4	11	21	37	40	
1906-07	1	20	5th	38	13	4	2	51	19	6	2	11	27	33	44	
1907-08	1	20	2nd	38	9	6	4	47	24	8	3	8	30	35	43	
1908-09	1	20	7th	38	8	7	4	31	22	6	3	10	27	34	38	
1909-10	**1**	**20**	**1st**	**38**	**17**	**2**	**0**	**62**	**19**	**6**	**5**	**8**	**22**	**23**	**53**	
1910-11	1	20	2nd	38	15	3	1	50	18	7	4	8	19	23	51	
1911-12	1	20	6th	38	12	2	5	48	22	5	5	9	28	41	41	
1912-13	1	20	2nd	38	13	4	2	57	21	6	8	5	29	31	50	**FAC Winners**
1913-14	1	20	2nd	38	11	3	5	36	21	8	3	8	29	29	44	*FAC Semi-finalists*
1914-15	1	20	13th	38	10	5	4	39	32	3	6	10	23	40	37	
First World War																
1919-20	1	22	9th	42	11	3	7	49	36	7	3	11	26	37	42	**FAC Winners**
1920-21	1	22	10th	42	11	4	6	39	21	7	3	11	24	49	43	
1921-22	1	22	5th	42	16	3	2	50	19	6	0	15	24	36	47	
1922-23	1	22	6th	42	15	3	3	42	11	3	7	11	22	40	46	
1923-24	1	22	6th	42	10	10	1	33	11	8	3	10	19	26	49	*FAC Runners-up*
1924-25	1	22	15th	42	10	7	4	34	25	3	6	12	24	46	39	
1925-26	1	22	6th	42	12	7	2	56	25	4	5	12	30	51	44	
1926-27	1	22	10th	42	11	4	6	51	34	7	3	11	30	49	43	
1927-28	1	22	8th	42	13	3	5	52	30	4	6	11	26	43	43	
1928-29	1	22	3rd	42	16	2	3	62	30	7	2	12	36	51	50	*FAC Semi-finalists*
1929-30	1	22	4th	42	13	1	7	54	33	8	4	9	38	50	47	
1930-31	1	22	2nd	42	17	3	1	86	34	8	6	7	42	44	59	

VILLA'S ALL-TIME LEAGUE RECORD – SEASON BY SEASON

Season	Div	Teams	Pos	P	W	D	L	F	A	W	D	L	F	A	Pts	Cup Honours
1931-32	1	22	5th	42	15	1	5	64	28	4	7	10	40	44	46	
1932-33	1	22	2nd	42	16	2	3	60	29	7	6	8	32	38	54	
1933-34	1	22	13th	42	10	5	6	45	34	4	7	10	33	41	40	FAC Semi-finalists
1934-35	1	22	13th	42	11	6	4	50	36	3	7	11	24	52	41	
1935-36	1	22	21st	42	7	6	8	47	56	6	3	12	34	54	35	
1936-37	2	22	9th	42	10	6	5	47	30	6	6	9	35	40	44	
1937-38	**2**	**22**	**1st**	**42**	**17**	**2**	**2**	**50**	**12**	**8**	**5**	**8**	**23**	**23**	**57**	FAC Semi-finalists
1938-39	1	22	12th	42	11	3	7	44	25	5	6	10	27	35	41	
Second World War																
1946-47	1	22	8th	42	9	6	6	39	24	9	3	9	28	29	45	
1947-48	1	22	6th	42	13	5	3	42	22	6	4	11	23	35	47	
1948-49	1	22	10th	42	10	6	5	40	36	6	4	11	20	40	42	
1949-50	1	22	12th	42	10	7	4	31	19	5	5	11	30	42	42	
1950-51	1	22	15th	42	9	6	6	39	29	3	7	11	27	39	37	
1951-52	1	22	6th	42	13	3	5	49	28	6	6	9	30	42	47	
1952-53	1	22	11th	42	9	7	5	36	23	5	6	10	27	38	41	
1953-54	1	22	13th	42	12	5	4	50	28	4	4	13	20	40	41	
1954-55	1	22	6th	42	11	3	7	38	31	9	4	8	34	42	47	
1955-56	1	22	20th	42	9	6	6	32	29	2	7	12	20	40	35	
1956-57	1	22	10th	42	10	8	3	45	25	4	7	10	20	30	43	***FAC Winners***
1957-58	1	22	14th	42	12	4	5	46	26	4	3	14	27	60	39	
1958-59	1	22	21st	42	8	5	8	31	33	3	3	15	27	54	30	FAC Semi-finalists
1959-60	**2**	**22**	**1st**	**42**	**17**	**3**	**1**	**62**	**19**	**8**	**6**	**7**	**27**	**24**	**59**	FAC Semi-finalists
1960-61	1	22	9th	42	13	3	5	48	28	4	6	11	30	49	43	***LC Winners***
1961-62	1	22	7th	42	13	5	3	45	20	5	3	13	20	36	44	
1962-63	1	22	15th	42	12	2	7	38	23	3	6	12	24	45	38	LC Runners-up
1963-64	1	22	19th	42	8	6	7	35	29	3	6	12	27	42	34	
1964-65	1	22	16th	42	14	1	6	36	24	2	4	15	21	58	37	LC Semi-finalists
1965-66	1	22	16th	42	10	3	8	39	34	5	3	13	30	46	36	
1966-67	1	22	21st	42	7	5	9	30	33	4	2	15	24	52	29	
1967-68	2	22	16th	42	10	3	8	35	30	5	4	12	19	34	37	
1968-69	2	22	18th	42	10	8	3	22	11	2	6	13	15	37	38	
1969-70	2	22	21st	42	7	8	6	23	21	1	5	15	13	41	29	
1970-71	3	24	4th	46	13	7	3	27	13	6	8	9	27	33	53	LC Runners-up
1971-72	**3**	**24**	**1st**	**46**	**20**	**1**	**2**	**45**	**10**	**12**	**5**	**6**	**40**	**22**	**70**	
1972-73	2	22	3rd	42	12	5	4	27	17	6	9	6	24	30	50	
1973-74	2	22	14th	42	8	9	4	33	21	5	6	10	15	24	41	
1974-75	2	22	2nd	42	16	4	1	47	6	9	4	8	32	26	58	***LC Winners***
1975-76	1	22	16th	42	11	8	2	32	17	0	9	12	19	42	39	
1976-77	1	22	4th	42	17	3	1	55	17	5	4	12	21	33	51	***LC Winners***

VILLA'S ALL-TIME LEAGUE RECORD – SEASON BY SEASON

Season	Div	Teams	Pos	P	W	D	L	F	A	W	D	L	F	A	Pts	Cup Honours
1977-78	1	22	8th	42	11	4	6	33	18	7	6	8	24	24	46	
1978-79	1	22	8th	42	8	9	4	37	26	7	7	7	22	23	46	
1979-80	1	22	7th	42	11	5	5	29	22	5	9	7	22	28	46	
1980-81	**1**	**22**	**1st**	**42**	**16**	**3**	**2**	**40**	**13**	**10**	**5**	**6**	**32**	**27**	**60**	
1981-82	1	22	11th	42	9	6	6	28	24	6	6	9	27	29	57	*EC Winners*
1982-83	1	22	6th	42	17	2	2	47	15	4	3	14	15	35	68	*ESC Winners*
1983-84	1	22	10th	42	14	3	4	34	22	3	6	12	25	39	60	*LC Semi-finalists*
1984-85	1	22	10th	42	10	7	4	34	20	5	4	12	26	40	56	
1985-86	1	22	16th	42	7	6	8	27	28	3	8	10	24	39	44	*LC Semi-finalists*
1986-87	*1*	*22*	*22nd*	*42*	*7*	*7*	*7*	*25*	*25*	*1*	*5*	*15*	*20*	*54*	*36*	
1987-88	2	23	2nd	44	9	7	6	31	21	13	5	4	37	20	78	
1988-89	1	20	17th	38	7	6	6	25	22	2	7	10	20	34	40	
1989-90	1	20	2nd	38	13	3	3	36	20	8	4	7	21	18	70	*FMC Area Finalists*
1990-91	1	20	17th	38	7	9	3	29	25	2	5	12	17	33	41	
1991-92	1	22	7th	42	13	3	5	31	16	4	6	11	17	28	60	
1992-93	P	22	2nd	42	13	5	3	36	16	8	6	7	21	24	74	
1993-94	P	22	10th	42	8	5	8	23	18	7	7	7	23	32	57	*LC Winners*
1994-95	P	22	18th	42	6	9	6	27	24	5	6	10	24	32	48	
1995-96	P	20	4th	38	11	5	3	32	15	7	4	8	20	20	63	*LC Winners/FAC SF*
1996-97	P	20	5th	38	11	5	3	27	13	6	5	8	20	21	61	
1997-98	P	20	7th	38	9	3	7	26	24	8	3	8	23	24	57	
1998-99	P	20	6th	38	10	3	6	33	28	5	7	7	18	18	55	

VILLA'S COMPLETE LEAGUE RECORD

	P	W	D	L	F	A	Pts
Home	1969	1135	427	407	4098	2243	2878
Away	1969	536	471	962	2502	3522	1640
Total	3938	1671	898	1369	6600	5765	4518

2pts for a win up to season 1980-8, 3pts for a win from season 1981-82

Other honours:

World Club Championship runners-up 1982-83

FA Charity Shield joint winners 1981-82

FA Charity Shield runners-up 1910-11, 1957-58, 1972-73

FAC = FA Cup; LC = League Cup; FMC = Full Members' Cup; EC = European Champions' Cup; ESC = European Super Cup.
Championship seasons in **bold** type, relegation seasons in *italics*.

BEING NEIGHBOURLY

While Villa eyes are primarily focused on the pitch, the club is also outward-looking, anxious to play its part in the community in which Villa Park is situated.

To this end, newly-appointed Community Services Officer Dave Ismay has spent the season working with local people and firms on numerous initiatives.

The club had previously dealt with community matters on an *ad hoc* basis, holding regular residents' meetings and organising Christmas parties for the local community.

Now it has also become involved in a campaign against racial harassment and is working with the Crimestoppers organisation and the Prince's Trust Volunteers, as well as local charities, schools and non-league football clubs, providing signed footballs and other prizes for fund-raising events.

VILLA'S RECORD IN EUROPEAN COMPETITIONS

1975-76 – UEFA CUP

| Sep | 17 | R1/L1 | A | Royal Antwerp (Belgium) | 1-4 | Graydon |
| Oct | 1 | R1/L2 | **H** | **Royal Antwerp** | 0-1 | |

Aggregate Score - Antwerp win 5-1

1977-78 – UEFA CUP

| Sep | 14 | R1/L1 | **H** | **Fenerbahce** (Turkey) | 4-0 | Deehan 2, Gray, Little |
| Oct | 1 | R1/L2 | A | Fenerbahce | 2-0 | Deehan, Little |

Aggregate Score - Villa win 6-0

| Oct | 19 | R2/L1 | **H** | **Gornik Zabrze** (Poland) | 2-0 | McNaught 2 |
| Nov | 2 | R2/L2 | A | Gornik Zabrze | 1-1 | Gray |

Aggregate Score - Villa win 3-1

| Nov | 23 | R3/L1 | **H** | **Athletic Bilbao** (Spain) | 2-0 | Iribar og, Deehan |
| Dec | 7 | R3/L2 | A | Athletic Bilbao | 1-1 | Mortimer |

Aggregate Score - Villa win 3-1

| Mar | 1 | R4/L1 | **H** | **Barcelona** (Spain) | 2-2 | McNaught, Deehan |
| Mar | 15 | R4/L2 | A | Barcelona | 1-2 | Little |

Aggregate Score - Barcelona win 4-3

1981-82 – EUROPEAN CHAMPIONS' CUP

| Sep | 16 | R1/L1 | **H** | **Valur** (Iceland) | 5-0 | Morley, Donovan 2, Withe 2 |
| Sep | 30 | R1/L2 | A | Valur | 2-0 | Shaw 2 |

Aggregate Score - Villa win 7-0

| Oct | 21 | R2/L1 | A | Dynamo Berlin (E. Germany) | 2-1 | Morley 2 |
| Nov | 4 | R2/L2 | **H** | **Dynamo Berlin** | 0-1 | |

Aggregate Score - 2-2, Villa win on away goals rule

| Mar | 3 | QF/L1 | A | Dynamo Kiev (USSR) | 0-0 | |
| Mar | 17 | QF/L2 | **H** | **Dynamo Kiev** | 2-0 | Shaw, McNaught |

Aggregate Score - Villa win 2-0

| Apr | 7 | SF/L1 | **H** | **Anderlecht** (Belgium) | 1-0 | Morley |
| Apr | 21 | SF/L2 | A | Anderlecht | 0-0 | |

Aggregate Score - Villa win 1-0

| May | 26 | | Final | N | **Bayern Munich** (W. Germany) | 1-0 | Withe |

Played at the 'De Kuip' Stadium in Rotterdam, Holland

1982-83 – EUROPEAN CHAMPIONS' CUP

| Sep | 15 | R1/L1 | **H** | **Besiktas** (Turkey) | 3-1 | Withe, Morley, Mortimer |
| Sep | 29 | R1/L2 | A | Besiktas | 0-0 | |

Aggregate Score - Villa win 3-1

| Oct | 20 | R2/L1 | A | Dinamo Bucharest (Romania) | 2-0 | Shaw 2 |
| Nov | 3 | R2/L2 | **H** | **Dinamo Bucharest** | 4-2 | Shaw 3, Walters |

Aggregate Score - Villa win 6-2

| Mar | 2 | QF/L1 | H | **Juventus** (Italy) | 1-2 | Cowans |
| Mar | 16 | QF/L2 | A | Juventus | 1-3 | Withe |

Aggregate Score - Juventus win 5-2

1982-83 – EUROPEAN SUPER CUP

| Jan | 19 | L1 | A | Barcelona (Spain) | 0-1 | |
| Jan | 26 | L2 | H | **Barcelona** | 3-0 | Shaw, Cowans (pen), McNaught |

Aggregate Score - Villa win 3-1

1982-83 – WORLD CLUB CHAMPIONSHIP

| Dec | 12 | | – | N | Penarol (Uruguay) | 0-2 | |

Played in Tokyo, Japan

1983-84 – UEFA CUP

| Sep | 14 | R1/L1 | A | Vitoria Guimaraes (Portugal) | 0-1 | |
| Sep | 28 | R1/L2 | H | **Vitoria Guimaraes** | 5-0 | Withe 3, Gibson, Ormsby |

Aggregate Score - Villa win 5-1

| Oct | 19 | R2/L1 | A | Spartak Moscow (USSR) | 2-2 | Gibson, Walters |
| Nov | 2 | R2/L2 | H | **Spartak Moscow** | 1-2 | Withe |

Aggregate Score - Spartak win 4-3

1990-91 – UEFA CUP

| Sep | 19 | R1/L1 | H | **Banik Ostrava** (Czechoslovakia) | 3-1 | Mountfield, Platt, Olney |
| Oct | 2 | R1/L2 | A | Banik Ostrava | 2-1 | Mountfield, Stas og |

Aggregate Score - Villa win 5-2

| Oct | 24 | R2/L1 | H | **Inter Milan** (Italy) | 2-0 | Neilson, Platt |
| Nov | 7 | R2/L2 | A | Inter Milan | 0-3 | |

Aggregate Score - Inter win 3-2

1993-94 – UEFA CUP

| Sep | 15 | R1/L1 | A | Slovan Bratislava (Slovakia) | 0-0 | |
| Sep | 29 | R1/L2 | H | **Slovan Bratislava** | 2-1 | Atkinson, Townsend |

Aggregate Score - Villa win 2-1

| Oct | 19 | R2/L1 | A | Deportivo La Coruna (Spain) | 1-1 | Saunders |
| Nov | 3 | R2/L2 | H | **Deportivo La Coruna** | 0-1 | |

Aggregate Score - Deportivo win 2-1

1994-95 – UEFA CUP

| Sep | 15 | R1/L1 | A | Inter Milan (Italy) | 0-1 | |
| Sep | 29 | R1/L2 | H | **Inter Milan** | 1-0 | Houghton |

Aggregate Score - 1-1, Villa go through after a penalty shoot-out

| Oct | 18 | R2/L1 | A | Trabzonspor (Turkey) | 0-1 | |
| Nov | 1 | R2/L2 | H | **Trabzonspor** | 2-1 | Atkinson, Ehiogu |

Aggregate Score - 2-2, Trabzonspor win on away goals rule

1996-97 – UEFA CUP

Sep	10	R1/L1	**H**	**Helsingborgs IF** (Sweden)	1-1	Johnson
Sep	24	R1/L2	A	Helsingborgs IF	0-0	

Aggregate Score - 1-1, Helsingborgs IF win on away goals rule

1997-98 – UEFA CUP

Sep	16	R1/L1	A	Girondins de Bordeaux (France)	0-0	
Sep	30	R1/L2	**H**	**Girondins de Bordeaux**	1-0	Milosevic

Aggregate Score - Villa win 1-0

Oct	21	R2/L1	A	Athletic Bilbao (Spain)	0-0	
Nov	4	R2/L2	**H**	**Athletic Bilbao**	2-1	Taylor, Yorke

Aggregate Score - Villa win 2-1

Nov	25	R3/L1	A	Steaua Bucharest (Romania)	1-2	Yorke
Dec	9	R3/L2	**H**	**Steaua Bucharest**	2-0	Milosevic, Taylor

Aggregate Score - Villa win 3-2

Mar	3	R4/L1	A	Atlético Madrid (Spain)	0-1	
Mar	17	R4/L2	**H**	**Atlético Madrid**	2-1	Taylor, Collymore

Aggregate Score - 2-2, Atlético Madrid win on away goals rule

1998-99 – UEFA CUP

Sep	15	R1/L1	**H**	**Strømsgodset** (Norway)	3-2	Charles, Vassell 2
Sep	29	R1/L2	A	Strømsgodset	3-0	Collymore 3

Aggregate Score - Villa win 6-2

Oct	20	R2/L1	A	RC Celta Vigo (Spain)	1-0	Joachim
Nov	3	R2/L2	**H**	**RC Celta Vigo**	1-3	Collymore (pen)

Aggregate Score - Celta Vigo win 3-2

CLARET & BLUE

THE OFFICIAL MAGAZINE OF ASTON VILLA F.C.

Forty-eight full-colour pages devoted entirely to events at Villa Park – on the field and behind the scenes. A publication just too good to miss.

Ensure you do not miss a single copy by taking a 6-issue subscription

Contact: Sports Projects Ltd,
212 Broad Street, Birmingham B15 1AY. Tel: 0121-643 2729. Fax: 0121-633 4628.
e-mail: info@sportproject.u-net.com
web site: http://sportsprojects.com

Cheques to be made payable to: Sports Projects Ltd.

SUBSCRIBERS ROLL CALL

001	Neil Gallagher	056	Oliver Eagle	111	Anthony Woolley
002	In Memory of Peter Bishop	057	Derek Day	112	Conner Wild
003	Thomas Keightley (1911-1998)	058	Kerry Day	113	Lee Day
004	Stuart James Dyke	059	Carly Day	114	Ben Taylor
005	David Watson	060	Jean Day	115	Susan Pudge
006	David Watson Jnr	061	J. R. Meek	116	Martin Lockley
007	John (Villa) Power	062	Elizabeth Dunbar	117	Stephen Paul Naylor
008	Sarah Jane Wall-Power	063	Lynsey Dunbar	118	Colin Brown
009	Jonathan Simon Power	064	Joe Ridout	119	Gerald Leek
010	Wayne Watson	065	Keith Ridout	120	Terry Wright
011	Ian Sutherland	066	Emily Ridout	121	Neal Sawyer
012	Ben Sutherland	067	Paul J. Edwards	122	John A. Gould (1934)
013	Mr V. A. P. Kiery	068	Ralf Schulz	123	Stephen Gould
014	Paul Bailey	069	Philip Gray	124	Mark Underwood
015	Jenny Bailey	070	Angela Mead	125	Adrian Hill
016	Gareth C. Jones (Bones)	071	The Fairfield Family (Lancaster)	126	Lisa Hill
017	Nigel Renshaw	072	Alison Jones	127	Paul Kenna
018	Norman Renshaw	073	Stephen J. Lammas	128	Baldrick E4
019	Stephen (Rennie) Renshaw	074	E. Oldham	129	Kal Cook
020	Dan (The Villa Man) Renshaw	075	Geoff Baker	130	Mr Robert Banks
021	Simon Renshaw	076	Tony C. Dacey	131	Janet Morgan
022	Dr Mark Wilson	077	Paul Nicholas Randle	132	Matthew Bridges
023	Helen Louis Sutton	078	Christine Rossiter	133	Ross Griffith
024	Warren H. McDivitt	079	Ian Rossiter	134	Martin K. James
025	Karen F. McDivitt	080	Bob Peach	135	Clive Platman
026	Harry W. McDivitt	081	Kenneth J. Marriott	136	Michele Platman
027	Ellie S. McDivitt	082	Stuart T. Swann	137	Kevin Wheatly
028	Brian C. Seadon	083	Dave Skinner	138	L. E. Osborn
029	Sam Boot	084	Peter Lee Maddocks	139	The Hitchmans
030	Karen Barlow	085	Robin D. Wilkes	140	R. E. Garratt
031	Lesley Smith	086	Brig Flounders	141	Richard M. Merker
032	David Hodges	087	Emily Kender	142	Mark Ford
033	Steve Smith	088	Martin Kender	143	Ashley Davis
034	David Woodley	089	Darren Bedford	144	Charlotte Davis
035	Alexander Berwick	090	Lisa Palmer	145	Paul Ford
036	Daniel Berwick	091	Paul Palmer	146	Michael Caiden
037	Paul Berwick	092	Thomas Palmer	147	Paul Caiden
038	Andrew Eades	093	John Knight	148	Nigel Groves
039	Phillip Robin Haynes	094	Dave 'AVFC' Knight	149	The Blythe Family
040	Tony Spraggon	095	Jayne Margetts	150	Matthew John Collinge
041	Roger Levicki	096	Tony Margetts	151	Andrea Warren
042	Tim Levicki	097	Lauren Margetts	152	Diane Swales
043	Andrew Levicki	098	Sam Margetts	153	Charles Wheadon
044	Mark Glyn Jones	099	Terry Knight	154	Darren Ewen
045	David Ian Jones	100	Jacky Atkinson Monks	155	Ian Ross
046	Glyn Jones	101	Simon 'Wilf' Wheeler	156	Roger 'Tamworth' Nicklin
047	Michael Halaj	102	Andrew Collins	157	Craig Ramsey
048	Glyn Richards	103	Gido Kirfel	158	Michael Rose
049	Lorraine Richards	104	Doyle Family	159	Luca Mancini
050	Caerwyn Richards	105	Thomas Johansson	160	Adam Rose
051	Cellyn Richards	106	Jason Paul Kennedy	161	Sue Tilt
052	S. J. Lavery	107	Kasper Holst	162	Mick Tilt
053	Frank MacDonald	108	Tom Sedgwick	163	Adam Tilsley
054	David Eagle	109	Ian R. Wilson	164	Robert Tilsley
055	Susan Eagle	110	Pete Abrahams	165	Geoff Underhill

166	Mick Thomas	221	Martyn Thomas	276	Leo Pinnock
167	Joshua Greaves	222	Peter D. Jones	277	Neil Hunt
168	Mark Pearce	223	Edward J. Howard	278	Edward Knott
169	Adam France	224	Martin Dillingham	279	Sue Ford
170	Richard Shutt	225	Gingerpud and Cadbury	280	Dan Ford
171	Keith Gleadall	226	Alan Gee	281	Richard Ford
172	Frank Antram	227	Wendy Samantha Jordan	282	Sarah Mills
173	Ben Antram	228	Jennie Taylor	283	Julie Harrison
174	Martin Dillingham	229	James Daly	284	Mark David Goodwin
175	Carly Spearing	230	Colin Daly	285	Gareth Tidey
176	Damian Barrow	231	Kieran Oakes	286	Martin Ward
177	Mark Barrow	232	Geoffrey Wright	287	James Ward
178	Kevin Stratford	233	Philip John Shakespeare	288	Fordon Parton
179	R. A. Jones	234	Valerie Shakespeare	289	Lars Nilsson
180	Roger Winn	235	Thomas Shakespeare	290	Steve Crump
181	Louisa Winn	236	Andrew Webster	291	Paul Dann
182	Davin John Edward Clayton	237	Julie Angela Richardson	292	Denise Dann
183	Jemma Clayton	238	David Warman	293	Michael English
184	Sarah Clayton	239	Darren Woodfield	294	Nicholas English
185	Matthew Clayton	240	Debbie Hill	295	Y. A. Graves
186	Laura Clayton	241	Van De Sÿpe Iggy	296	Julian M. Turner
187	Andy Perry	242	Van De Sÿpe Lorenzo	297	Alun Llywelyn Parish
188	Robert Gough	243	David Tansey	298	Philip J. Etheridge
189	Derek T. Hough	244	M. A. Cooper	299	Stephen Dickens
190	Paul McKenna	245	Steve Talbot	300	Stephen Hill
191	Keith Stubbs	246	Douglas Talbot	301	Sim and Jess (Holtenders)
192	Natalie Stubbs	247	Simon Kerr-Edwards	302	Christopher Sanderson
193	Vicki Stubbs	248	Brian Etheridge	303	Paul Sanderson
194	John Cullen	249	Richard McCallum	304	Roger Sanderson
195	Kevin Larkin	250	Sue Glaves	305	Peter Brett
196	Malcolm Cooper	251	Dr Stephen C. Tovey	306	Barrie Bailey
197	Sharon Cooper	252	Chris Bale	307	Lee Pritchard
198	Dave Buet	253	Daren Reynolds	308	Callum Fenlon
199	Paul Buet	254	Mark Lench	309	Martin Greenslade
200	Marg Buet	255	Stephen Morris (France)	310	Gerald Murphy
201	Mrs Lilian Cemm	256	Karen Ellis	311	Ian Tate
202	Amanda Bonas	257	Dean Shepherd	312	Bridget Tate
203	Susan Bonas	258	Joseph Shepherd	313	Scott Hamblett
204	Patrick Fenelon	259	Mestre Didier	314	Andrew Gerrard
205	Gabrielle Fenelon	260	Carl Pell	315	Kevin Gledhill
206	Mark Napier	261	Christopher Godson	316	Peter Gledhill
207	Rob Wardle	262	Gary Godsen	317	Richard Gledhill
208	Karen Wardle	263	Andy Congrave	318	Andrew Gledhill
209	Robert Wardle Junior	264	Helen Hollywell	319	Sean Christopher Starrs
210	Samantha Wardle	265	Simon Dyke	320	Graham N. Willetts
211	Alexander Wardle	266	Becky Vizor	321	John R. Ward
212	Ranting Robert	267	S. Boddy	322	Adam Shaffrey
213	Richard Baker	268	Paul Perry	323	Raymond Warr
214	Steven Baker	269	Sophie Parkin	324	Lewis Carter
215	Jenny Baker	270	Alex Groemminger	325	Matthew Kenny
216	Malcolm Taylor	271	James Flynn	326	Andrew Kenny
217	Reine Bladh	272	Kate Turner	327	Glyn Howell
218	Henrik Bladh	273	Mark Ferriday	328	Brendan Shields
219	Mr Jason Webb	274	Andrew Brooks	329	Neil Harvey
220	Michael Ault	275	Jack Pinnock	330	Louise Roberts

331	Dean Strange	386	Russell S. J. Goodman	441	Jim McDonald
332	Maria Ganner	387	Michael Bateson	442	Thomas McDonald
333	Emma Ganner	388	Kirsty Nicholls	443	Antony McAllister
334	Clare Ganner	389	John Henry Lane	444	Sarah Kinsman
335	Peter Bullock	390	Shirley Blizard	445	Kevin A. Williams
336	Stewart Ray	391	Geoff Blizard	446	D. S. Willetts
337	John Peter Reidy	392	Carol Maguire	447	Henry Philip Jones
338	Paul Alphouse	393	Steven Ward	448	Martin 'Statto' Jenkins
339	Gordon Reynolds	394	John Simmonds	449	Antony Richard Joyner
340	Frank Allen	395	Paul Jarvis	450	Alan Stephen Jones
341	Andrew Friel	396	Sab Gatrad	451	Simon Phillips
342	Tony Friel	397	Malcolm Fazakarley	452	Jenny Balmforth
343	Bob Daniels	398	Brett Moss	453	Gordon W.
344	Roy Farmer	399	Rachel Townsend	454	Malcolm P. Price
345	Erica Farmer	400	David Poole	455	Peter Curry
346	Chris Newton	401	Nicholas Cox	456	Adrian Paul Broad
347	Ian Edward Beesley	402	Simon A. J. Burley	457	Norman D. Crandles
348	Susan Beesley	403	Adrian Batsford	458	Paul Rostance
349	Alex Williams	404	Anthony Robert Bevington	459	Jason Davis
350	Stephen Evans	405	Dave Alan Turner	460	Bruce Maciver
351	Roger Collett	406	Gary Bick	461	Katrina Maciver
352	William Alexander	407	Rheanne Bick	462	Gavin Maciver
353	W. A. Harvey	408	Lauren Bick	463	Scott Maciver
354	Dejan Tomic	409	Callum Bick	464	Anne (Kop) Clark
355	David Peachey	410	Robert Bick	465	Emma Jones
356	Tony Broadhurst	411	Karen Bick	466	Samantha Jones
357	John Brealey	412	Kevin Lowbridge	467	Phil R. Jones
358	James Michael Deeley	413	Mark Bradshaw	468	Robin Peck
359	Mark C. Hall	414	Gavin Dutton	469	Michael Morgan
360	Teeni Smith	415	James Villans and Mathew 99	470	Roger Fullbrook
361	Nigel Iwanski	416	Neil Stevens	471	Mark Fullbrook
362	Ross Iwanski	417	Martin Colin Roberts	472	Andrew C. Dawes
363	Vera Ellen Ragsdale	418	Charlotte Louise Briggs	473	John Donohoe
364	Morten Esbjerg	419	S. W. Walton	474	David Musson
365	L. B. Reading	420	Vernon Grove O.B.E.	475	Charlotte Rollason
366	James Davis	421	Chris Deakin	476	Gavin Harris
367	Andrew Mason	422	Arthur Bent	477	Katrina Harris
368	M. Asson	423	Matthew Dale	478	K. W. Powell
369	Bernard Dain	424	Amanda Jane Brampton	479	Rod Evans
370	Derek Hollis	425	Peter Boam	480	Ron Gamble
371	Alan F. Jasper	426	Antony Michael Millas	481	Becky Nines
372	Bob Harvey	427	Scott Davidson	482	Nigel Ainge
373	Michael (Mick) O' Brien	428	David Clatworthy	483	Adrian J. Mullis
374	Veronica McCormack	429	Iris Barford	484	Jon Noden
375	Chris McCormack	430	John Kennedy	485	West Heath Villa
376	Beryl Stanyard	431	Tina Rees	486	Chris Russell
377	Neil Byrne	432	Ian Symes	487	Bob Nicholls
378	Judith Bellingham	433	Paul Wheeler	488	Clive Nicholls
379	Roger Bellingham	434	Gordon Cull	489	Stephen Drew
380	Mark Wheeler	435	Antony Rogers	490	Martyn Walker
381	G. Jinks	436	Michelle Diggins	491	Richard Carter
382	M. T. Randle	437	Carl Davies	492	Jason Norbury
383	S. F. Randle	438	Luke Davies	493	Julie Edkins
384	Arthur Lockyear	439	Chris Clutterbuck	494	Dave Edkins
385	DJ Matt E. Pugh (on his debut)	440	Owen Suter	495	Jason Russell Perry

496	Adrian Paul Rogers	551	Andrew Williams	606	Hayden Wakeling
497	Andy Campkin	552	Gordon Williams	607	Edmund Gajny
498	Rob Vincent	553	Matthew Barrie Claridge	608	Jan Parkinson
499	Chris Marcantonio	554	Martin Lane	609	The Late Dublin Con Portley
500	Jim Marcantonio	555	Ian Robert Lane		and Family
501	Ryan Cox	556	Debbie Reynolds	610	John W. Daw
502	Kelvin Cox	557	Mark Stoneman	611	Simon and Bev Stringer
503	David Huxtable	558	Mark Attwood	612	Sacha and Luca Molin
504	Samuel York	559	Julia Attwood	613	Roy Stringer
505	Richard Hinton	560	Tracey Roberts	614	Nicholas Jones
506	Pamela Wood	561	Robert Smyth	615	Allen Souch
507	Tracey Hatfield	562	Terry Smyth	616	Michael David Bromwich
508	Roy Hatfield	563	Andrew Smyth	617	Carol Smith
509	Anna C. Calver	564	Craig Roberts	618	John Millward
510	Warren Carvell	565	Gavin Roberts	619	Ruth Millward
511	Paul Rostance	566	Ron Dovey	620	Bethany Millward
512	The Butler Family	567	Chris Dovey	621	Jansen King
513	Darryl Michael Sankey	568	Paul Dovey	622	Julie King
514	Paul Tooby	569	Keith Dovey	623	Heather King
515	Matthew Harris	570	Andrew Dovey	624	Jamie King
516	Brian Harris	571	Dave Dovey	625	Brandon King
517	Nicholas Harris	572	Shaun Hall	626	Debbie Sanders
518	Patrick F. J. O'Reilly	573	Shareen	627	Roy Sanders
519	Matthew Bond	574	John Murphy	628	Emma Sanders
520	Martin J. Watson	575	Geraldine Coffey	629	Paul Sanders
521	Vincent J. McKenna	576	Cheryl Voake	630	George Sanders
522	Ian Harrison	577	Adam Voake	631	John Hartley
523	Simon Harrison	578	Gareth Hubbard	632	Trevor Hartley
524	John Lacey	579	Maggie Dove	633	Catherine Hartley
525	Neil Jones	580	Joanna Branson	634	David Hartley
526	Antonio Durante (Rome, Italy)	581	Steve Hartwell	635	Andrew Hartley
527	Benjamin Wiseman	582	Matthew Blood	636	Steve Farr
528	David Beddard	583	Anna Tidmarsh	637	Martin Farr
529	Jamie Beddard	584	Michael Burbage	638	Vic and Jan Millward
530	James W. Johnstone	585	Paul Robert Eccles	639	Frank and Edie Beach
531	G. S. Clarke	586	Chris Abraham	640	Phil Lees
532	Robert Cooper	587	Paul Abraham	641	Nadine Goldingay
533	Ian J. Walker	588	Helen Corcoran	642	James Allsop
534	Chris Henman	589	Elizabeth Erickson	643	Claire Allsop
535	Mary Henman	590	Stephen Bristow	644	Dave Bridgewater
536	Richard Henman	591	Michael Siddons	645	Pam Bridgewater
537	Alexander Berry	592	Madeline Smith	646	Bill Willcox
538	Thomas Berry	593	Declan Swallow	647	Kate Atkins
539	Mrs Susan Byrne	594	Peter Miles	648	Barry Atkins
540	N. Salter	595	Christian M. Salter	649	Dot Flowers
541	Daniel Evans	596	Nicholas M. Salter	650	Robert Pittaway
542	Kayleigh Evans	597	Ken Noon	651	Molly Pittaway
543	Jonathan Muir	598	Paul Noon	652	Roger Pemberton
544	Alex Ashford	599	Peter Noon	653	Malcolm Vale
545	Clive Foster	600	B. R. Veale	654	Neil Warner
546	Mark Lander	601	Thomas Hill	655	Betty Armstrong
547	David Cox	602	Ralph Willis	656	Neil Armstrong
548	Scott Bradley	603	Emma Gregory	657	Robert Dobson
549	Emma Powell	604	Scott Bradley (Evesham)	658	Anne Dobson
550	Joanne Potter	605	Adam Thomas Barrett	659	Keith 'Laurie' Firth